CW00765296

JIM HENSON'S
IMAGINATION
ILLUSTRATED

the
MUPPETS

JIM HENSON'S

IMAGINATION ILLUSTRATED

BY KAREN FALK
INTRODUCTION BY LISA HENSON
FOREWORD BY RON HOWARD

SAN RAFAEL • LOS ANGELES • LONDON

PO Box 3088
San Rafael, CA 94912
www.insighteditions.com

Find us on Facebook: **www.facebook.com/InsightEditions**
Follow us on Instagram: @insighteditions

Published by Insight Editions, San Rafael, California, in 2024.

ISBN: 979-8-88663-614-7

Publisher: Raoul Goff
VP, Group Publisher: Vanessa Lopez
VP, Creative: Chrissy Kwasnik
VP, Manufacturing: Alix Nicholaeff
Art Director: Stuart Smith
Executive Editor: Paul Ruditis
Editorial Assistant: Jennifer Pellman
VP, Senior Executive Project Editor: Vicki Jaeger
Senior Production Manager: Greg Steffen
Senior Production Manager, Subsidiary Rights: Lina s Palma-Temena

Page 189 constitutes a continuation of the copyright page.

Insight Editions, in association with Roots of Peace, will plant two trees for each tree used in the manufacturing of this book. Roots of Peace is an internationally renowned humanitarian organization dedicated to eradicating land mines worldwide and converting war-torn lands into productive farms and wildlife habitats. Roots of Peace will plant two million fruit and nut trees in Afghanistan and provide farmers there with the skills and support necessary for sustainable land use.

Manufactured in China by Insight Editions

10 9 8 7 6 5 4 3 2 1

Lisa Henson is CEO of The Jim Henson Company, where she oversees all television and feature film production, from early development through post-production. The eldest daughter of Jim Henson, she graduated summa cum laude with a degree in Folklore and Mythology from Harvard University, where she was the first female president of *The Harvard Lampoon*.

Ron Howard is an Academy, Golden Globe, Emmy, and Grammy award-winning director, actor, screenwriter, and producer whose career has spanned over 60 years. He has created some of Hollywood's most memorable films, including the award-winning and critically acclaimed *A Beautiful Mind*, *Apollo 13*, *Thirteen Lives*, *Parenthood*, and *Splash*. In recent years, Howard has also expanded into documentary filmmaking, achieving great success with films such as the Emmy-nominated *We Feed People*, profiling the humanitarian work of renowned chef José Andrés and his World Central Kitchen, and the Grammy-winning Best Music Film, *The Beatles: Eight Days a Week*. Howard's next highly anticipated film will be *Jim Henson: Idea Man*, a documentary that will serve as the definitive portrait of Jim Henson's life. Howard founded Imagine Entertainment in the early '80s with longtime partner and collaborator Brian Grazer, which they continue to run together as executive chairmen. In 2021, he published his memoir, *The Boys: A Memoir of Hollywood and Family*.

CONTENTS

FANFARE

FOREWORD

I met Jim Henson only one time. We crossed paths on the set of a talk show on which we were both scheduled as guests. This was the early '70s. Jim and his puppeteers were there to perform. With their beards and their long hair, I first thought they were a rock band. I don't remember what Jim and I talked about, but I remember being struck by his gentle soft-spokenness, which was in such stark contrast to the big personalities of his characters. Little did I know then that, some forty-odd years later, I would be entrusted by the Henson family to bring Jim's extraordinary life to the screen.

The book you are holding now provided much of the initial inspiration that guided our team in the process of creating our film: *Jim Henson: Idea Man*. Its author, Karen Falk, intrepid keeper of the Henson archive, did much of the hard work years before our film, organizing and curating Jim's massive archive. She continued to be an invaluable resource to us throughout the making of the film.

The sheer breadth of Jim's work is, as you can see in the following pages, simply astonishing. The early sketches, the whimsical paintings, the notebooks chock-full of ideas for characters and stories, even musical notations—it all adds up to a portrait of a guy who was positively bursting at the seams with ideas.

There's no denying that Jim was a genius. That's a word that came up in many of the conversations I had with those who knew him best. But what exactly was Jim's genius? Is it even possible to define? There was, of course, the brilliance of his artistic vision. There was also his knack for assembling talented and like-minded people and leading them, in his own quiet way, toward seemingly impossible goals. Many I spoke to mentioned his sense of fun and play, the joyfulness that went into every act of creation.

One thing I wasn't expecting to discover was the sense of urgency with which Jim worked. It was only when I began speaking to his closest collaborators that the full scope of his relentlessness came into focus. What struck me most was Jim's fascinating relationship with time. You see it in his work, in the continual motif of ticking clocks. You see it in his journals which reveal a man aware that he would never have enough time to do all he wanted to do, but determined to accomplish as much as he could in the paltry window of time he was allotted. One way or another, we're all the beneficiaries of that willful spirit and remarkable determination of Jim's.

Jim never stopped pushing, even when the odds were against him. And when he found success, he continued to challenge himself, exploring new forms, new styles, new ways of communicating. That peculiar combination of playfulness and determination—what Muppets head writer Jerry Juhl once referred to as Jim's "whim of steel"—that, to me, is the essence of what made Jim and his work so special. And it's my hope that, in looking back on Jim's life, whether in this book or in our film, a little of that whimsy and a little bit of that steel might rub off on the rest of us.

—Ron Howard

INTRODUCTION

Everyone knows that Jim Henson created the Muppets,

and that he performed the most famous Muppet of all, Kermit the Frog. Many people also know about his other popular television productions, such as *Fraggle Rock,* and his work on Sesame Street. And his devoted fans are aware of the groundbreaking fantasy films *The Dark Crystal* and *Labyrinth,* into which he poured so much imagination and craft.

What no one really understands is how much other creative stuff was going on in my father's mind. Jim spent almost all of his waking hours in some form of creative activity, which was as natural for him as smiling and walking are for other people. What he produced was only a fraction of all the ideas that he had, and what we generally see today is only a fraction of what he produced. He packed so many projects into a single year that it was hard for anyone to keep up with him, and it was even harder for him to remember exactly what had happened when. Thus his keeping of the little red book.

My father used the book to remember family milestones, such as what year we went to Hawaii, or bought the station wagon, or when the baby started school, but he also wanted to remember how many commercial campaigns he did in a year, and when each puppeteer came to work for the Muppets. He wanted to remember when the family got a new dog as well as when the Valentine's Day special with Mia Farrow was shot. He kept all of those dates in a simple chronology, mixing family and projects indiscriminately. It shows how blurry the boundaries were in his mind between his creative and family life, and these juxtapositions are interesting on a very personal level. For instance, by reading his chronology, I discovered that I was born five years to the day after his show *Sam and Friends* premiered. When I was six, he flew home from performing in Anaheim with Jimmy Dean for my birthday party. And in both 1976 and 1977 he celebrated my birthday on the ship *QE2* on his way to England for *The Muppet Show.* He also documented each and every time that I visited him after I went to college. He was a devoted father, and his journal is full of references to special family trips and one on one time spent with each of his five children.

While my father was not a diarist and he was not much of a letter writer, he did think it was

important to keep records. He began to have the company preserve important, as well as seemingly unimportant, works of art, design, and planning. As he got older, he became aware of the significance of his own work, and he and my mother Jane Henson took care to maintain these files of photography and art, including not just his own art but the beautiful work of designers Michael Frith and Brian Froud, the charming character designs by puppet builders Don Sahlin, Bonnie Erickson, and the creative work of many others.

It is from these materials that the incredible Karen Falk has created a proper archive and drawn from it to illustrate my father's journal excerpts, as presented here for the first time. She has unearthed rare tidbits of unproduced material, as well as quintessential items in the evolution of the famous Muppets. She has found thematic threads that connect projects many years apart, as well as kernels of ideas that germinated major productions. The great profusion of images, titles, and characters that she has used to illustrate my father's journal is a wonderful way to capture Jim's very busyness—his wildly creative mind. Because creativity is a process, it is also rewarding to focus on it more than the finished projects. In this book, you are able to see snapshots of my father's creative process, flashes of his inspirations and his memories of the milestones that were the highlights of his personal and professional life.

His was a life worth celebrating, and we are thrilled to share it with you.

—Lisa Henson

PROLOGUE

ON JUNE 7, 1965, Jim Henson, who would become celebrated the world over as the creator of the Muppets, sat down with a small, red cloth-covered book and began to document his first decade of professional accomplishments and personal highlights. A modest act at the time, this unique journal would eventually chronicle a creative odyssey that spanned almost forty years and five continents, and touched millions of lives.

At the age of twenty-eight, Jim had already garnered significant success with his own local Washington, DC, television show, numerous appearances on national variety shows, and hundreds of commercials. He had dozens of projects in development and had connected with a myriad of talented people in the worlds of entertainment, puppetry, advertising, and animation. One of the concepts he was pursuing at the time was a film depicting the "Organized Brain," exploring how ideas and information are collected, and, more importantly, how they are filed away in the subconscious. Jim's journal was, in effect, an effort to organize his thoughts by writing them down, freeing up space in his crowded mind and making room to pursue new ideas while preserving access to the experiences, dates, and people collected along the way.

On hiatus from regular Rowlf the Dog appearances on *The Jimmy Dean Show*, Jim's hectic schedule was slightly lighter heading into those summer months, perhaps giving him a little more time at home to enjoy his children, including his recently born fourth child, John Paul, and his new Great Dane puppy, Troy, and to go back through his calendars and desk diaries to make the entries in his red book. Referring to himself in the third person, he noted down what had happened up until that point (labeling it "Ancient History"), as though reflecting on it all from an outside perspective. Moving forward, he recorded anything that he felt was worth noting, be it a television production or a child's graduation. In single-line entries, Jim described the range and variety of his work, the web of relationships he developed, the innovations he pursued, and the recognition he received in the ensuing years.

Jim made the entries in batches and developed a rhythm. According to his youngest daughter Heather, each January, referencing the previous year's appointment books, Jim logged his activities and milestones into his journal. While most of the entries, which run from 1954 through 1988, were made in a timely fashion, Jim made sure to fill in missing information later when he was too busy for his annual ritual. There are a few discrepancies

between dates in the book and dates as recorded on other documents and press clippings, possibly because of lapses in memory, but more likely because a scheduled event on Jim's calendar was moved to a different date but not revised on paper.

Jim often used blank books to sketch out ideas for specific projects or designs for characters, and once or twice, tried to start a diary containing longer accounts of events and his related feelings, but always set them aside after a short period. This journal is the only continuous effort of this sort, covering almost his entire adult life. It was a utilitarian document, kept in his New York office, and Jim's brief descriptions, sometimes accentuated with exclamation points or color marker, only hint at the riotous activity in his life. As a historical record, the journal is invaluable, providing a window into Jim's relationships, his ambitious imagination, and his inventive thinking. To Jim, however, leafing through it each year must have been a satisfying exercise, allowing him to take stock, savor his triumphs, and get a renewed sense for what he wanted to achieve in the future. As he completed each section, his mind cleared, ready to fill up again with new ideas and inspirations.

The following pages include Jim's handwritten entries in chronological order. Each major event is described and illustrated with artwork, notes, documents, memos, doodles, press clippings, and photographs that he saved and are now part of the Jim Henson Archives collection. Together, Jim's words and the related materials tell the story of an extraordinary man and the astonishing contributions he made over the course of a lifetime.

❶ The title page from Jim's journal. ❷ Jim in his New York office.

CHAPTER 1

THE WASHINGTON YEARS

1954–1962

BORN SEPTEMBER 24, 1936, in Greenville, Mississippi, Jim Henson lived in nearby Leland into his early teens, and the relaxed rhythms of the Delta provided the setting for his earliest explorations. His focus on the natural world, his friendships, and his family laid the groundwork for his budding creativity and his optimistic and curiosity-filled approach toward the world. Days spent catching tadpoles in Deer Creek or visiting his dad at the agricultural research station where he worked taught Jim to look around and notice how things grew and fit together. His imaginative play with his brother and schoolmates revealed a child's sense of possibility and the joys of collaboration. When the family moved to Hyattsville, Maryland, during his middle-school years, Jim discovered television, and he began to focus his creative impulses on expressing himself visually, first with still art and then with moving images.

Jim's years in the Washington, DC, area provided his professional foundation, establishing him first in the graphic arts and then in television production. At Northwestern High School, he took art classes, designed theater sets and programs, and drew cartoons and spot illustrations for student publications. His extended family shared their talents in storytelling, collaborative music-making, and handicrafts, all of which would prove to be integral to his future career.

Jim started performing on local Washington television in 1954 and, at the same time, enrolled in the University of Maryland, studying design. His first puppets lip-synched to popular records on various shows on the NBC affiliate, WRC-TV, and by spring 1955, Jim had his own five-minute show, *Sam and Friends*. His repertory company of Muppets, including an abstract lizard-like character named Kermit, became local celebrities, winning Jim an Emmy award and appearing as guests on the national broadcasts of *The Steve Allen Show, The Today Show*, and others. He also produced the first of hundreds of television commercials, establishing himself in the world of advertising.

By the time Jim moved to New York in early 1963, he had gathered together his core group of creative partners including his wife, Jane, his head writer Jerry Juhl, and puppet builder Don Sahlin. He traveled to Europe and across the country several times during those years and learned to use various still and moving-image cameras and animation equipment. His first two children were born in Washington, DC, and with the creation of Rowlf the Dog and a group of fairy-tale characters there, Jim was poised to expand to the national arena.

❶ Jim, Sam, Kermit, and Yorick at WRC-TV, Washington, DC, late 1950s.

Jim went to Northwestern High School graduated June 1954.
Jim – U. of Maryland started and graduated June 1960.

Jim made the most of the creative opportunities at his high school in suburban Maryland, providing covers, cartoons, and spot illustrations for student publications *Wildcat Scratches* and *The Midget Mag*. His talent for set design was showcased in school theater productions and the puppet shows of Les Petit Players, and he took on an occasional dramatic role. This set the pattern for his activities at the University of Maryland, just down the road from his parents' house. There, Jim studied art and graphic design, ran his own silk-screened poster business, designed sets, and took courses that ranged from landscape painting and public speaking to French, typography, and costume illustration.

❶ Jim as a high school senior. ❷ An unpublished cartoon by Jim. ❸ Ad for Jim's college poster business. ❹ Jim's cover art for *The Midget Mag*. ❺+❻+❼ Jim's program designs for the University of Maryland theater department.

THE
WINGET
MAG

4

Dark
of the
Moon

UNIVERSITY THEATRE
UNIVERSITY OF MARYLAND

5

ITWARD
OUND

UNIVERSITY THEATRE
UNIVERSITY OF MARYLAND

6

THE
UNIVERS
OF
MARYLA

Summer
Theatre
Workshop

7

STERS

3/5

In the summer of 1954, with Russel Wall
Jim began puppets on WTOP, Washington
DC – went to WRC-TV –
3 times a week starting July 31, 1954
met Jane September 1954 and began
working together Feb. 1955 "Afternoon" starts March 7, 1955

Jim's first television experience performing puppets with his friend Russell Wall on a short-lived program for WTOP, Washington's local CBS affiliate, led to work on various shows at the NBC station, WRC-TV. That fall, in a college puppetry class, Jim met his next partner and future wife, Jane Nebel. The intensity of the class gave Jim an opportunity to assess the talent around him, and he quickly saw that Jane had a lot to offer as a performer and artist. He invited her to start working with him that winter, and on March 7, 1955, they began performing as part of WRC's daytime variety show, *Afternoon*.

❶ Jim's photo behind the scenes at WRC's *Circle 4 Ranch*. ❷ Pierre, one of Jim's first puppets from 1954. ❸ Jim's sketches behind the scenes at WRC. ❹ Promotional postcard with Sam and his friend Kermit. ❺ Jim and Jane with Sam, Mushmellon, and Kermit. ❻ Sam appearing on WRC's Footlight Theater.

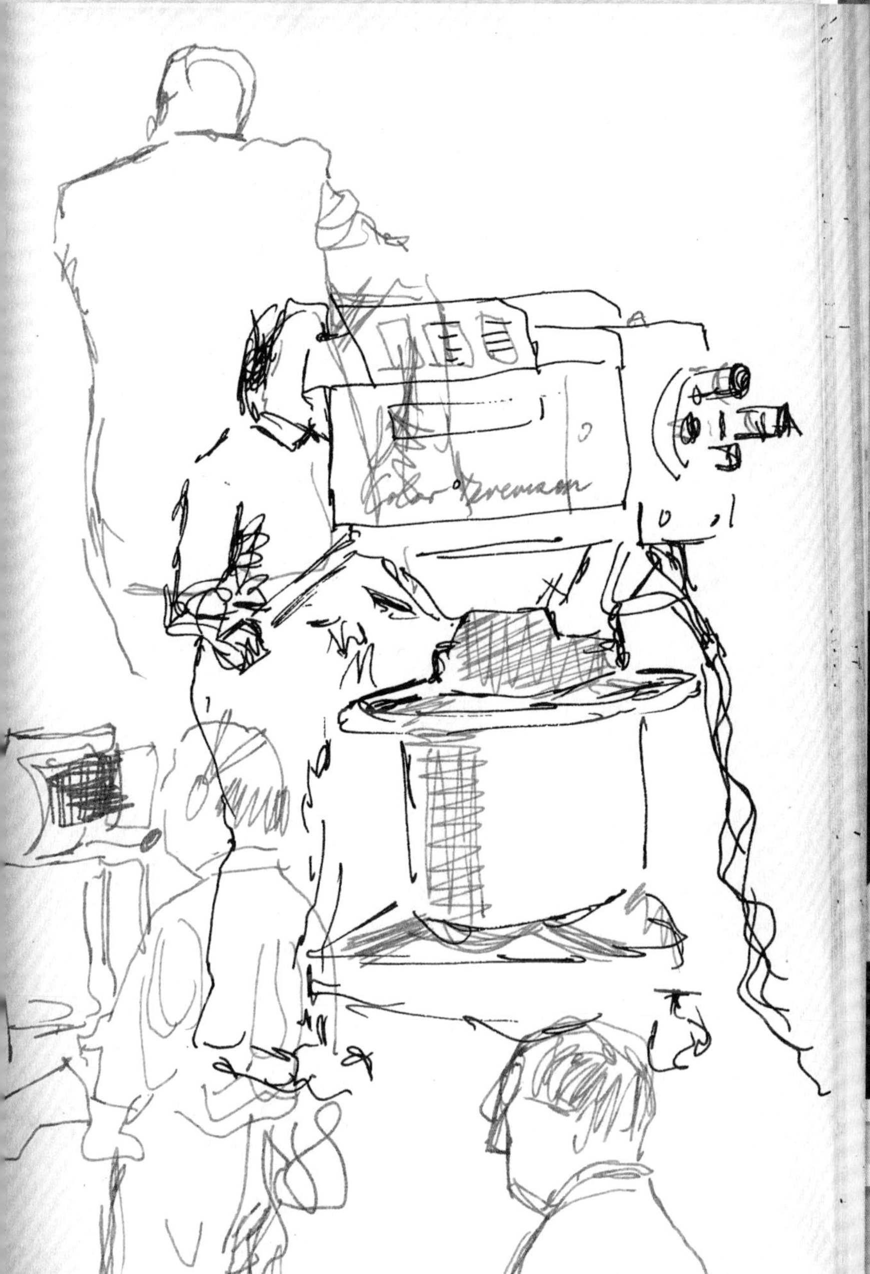

Cheerio!
from Sam and friends
and WRC-TV ~ 4

FOOTLIGHT
THEATER

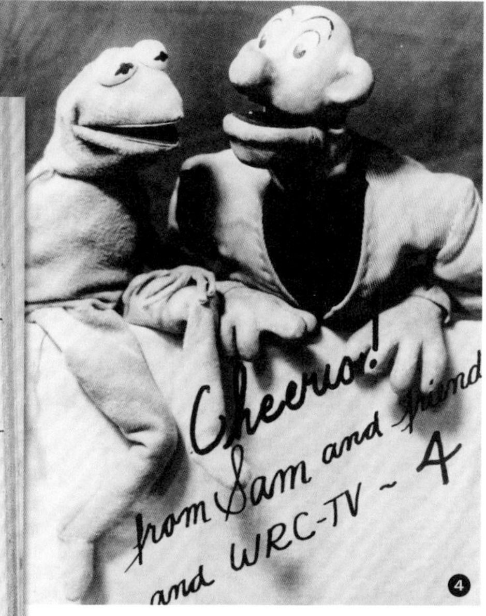

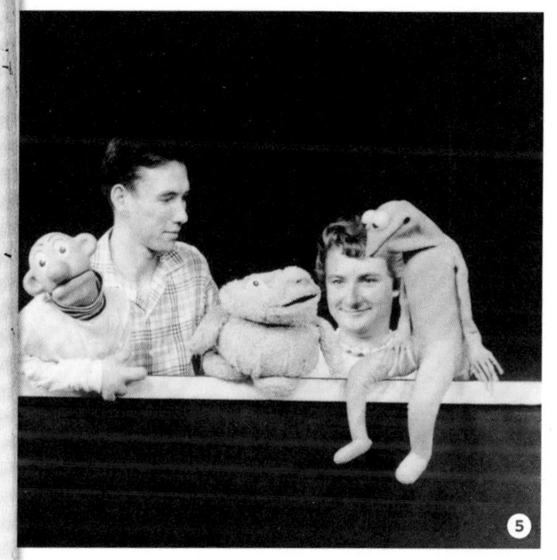

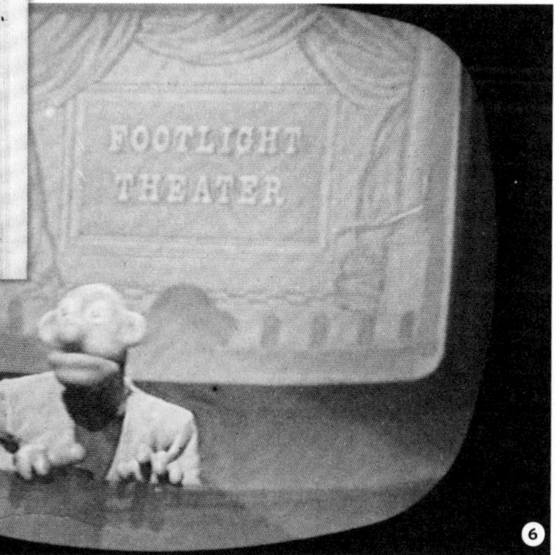

Sam + Friends on the Air MAY 9, 1955

The popularity of Jim's first characters, called Muppets from the start, prompted WRC executives to offer Jim his own program, *Sam and Friends*. The five-minute late-night show featured a repertory company of characters, including the nominal star Sam, a smartly dressed fellow whose unchanging face was set to constant surprise. One of Jim's earliest and more traditional puppets, Sam's face was frozen in a hard shell of papier-mâché. To create a more expressive character for the close-ups of the television camera, Jim made a puppet out of fabric and put it directly over his hand without any structure or stuffing. This was Kermit, and his flexibility allowed for incredibly accessible and believable performances.

❶ Early *TV Guide* ad featuring *Sam and Friends*. ❷ Sam. ❸ Jim and Jane with *Sam and Friends*. ❹ *Sam and Friends* title card drawn by Jim. ❺ Jim's sketch of Sam and Kermit.

❶

❷

SAM
and
FRIENDS

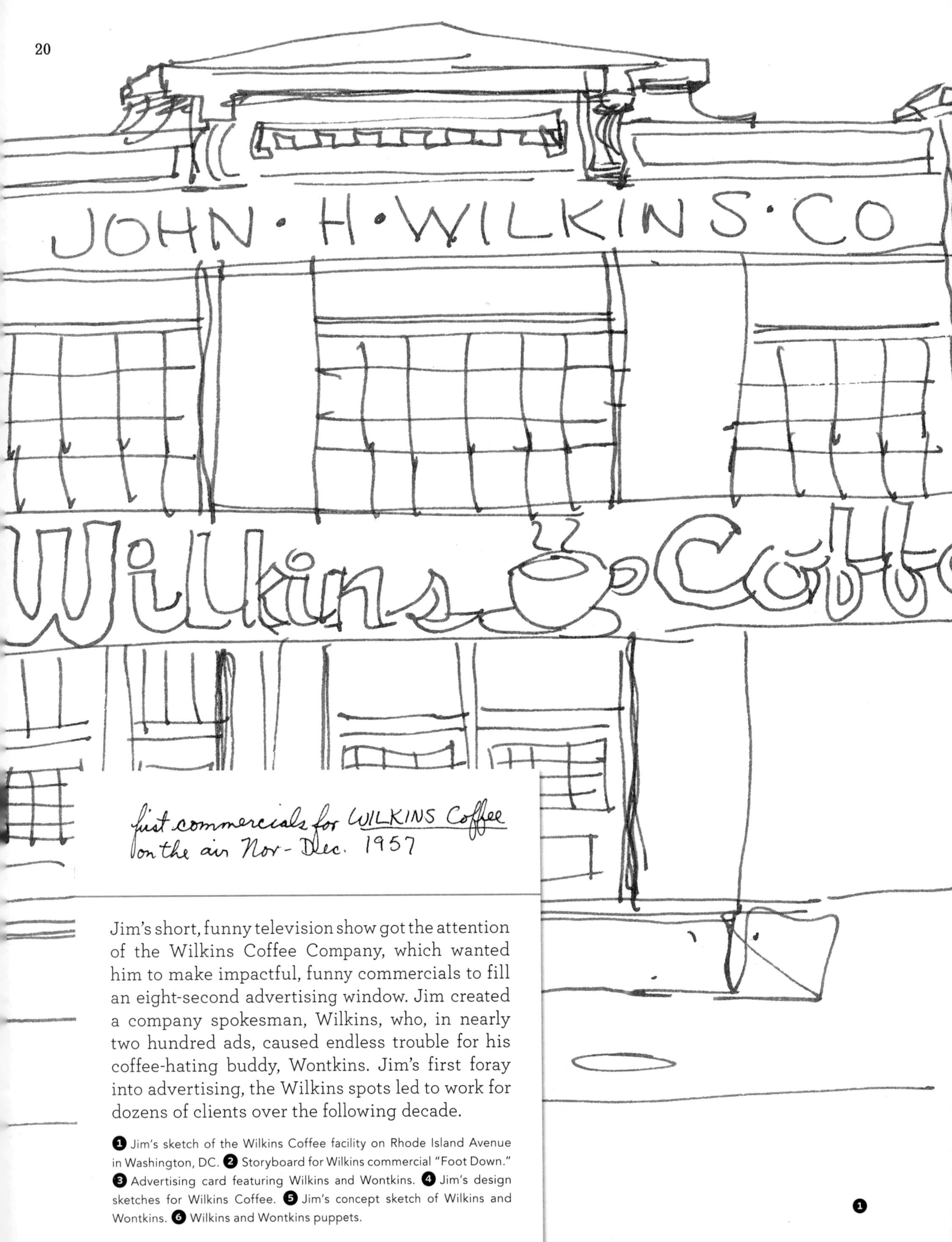

Jim's short, funny television show got the attention of the Wilkins Coffee Company, which wanted him to make impactful, funny commercials to fill an eight-second advertising window. Jim created a company spokesman, Wilkins, who, in nearly two hundred ads, caused endless trouble for his coffee-hating buddy, Wontkins. Jim's first foray into advertising, the Wilkins spots led to work for dozens of clients over the following decade.

❶ Jim's sketch of the Wilkins Coffee facility on Rhode Island Avenue in Washington, DC. ❷ Storyboard for Wilkins commercial "Foot Down." ❸ Advertising card featuring Wilkins and Wontkins. ❹ Jim's design sketches for Wilkins Coffee. ❺ Jim's concept sketch of Wilkins and Wontkins. ❻ Wilkins and Wontkins puppets.

❶

Wilkins
WILL:
WANT
A CUP OF
WILKINS COFFEE?

WONTKINS:
WHAT'LL MR. WILKINS
DO IF I DON'T?

165. FOOT DOWN
O.K.

(FOOT STOMPS ON
WONTKINS)
CRUNCH!

WILL:
OH, HE'LL
PROBABLY PUT
HIS FOOT DOWN.

"We're the Famous 'Muppets' As Seen
on WMAR-TV, CHANNEL 2!"
We Want to Remind You
to Remind Your Customers to Get
FAMOUS WILKINS COFFEE!
That's Right, Mr. Grocer, Be Sure That
Wilkins Regular Grind Coffee and
Wilkins Instant Coffee Are Always
Seen On Your Shelves . . .
Wilkins INSTANT coffee
Wilkins coffee REGULAR GRIND
Don't Miss Us "MUPPETS" Selling
For You On WMAR-TV, Channel 2,
Sunpapers Television

fres
fresh
Freshest coffee
taste in town

WILKINS

PAGE 8 NORTHERN VIRGINIA SUN

The Birth of a MUPPET

Jane and Jim Henson create a new Muppet—he's Theodore, an "announcer-type" character.

Photographed by Jack Hiller

(1) Jim checks out his idea.

(2) Mr. and Mrs. Henson discuss Theodore's dimensions.

1 (3) Cat George Washington wants in act.

(4) Character comes to life on paper.

2

June-Aug 1958 Jim trip to Europe
Local Academy TV arts + sciences Wash. D.C.
Best Local Entertainment Program 1958
Jane + I married May 28, 1959
MAY 9, 1960 - Lisa Marie Henson

Along with Jane, Jim brought in his friend Bob Payne to help with the many hours of planning, rehearsing, and puppet-making that went into each daily five-minute *Sam and Friends* show. Jim took a trip to Europe in 1958, literally leaving *Sam and Friends* in Jane and Bob's hands for a couple of months, and after returning, learned that his show had been nominated for a local Emmy award. Around that time, Jim and Jane became romantically involved, and they were married on May 28, 1959. Their first child (of five), Lisa, was born a year later.

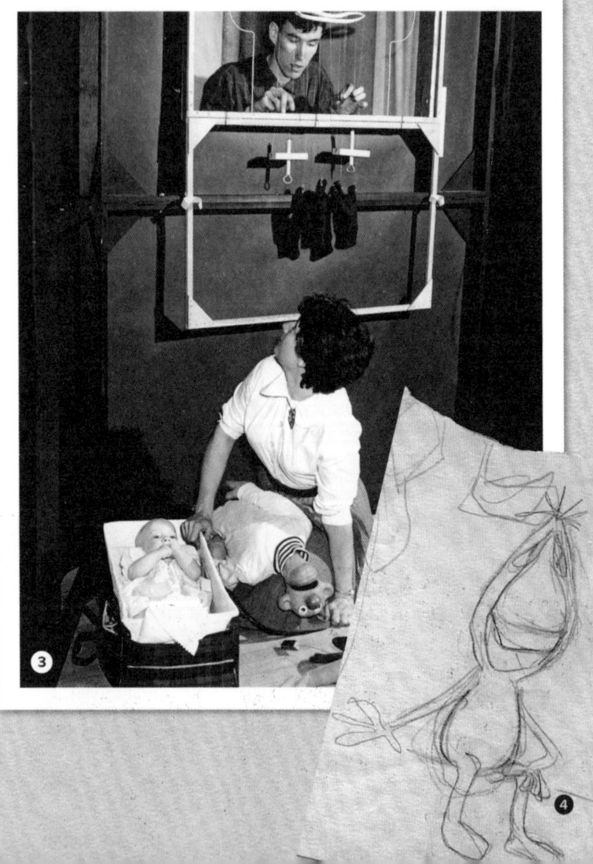

3

4

1 *The Northern Virginia Sun*'s story on Jim, Jane, and the creation of a Muppet. 2 Jim and Jane on their wedding day. 3 Jim and Jane with baby Lisa. 4 Jim's design for Chicken Liver, otherwise known as Theodore. 5 Jim's concept for his pr`omotional brochure.

ABSOLUTELY GREAT ★★ HILARIOUS
SOPHISTICATED.. CLEVER.. WITTY..
UNIQUE - REALLY SWELL
APPEALING
WAY OUT.. HYSTERICALLY FUNNY
LOVABLE
NEW AND DIFFERENT
LOVABLE
FASCINATING
NICE
INGENIOUS -
WHIMSICAL
INTELLECTUAL - WARM + CUDDLY
INCREDIBLY COMICAL
SUPERLATIVE
CUTE
EXPENSIVE
UNPRECEDENTED
INCOMPARABLE
PEACHY KEEN
MUPPETS

5

June 1960 - Vacation - first trip to Calif. - Disneyland - animation equipment.

After a busy first year of marriage that included their daily show, a myriad of commercials, the birth of their first child, and Jim's college graduation, the Hensons took a much-needed vacation. A huge Disney fan, Jim was excited to visit the theme park in Anaheim and see the work in three dimensions. Around the same time, he bought an animation stand and related equipment which he set up in their Bethesda, Maryland, home workshop. This allowed Jim to explore a medium beyond puppets, animating with paint under the camera or moving cut paper to a music track, and he launched a parallel career in experimental film.

❶ Cut-paper animation element for a musical short Jim called *Look Jazz, See Jazz.* ❷ Jim working at his animation stand. ❸ Jim's unrealized character concepts from 1960. ❹ Jim's notebook used to chart the animation to the soundtrack of *Time Piece.* ❺ Jim, Jane, and Lisa Henson in front of their Bethesda home. ❻ Jim's sketch of his Maryland home where he had his workshop. ❼+❽ Elements from an animated short about an ambitious grape, produced by Jim with Bob Payne.

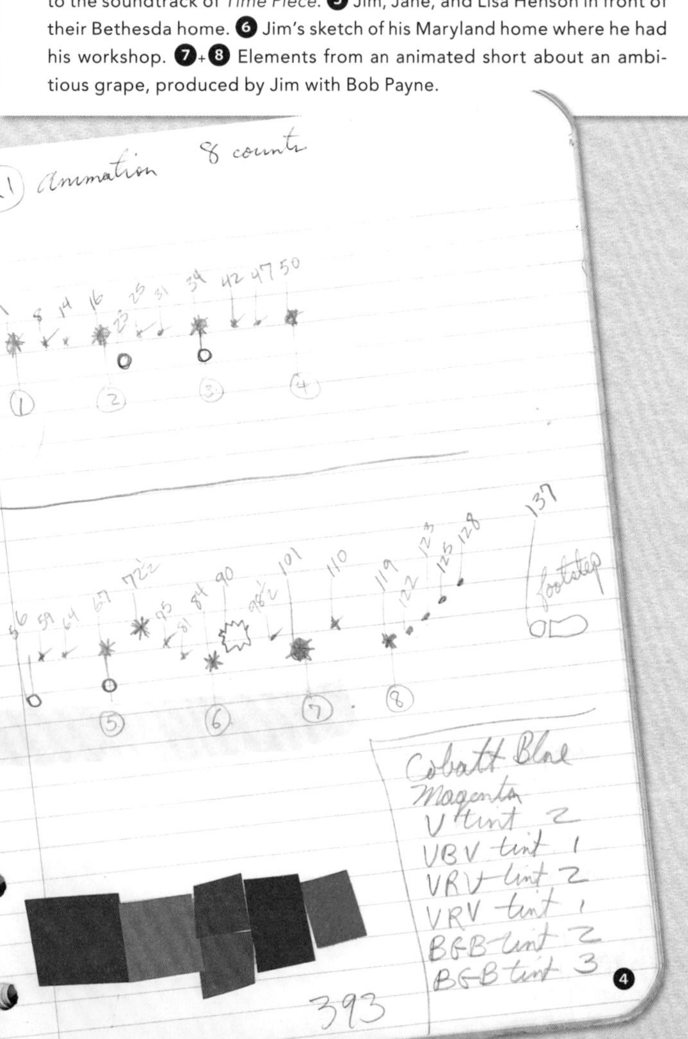

AUGUST 7, 1961 Cheryl Lee Henson

6

1

ALEXANDER
THE
GRAPE

TITLES

2

NARR: ONCE THERE WAS
A LITTLE GRAPE NAMED
ALEXANDER ----

7

ALEXANDER
THE
GRAPE

8

With a second child on the way, Jane limited her performing, and Jim was eager to fill the void. At the annual Puppeteers of America festival in Asilomar, California, he recruited Jerry Juhl who gladly moved east, working first as a puppeteer, but quickly moving into the head writer role. They traveled to Germany on behalf of the USDA and spent an intense ten days performing their inventive routines. Jim knew immediately that he had found an ideal collaborator in Jerry—their comic sensibilities and overall sense of decency matched well, and in the ensuing years, they would develop characters, stories, and worlds together.

❶ Jim's sketch of Jerry in Berlin. ❷ Jerry, Jim, and Jane with the *Sam and Friends* gang. ❸ Jim's snapshot of Jerry in Berlin. ❹ Jim and Jerry with the mechanical puppet they performed in Germany.

❶

2

3
FEB · 62 ·

Sam & Friends - Last show: Dec. 15, 1961

Videotaped "Tales of the Tinkerdee"
Atlanta June 1962

After *Sam and Friends,* Jim was eager to pursue longer-form programs. He saw the comic possibilities in combining traditional characters and stories with the Muppet sensibility and began to sketch witches, kings, princesses, and noblemen. In collaboration with Jerry Juhl, Jim made *Tales of the Tinkerdee,* a pilot for a series chronicling the activities of the court of King Goshposh as narrated by a minstrel played by Kermit. While it never aired, Jim continued to pitch projects in this vein, eventually using the characters in an industrial sales film and in the television specials, *Hey Cinderella!* and *The Frog Prince.*

❶ Shrinkel, Stretchel, and Taminella Grinderfall from a Pak-Nit industrial sales film. ❷ Jim's Hansel and Gretel puppets, late 1950s. ❸ Storyboard panel for *Rumple Wrinkle Shrinkel Stretchl Stiltzkin* industrial sales film for Pak-Nit. ❹ Jim's sketchbook concepts for Tinkerdee characters. ❺ Storyboard panel of Tinkerdee Kermit. ❻ Jim's set design for *Hansel and Gretel.* ❼ Jerry Juhl's script for *The Land of Tinkerdee*, 1964.

1

2

#3 (First episode)

2

dissolve

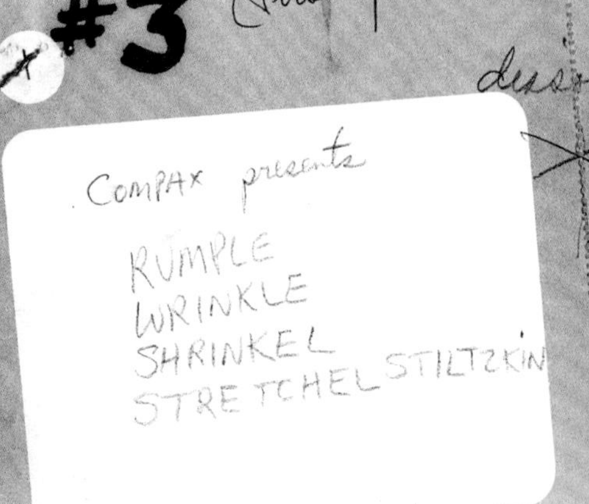

ANNCR: And now, Compax presents the Paknit Muppets in the story of ..
Rumple Wrinkel Shrinkel
Stretchelstiltzkin.

(MUSIC UP AND UNDER)

tomkins telapad — copyright 1950 Arthur Brown & Bro., Inc. N.Y.

Once upon a time, a king named Impossible the Third, threw a poor damsel into a dungeon
(SOUND EFFECT: GRUNT - THUD)
and said,

tomkins telapad — copyright 1950 Arthur Brown & Bro., Inc. N.Y.

3

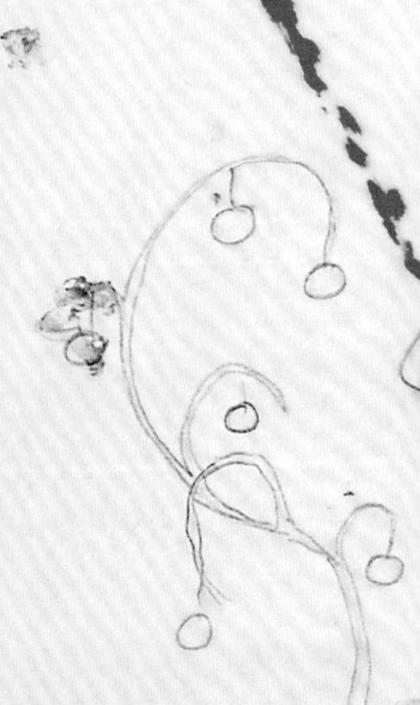

4

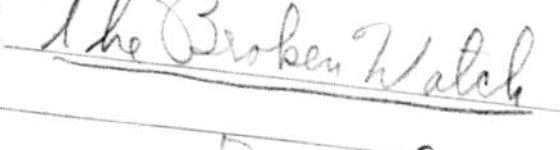

7

The Broken Watch

Parsyll greets the audience. He and
Rufus chat briefly. Then the King arrives.
He has brought with him a priceless ~~old~~ gold
watch which is a rare old family heirloom.
He asks Parsyll to clean it. He leaves.
Parsyll and Rufus examine the watch.
Then Parsyll discovers that he is out of
oil – so he goes to the store for some.
While Parsyll is gone Rufus tinkers
with the King's watch. The bell at the
town gate rings and Rufus goes outside
to answer it. Tammy is at the gate. She
wants to come in – she has to buy
some groceries. Rufus lets her in – but
warns her not to start any trouble.
Rufus goes back inside & toys with
the watch some more. Suddenly it slips
out of his hand and falls to the floor.
Rufus looks at the broken watch in horror.
Just then Parsyll returns. He asks Rufus
what happened. Rufus hems and haws
and finally says that Tammy did it.
He tells a wild tale of ~~Tam~~ the witch
suddenly appearing and smashing the
watch in anger. Parsyll thinks it
strange, but he believes Rufus.

5

6

ROWLF built - Nov-Dec. 1962

Moved to New York Jan. 23, 1963

Don Sahlin started to work regularly Feb. 1963

The creation of Rowlf, a laid-back philosophical hound, for a Purina Dog Chow commercial marked the further expansion of Jim's team and access to bigger opportunities. Puppet builder Don Sahlin was hired to interpret Jim's designs and create an expressive character. Don used the gloved-hand style pioneered by Jim for his *Tinkerdee* program instead of arm rods, enabling Rowlf to gesture naturally and hold props. Jim took to him immediately and developed a personality that made Rowlf irresistible to audiences. National television beckoned, and the whole Henson team made the move to New York, with Rowlf tugging at the leash.

❶ Jim and Jane Henson on the set of the Purina commercial. ❷ Jim's New York view, around the corner from his future apartment. ❸ Jim's sketches of Rowlf. ❹ Rowlf with his builder, Don Sahlin. ❺ Onky, another gloved-hand puppet made in 1962.

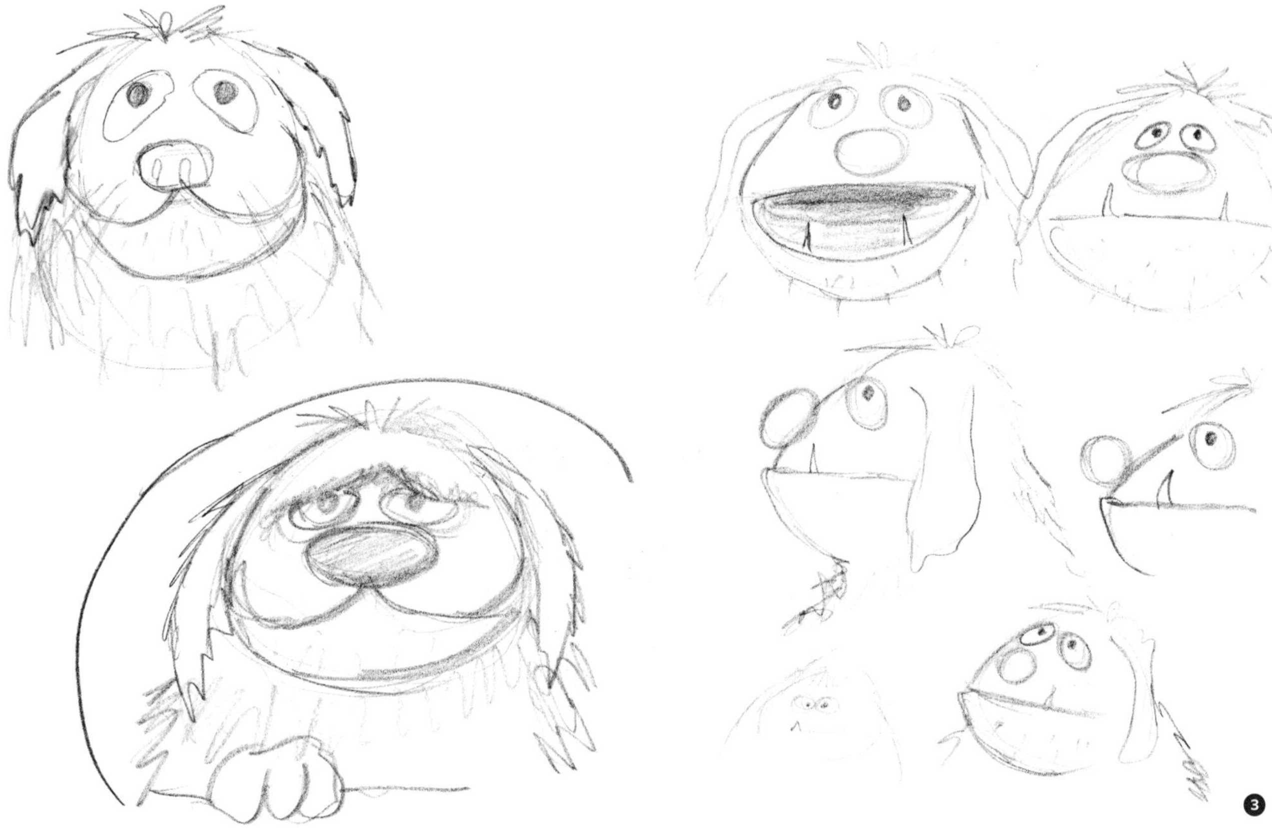

ON-COR
FROZEN FOODS
ON-COR
FAMILY-PACK
Gravy & Sliced Beef

NEW YORK AND NEW DIRECTIONS

1963–1969

JIM'S MOVE TO NEW YORK marked the start of an expansive period in his artistic and professional development. Audiences from coast to coast appreciated the subversive, offbeat humor of his characters' appearances on popular shows like *Today, The Jimmy Dean Show, The Tonight Show,* and *The Ed Sullivan Show*. Rowlf the Dog, Jim's laid-back alter ego, was everywhere—on variety shows, in industrial sales and meeting films, as a licensed toy, and, in 1967, as the host of his own summer show. Viewers responded warmly to Rowlf with fan mail and positive reviews, affirming Jim's talent for creating believable characters with expressive personalities. The press clamored to cover the Muppets, and the networks recognized the possibilities for longer-form television specials featuring Jim's creations.

Hundreds of short, anarchic commercials had been produced in Washington, DC, by Jim starting in 1957, providing an entrée into the world of Madison Avenue and its creative agencies. This led to a variety of lucrative advertising and industrial film work that allowed Jim to develop new types of characters with surprising personalities and to experiment with state-of-the-art technologies, a range of puppetry techniques, and novel thematic approaches to selling a product.

The Henson team was further expanded by the addition of two puppeteers—a teenage Frank Oz, who started in 1963 by performing Rowlf's right paw and would become Jim's closest performing partner and best friend; and in 1965, Jerry Nelson, a virtuoso actor, voice artist, and singer whose puppetry came naturally and whose relaxed personality meshed well with the group. Jim was the ringleader, and working together, the group realized Jim's vision in three dimensions and on the screen.

Along with the Muppets, Jim had a parallel outlet for his creative energies. Having acquired a Bolex 16mm camera and animation equipment, Jim eagerly pursued other methods of expressing himself on film. He painted under the camera, filmed cut paper as it danced to jazz riffs and syncopated rhythms, and shot abstract footage of lights, trees, and city streets. This led to existential live-action shorts, including *Time Piece* in 1964, which was nominated for an Oscar, and hour-long documentary or dramatic pieces that aired as *Experiment in Television*. Tempted to focus on his live-action filmmaking career and pursue grown-up projects like a psychedelic nightclub, the decade ended with a tug back to puppets. Jim was invited to participate in the development of a revolutionary children's show, *Sesame Street*, which premiered in November 1969.

1 Jim's concept for a Halloween special, c. 1969.

aug. 1963 - FRANK OZnowcy started to work

aug 29, 1963 taped Show A - Jimmy Dean
JIMMY DEAN SHOW - Sept 1963

Having met Jim back in 1961, Frank Oz was now nineteen and ready to accept Jim's job offer and join him in New York. For the launch of *The Jimmy Dean Show* on ABC, Frank began performing Rowlf's right paw while Jim performed the head and left paw. This marked the start of an extraordinary partnership resulting in some of the most inventive comic duos developed for television: Ernie and Bert, Kermit and Miss Piggy, and the head and hands of the Swedish Chef. But Rowlf led the way. From the first show, the network received piles of fan mail for Rowlf and signed a long-term commitment. Rowlf was an immediate star, integral to the show's successful three-year run.

❶ Early press highlighting Rowlf's popularity, 1963. ❷ Frank Oz, Rowlf, and Jim, mid-1960s. ❸ Rowlf with Jimmy Dean, about 1964. ❹ *Jimmy Dean Show* script for Rowlf by Frank Peppiatt and John Aylesworth. ❺ Rowlf and Jimmy Dean, 1964. ❻ The Hensons' house in Greenwich, Connecticut.

He's a Hound for Fun

Rowlf, the Muppet hound, did one guest shot on The Jimmy Dean Show on ABC-TV, and he was in like Flynn. Now he's a regular who outstrips Star Dean in the fan mail department. He is the creation of Jim Henson, bearded Muppet-producing puppeteer. Henson is Rowlf's voice and works his left arm. The right arm is worked by Puppeteer Frank Oznowicz. Rowlf is madly in love with Lassie, who has twice appeared on the show with him.

❶

❷

❸

Oct. 17, 1963

51

You're Just in Love

JIMMY & ROWLF

ROWLF:

I'M IN THE MOOD FOR LOVE
SIMPLY BECAUSE SHE'S NEAR ME
(CAMERA PULLS BACK REVEALING
JIMMY SEATED BESIDE ROWLF.)

JIMMY:

Hi, Rowlf. You sound mighty happy.

ROWLF:

Well, I am ... and I'm not! I've got problems of the heart.

JIMMY

(POINTEDLY) You mean -- !?

ROWLF:

(SADLY) Yes, Jimmy .. I'm in love.

JIMMY:

Why, that's wonderful, Rowlf. But are you sure it's not just puppy love?

ROWLF:

No, Jimmy, it's definitely not puppy love.

JIMMY:

Why not?

ROWLF:

'Cause Im in love with a cat, that's why.

4

5

6

sept 1963 - build Rufus

Nov 3 - Brian born

MOVED TO GREENWICH, CONN.
April 6-7, 1964

A bearded man's head is served on a platter in
TIMEPIECE
Academy Award Nominated Short Film

A bearded man flies like a bird in
TIME PIECE,
Academy Award Nominated Short Film.

A bearded man pogo sticks through heavy traffic in
TIMEPIECE
Academy Award Nominated Short Film

A bearded man dressed like Tarzan runs up Fifth Avenue in
TIME PIECE,
Academy Award Nominated Short Film. ❶

TIME PIECE ❷

began TIMEPIECE May, 1964

Working from his elaborate hand-drawn twenty-four-page storyboard, Jim began production on an eight-and-a-half-minute experimental film, *Time Piece*, which would earn him a 1965 Academy Award nomination. Without dialogue but painstakingly timed to a rhythmic soundtrack, Jim's comedic drama focused on the frustrations of the Everyman as he raced with the clock while facing the challenges of modern life. Jim was producer, director, writer, and star, presenting his vision with quick-cut editing, animated sequences, and touches of irreverent humor. Jim's core team worked with him on the project, but all agree that this was a very personal effort.

april 25, 1965 - John Paul Born

❶ Attention-grabbing ads for *Time Piece* that ran in *Variety* during the Oscar race. ❷ Promotional brochure featuring a winged Jim. ❸ Jim's planning notes. ❹ Jim after diving into a pool for a scene from *Time Piece*. ❺ *Time Piece* storyboard panel. ❻ Jerry Juhl and Frank Oz on location in New York.

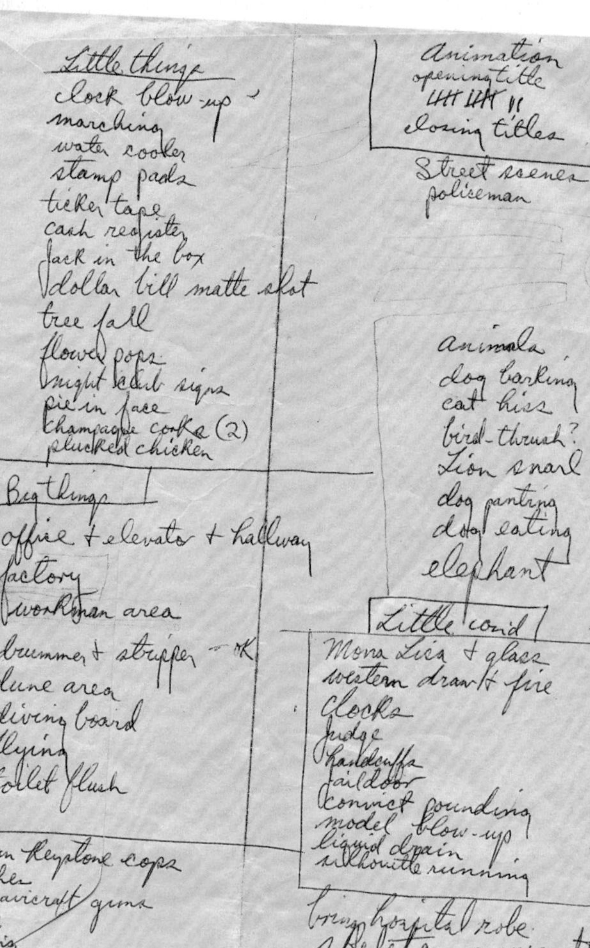

Little things
clock blow-up
marching
water cooler
stamp pads
ticker tape
cash register
jack in the box
dollar bill matte shot
tree fall
flower pops
night club signs
pie in face
champagne corks (2)
plucked chicken

Big things
office + elevator + hallway
factory
workman area
drummer + stripper – ok
dune area
diving board
flying
toilet flush

...ian Keystone cops
...ther
...-aircraft guns
...e
...nis
...k in mud

Animation
opening title
HHT HHT II
closing titles

Street scenes
policeman

animals
dog barking
cat hiss
bird-thrush?
Lion snarl
dog panting
dog eating
elephant

Little cond
Mona Lisa + glass
western draw + fire
clocks
judge
handcuffs
jaildoor
connect pounding
model blow-up
liquid drain
silhouette running

bring hospital robe
skeleton marionette

3

4

May 6, 1965 first screening of
★ TIMEPIECE ★
Museum of Modern art

July 8 +
July 28 – tape 3 Al Hirt "Fanfare"

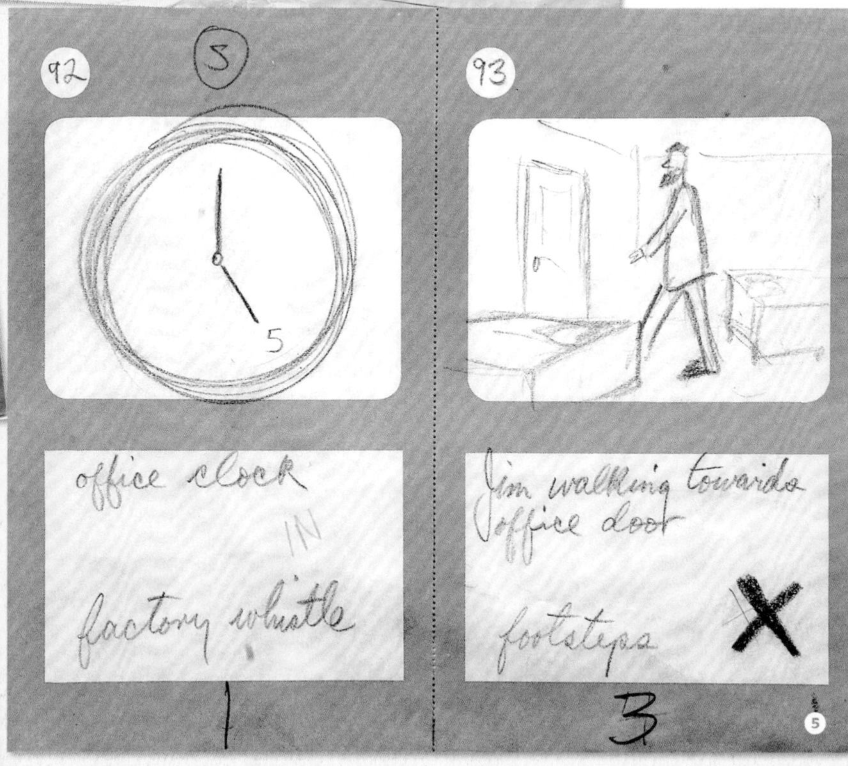

5

6

1965

Aug 23 - 27 - shoot 6 commercials for WILSON'S MEATS and a sales film also shoot 8 commercials for CLAUSSEN'S BREAD - all COLOR

Sept 27 - 29 shoot 8 spots for Southern Bread - 35mm color

Oct 31 - Nov 2 - shoot presentation film + 7 spots for La Choy

Nov. 22 - 24 shoot 4 spots for Aurora using Jane's hand

By the mid-1960s, Jim was fully engaged in the world of advertising, transforming his local Washington, DC, coffee commercials into campaigns for numerous clients. Along with the eight-second ads that had been so successful, Jim began to explore longer formats, using an array of distinctive characters and offbeat techniques. For Wilson's Meats of Chicago and the Carolina-based Claussen's Bakeries, Jim followed his original "buy it or else" formula. He also created a Southern Colonel character who took great risks on behalf of the Southern Bakery and a clumsy but enthusiastic dragon for La Choy. For the delicate job of selling Aurora brand toilet paper to TV audiences, Jim took a more abstract approach featuring an expressive gloved hand.

❶ Jim's storyboard for a Wilson's Meats commercial with the requisite bad pun. ❷ Don Sahlin and Jerry Juhl help the La Choy Dragon breathe fire. ❸ Jim's design for the La Choy dragon. ❹ Jim's design for the Southern Colonel. ❺ The Southern Colonel braves the train tracks for Southern Bread. ❻ Photo storyboard for Aurora bath tissue showing the gloved hand.

Dec 1 + 5 tape 2 Dean shows in Hollywood with Jerry Nelson

Dec 12 - tape Perry Como Christmas Show with 5 Reindeer - fairly good

American Can Company (Consumer Products Sales Division)
Aurora Bath Tissue
NAT-30-539 "Discovering" :30

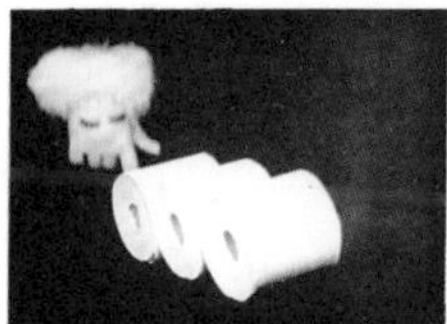

2. (Music under, Wm VO) Don't let ...

3. ...anything ...

4. ...stop you ...

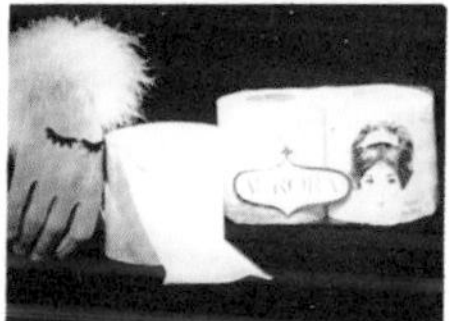

5. ...from discovering the softness of Aurora.

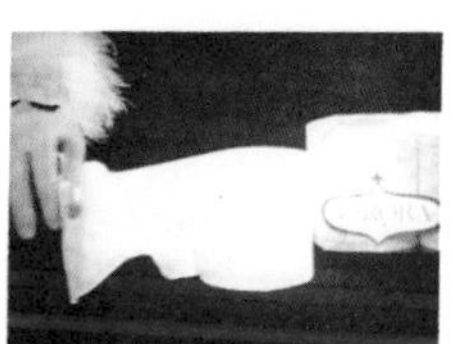

6. Two layers of softness.

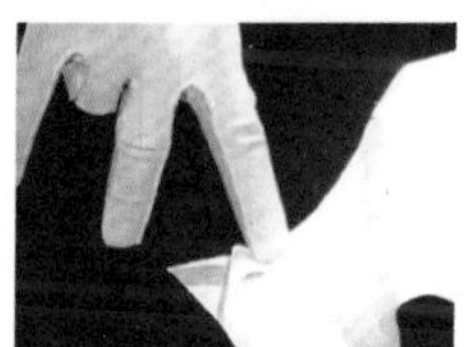

7. One layer a pretty pastel, ...

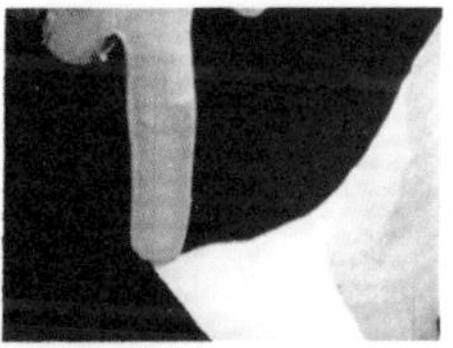

8. ...the other – purest white.

9. Soft to the touch.

10. Softly scented, too.

11. (Music)...

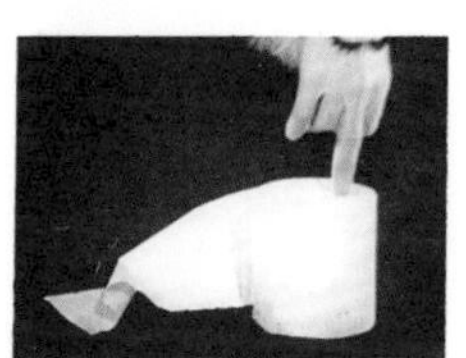

12. ...

13. The whole point is...

14. ...Aurora ...

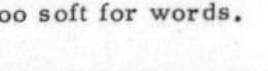

15. ...is too soft for words.

1965
Dec 31 - New Years Eve - Tonight Show (live)
Let Me In + Glow Worm - fair
1966
Jan 13 - Tonight Show - Money + Sclrap Flyap

Dec 29 pick up New Pontiac Station Wagon (1966) and drive to Washington to visit Mom + Dad overnight

Jim felt at home on late-night television, having performed his Washington, DC, show in the 11:25 p.m. time slot, leading right into *The Tonight Show*. Steve Allen, the first host of *Tonight*, was quick to see the Muppets' tremendous appeal and hosted them as early as 1956. Jim returned to the show at least seventeen times, rotating various bits from his repertoire. A staple was "Glow Worm," in which Kermit tried to eat a small worm that turned out to be the nose of a very hungry monster. "Sclrap Flyap" was an abstract piece featuring three exploding creatures in a smoky, extraterrestrial landscape, and the Stan Freberg song "Money" was a send-up of the money-hungry, parodying the quest for the Almighty Dollar.

❶+❷+❸ Jim's character designs for "Sclrap Flyap." ❹ Jim's lyric sheet for "Money" with notes regarding props. ❺ Jim's 45 rpm record of "Money." ❻ Jim and his tongue-in-cheek sculpture, *Shrine to the Almighty Dollar*. ❼ Jerry Juhl, Don Sahlin, and Jane Henson perform "Sclrap Flyap" on *The Today Show* in 1963. ❽ The "Sclrap Flyap" puppets.

❶

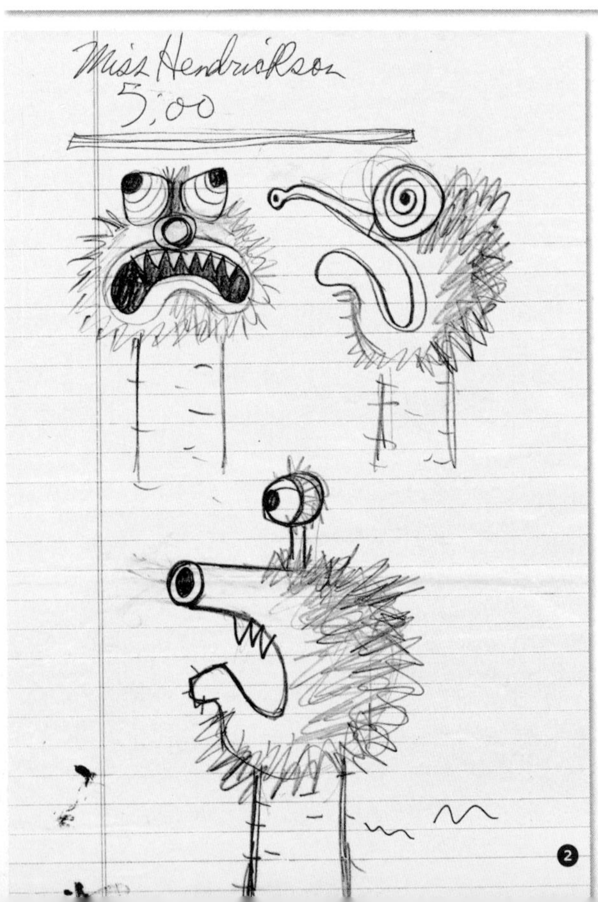

❷

❸

_ _ _ Y

COINS
Don't want no lovin' - don't want no kissin',
Don't want no gal to call me "Honey".
Don't want my name in the Hall of Fame,
Just want a big fat pile of money.

DOLLAR
Give me that almighty dollar; for that lettuce hear me hollar,
Give me buckets full of ducets, let me walk around and waller
In mazooma, el dinero; want to be a millionero,
Give me money, money, money, money, money.

WALLET
I want that green ammunition, that's the stuff for which I'm wishin',
Fill my closets with deposits - I'm a demon in addition,
Give me sheckels, give me pesos - let me see their smilin' faceos.
Money, money, money, money, money.

PIGGY BANK
I want to get me a suit, that's made out of loot,
And whistle the "Wearin' of the Green".
I've got that monetaryitus, like to be just like King Midas,
Want that golden touch is what I mean.

SHIRT
Give me that old double eagle, want that tender that is legal,
And financially, substantially any sum I can inveigle.
Want to live in regal splendor, with that lovin' legal tender,
Give me money, money, money, money, money.

BANK BAG
I'm a greenback collector, I'm a paper bill inspector,
I'm a savage for that cabbage; Man, to me it's golden nectar.
Pour that filthy lucre on me, spread those lovin' germs upon me,
Give me money, money, money, money, money.

EVERY-WHERE
Just let me roll 'round upon it, stuff those bank rags in my bonnet,
Any kind, just so some president has got his picture on it.
Let me feel it, let me hold it, let me sit there and fold it,
Give me money, money, money.

PLATE
And if they ever plant trees of e pluribus unum,
I want to be the guy that they send out to prune 'em,
Money, money, etc.

4

5

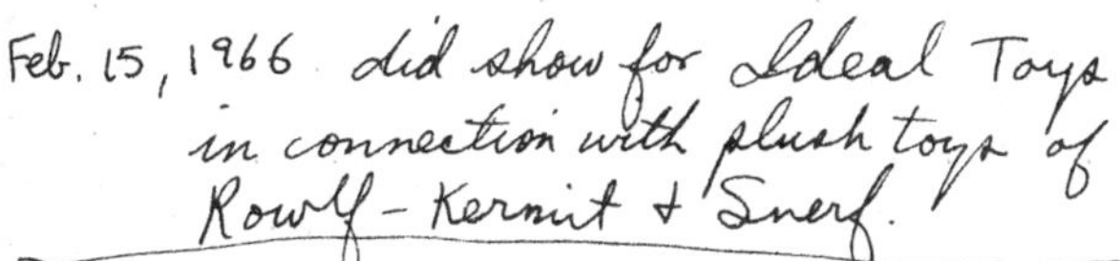
Feb. 15, 1966 did show for Ideal Toys in connection with plush toys of Rowlf - Kermit + Snerf.

FEB. 17 - heard that TIMEPIECE Nominated for Academy Award

6

7

8

1966

FEB. 21 - filmed one minute pilot commercial for Wheels, Crowns + Flutes.

The request from General Foods Canada to make a test commercial for their snack products Wheels, Crowns, and Flutes inspired Jim to design an array of monsters who could eat convincingly on camera. He wanted his big-eyed Wheel Stealer to be "able to feed himself," so builder Don Sahlin made it possible by combining Rowlf's gloved-hand puppet style with a tube down the puppeteer's sleeve. They also created the Crown Grabber and the Flute Snatcher in contrasting shapes, but it is the Wheel Stealer that has enjoyed the longest life—after several incarnations for other commercials, he evolved into our favorite insatiable eater, Cookie Monster.

❶ Jim's design of two monsters, the Flute Snatcher and the Wheel Stealer, for General Foods. ❷ The Wheel Stealer, the Flute Snatcher, and the Crown Grabber created for General Foods. ❸+❹ The monster that ate the machine in Jim's 1968 IBM meeting film. ❺ Jim's 1963 idea for a big-eyed monster. ❻ Jim's sketch of a fuzzy monster in an alien landscape from 1963. ❼ Storyboard panel featuring Arnold the Munching Monster for a Munchos commercial for Frito-Lay.

Video:

(D)

(ARNOLD SMASHES A HOLE IN
Audio: WALL IN FRUSTRATION)

ARNOLD: <u>LOVE</u> MUNCHOS!

MARCH 1-6 - in Los Angeles - tape
2 spots on Hollywood Palace.
"Music Hath Charms - Air March 19
"Glow Worm - Air - April 30

DEAR MOM. IT'S HARD TO BELIEVE THAT I'VE BEEN WITH IBM FOR 9 FULL MONTHS. YOU KNOW, I REALLY WANT TO GET AHEAD IN THIS COMPANY.

SO I'VE BEEN WORKING NIGHTS ON AN IDEA FOR THEIR TELEVISION ADVERTISING. OF COURSE, THIS IS SOMETHING I'VE BEEN DOING ON MY OWN, BUT I'VE WORKED OUT A WHOLE SERIES OF COMMERCIALS FOR THEM.

SCRIPT NO: One
TITLE: IN WHICH ROWLF TAKES ON A NEW CHALLEN
FINDS HAPPINESS IN AN ET/DE SALES MAN
TIME: Approximately 2:30
FOR: IBM
DATE: 2nd Feburary 1966
303 EAST 53RD STREET NEW YORK 22 PL. 2 1949

(Rowlf is seated at an ancient battered typewriter pounding out a letter. He speaks the words as he type

ROWLF: (Narrating)

Dear Mom.

I have wonderful news. Your son, Rowlf, has a new job. Now I know you're used to thinking of me as a big TV star . . .

(Camera has zoomed into page being typed. Dissolve to a series of quick shots showing Rowlf performing on THE JIMMY DEAN SHOW, the audience applauding, Rowlf stepping out of theatre and signing autographs, climbing into limousine and lighting a cigar with a ten-dollar bill)

. . . leading a life of excitement, fame, riches . . .

(Dissolve back to Rowlf at typewriter)

. . . But now I have a really interesting job. — I'm a salesman for IBM!!! Believe me, it's a wonderful feeling. Now when you're hired by IBM, before you start working as a salesman . . .

(Zoom into page. Dissolve to Rowlf in front of IBM Training Center)

Continued . . .

1966

around MARCH 21 – deliver final prints to IBM of 4 short films, starring Rowlf. IBM ecstatic

The four short films that Jim delivered marked the start of a long relationship with IBM and the beginning of a professional collaboration and friendship with David Lazer, IBM's audio-visual program manager. Rowlf was recruited as an IBM salesman, and over the course of those four films made to liven up a sales meeting, he progressed from an ancient battered typewriter to an IBM Selectric, then the speedy MT/ST, and finally an IBM portable dictation machine, enthusiastically damaging equipment along the way. He starred in additional films for IBM in the ensuing years, entertaining the sales force, destroying more products, and opening doors to other Henson work for the company.

❶ Panels from Jim's storyboard for an IBM film. ❷ The first Rowlf IBM script written by Jerry Juhl. ❸ Jim on set for IBM with a guitar he decorated for Rowlf. ❹ The astrological chart drawn by Jim and used by Rowlf in his role as Lorenzo Shazam in 1970. ❺ David Lazer with Rowlf, Jim, and Jerry Juhl.

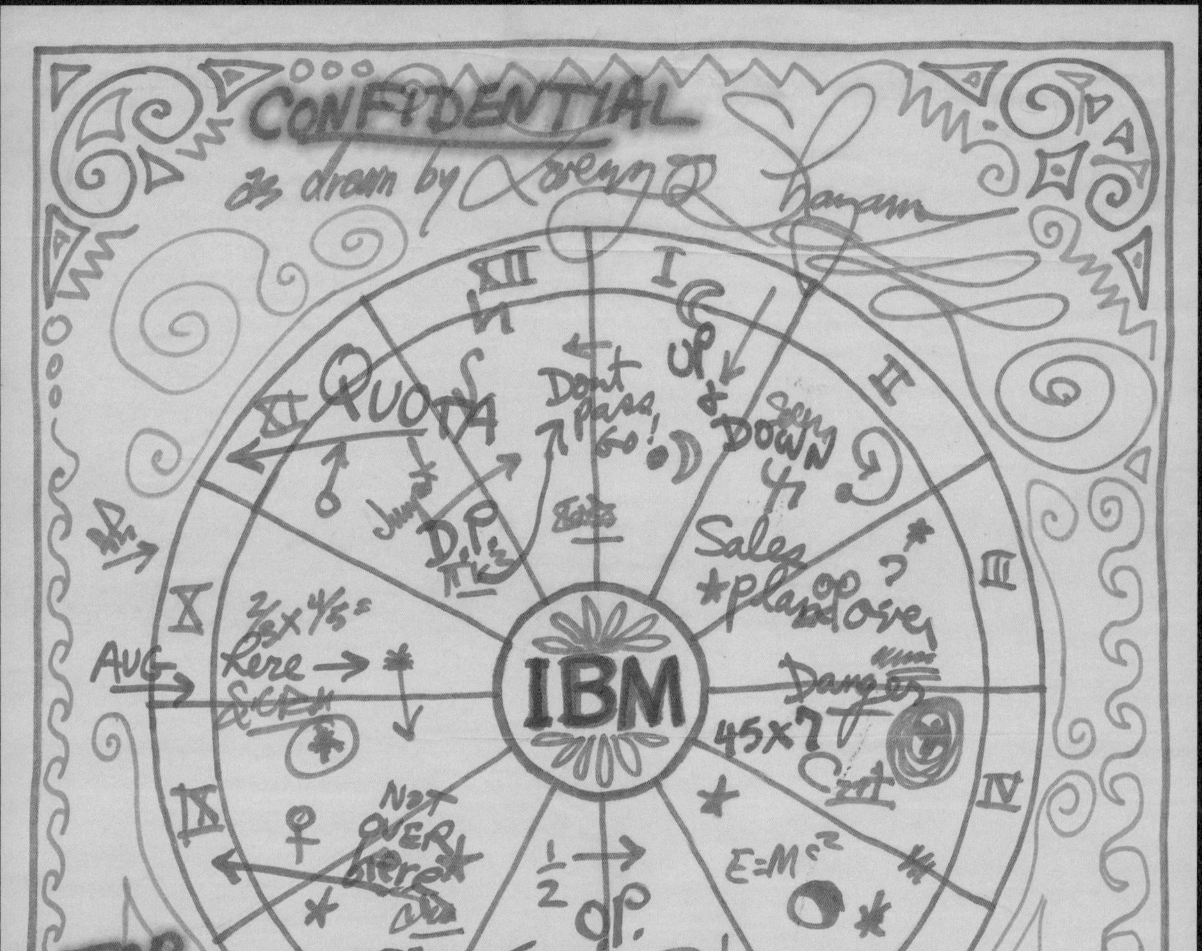

CONFIDENTIAL

QUOTA

Don't Pass GO!

UP & DOWN

Sales plan

IBM

Danger

45 x 7

AUG

NOT OVER here

E=MC²

½ OP.

NOTE

NO LEFT TURN

TOP SECRET

1970 - Horoscope
14 Lat 3° NxNW

4

5

MARCH 25, 1966 - tape our last Jimmy Dean Show

April 18. Oscars - in L.A. with Jane

MAY 10 - 12 in Nassau with Jerry + Jerry to do appearance with Rowlf + his Mother for IBM Golden Circle - (won $75 gambling)

1966

Commercials-June-July Aug-FHA-Southern
Wilson's-Southern Bell-RC.
Jerry writing Santa Claus Switch

The Washington, DC, airwaves put Jim in the sights of a steady advertising client, the Federal Housing Administration, and he made numerous public service announcements for them. The earliest were eight-second spots, but he quickly branched out to thirty and sixty seconds and created an array of new characters like a talking house (inspiring a *Muppet Show* sketch a decade later) and a ghoulish monster. Performer Jerry Nelson, with his impressive musical talent, joined the team, allowing for more complex situations for a range of other advertisers including the Southern Bell Telephone Company and Royal Crown Cola. In the meantime, Jerry Juhl began to rewrite a 1963 script for an original Christmas special that would eventually shoot and air in 1970.

❶ Jim's Falling Down House character designed for an FHA public service announcement. ❷ Jim and Don Sahlin on set with executives from the FHA. ❸ Jim's FHA public service announcement storyboard. ❹ Jim's FHA idea for a character that anticipates a certain grouch on *Sesame Street*. ❺ Nutty Bird designed by Jim for the Royal Crown Cola campaign.

❶

❷

❸
#3-"FALLING HOUSE"

SCOOP: (DRIVING UP)
SAY FELLA, ...YOUR HOUSE COULD USE SOME REPAIRS.

SKIP:
I KNOW. BUT I CAN'T AFFORD IT.

SCOOP:
DON'T BE TOO SURE. FHA INSURED HOME IMPROVEMENT LOANS ARE ECONOMICAL AND EASY TO GET.

FOR A
CONSUM
WRITE -
IMPROV
DEPART
FHA,

#3
FHA
SKIP:
BY GEORGE, I WILL....
(HE RUNS INTO HOUSE)
FHA
SKIP:
....BEFORE IT'S TOO.... (STILT BREAKS)
LAAAATTTTEE EEE
FHA

Sept 18, 1966 – 1st Ed Sullivan Show – Rock + Roll Monsters

The Muppets' popularity on variety shows made it inevitable that Ed Sullivan would tap them for his highly visible program. For the first of what would be twenty-five appearances, Jim and his team created a three-headed monster (requiring three puppeteers) that played rock 'n' roll. He rounded out a diverse program that included an opera duet, the comedy of both Red Buttons and Jackie Mason, Polynesian dancing, and popular music performed by Herman's Hermits and the bilingual Nancy Ames. Over the ensuing years, this eclectic mix inspired Jim to present both classic bits from his *Sam and Friends* days and to try out new characters like the abstract Java or the hipster Mahna Mahna on the show.

❶ Ed Sullivan with Jim and Kermit. ❷ Jim's drawing of the dryer-hose puppets performing to Al Hirt's rendition of "Java." ❸ A selection of characters from Jim's variety show repertory company. ❹ Jim's design for the Rock 'n' Roll Monster. ❺ Jim's idea for a father and son monster bit. ❻ Another *Ed Sullivan Show* bit, The String Quartet.

❶

Oct 9 - Shooting Cyclia footage - Gabi
Oct. - wrote "The Cube" with Jerry - NBC rejected
Oct 23 - Sullivan - "Father + Son Monster"?
Oct 25 - shoot Big La Choy Dragon in Wash
Nov 27 - Sullivan - "Glow worm?"
Nov 28 - film more aurora - used Lisa in one

1967 shooting 2 competition shorts for Expo film festival—"Wheels" & "Ripples" →

March-6- filming LINIT

March-April - pitching Santa Claus Switch everybody rejects

In several commercials, the charming Sir Linit, with his iron-shaped feet and pseudo-Elizabethan tongue, skated across the ironing board, making quick work of wrinkled clothes. Built as both a hand puppet and a marionette by Don Sahlin, Sir Linit promised, "Forsooth, one merely sprayeth and ironeth. The iron sticketh not and it scorcheth not." Ad executive Bill Ballard originally suggested a character called "Linit-Man," "a Johnny-on-the-spot like a minuteman." Jim and Jerry Juhl put their heads together and came up with, "a sort of parody of the White Knight, blowing his trumpet (always flat), and speaking with 'forsooths,' 'odds bodkins,' 'whence cometh,' 'hey, nonny nonny,' etc." The agency liked it and Sir Linit was born.

❶ Stop-motion knights created by Jim and Don Sahlin for a *Sesame Street* counting film in 1970. ❷ As a teenager, Jim drew this cartoon featuring his idea of a heroic knight. ❸ Jim's design for Sir Linit. ❹ Sir Linit with his namesake product. ❺ Sir Linit in action.

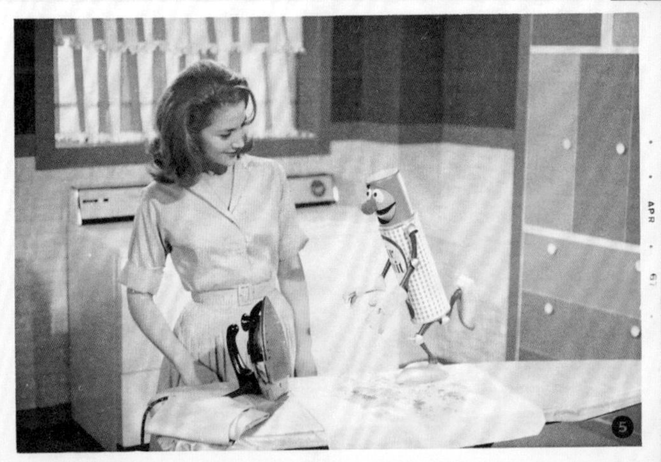

april-May-June-10 "Our Place" Show with Doodletown Pipers, Burns & Schreiber
June 4- Sullivan.
Visual Thinking
June 3- do thing for Bristol Myers-

July 1967 – Jim in L.A. with Barry C. showing Cyclia

Along with film and television, Jim sought other ways to integrate sound, light, and movement while exploring the bold graphics, revolutionary music, and psychedelic styles of the mid-'60s. For several years, he worked on Cyclia, a dome-shaped multimedia nightclub, where patrons would enjoy a full sensory experience of music synchronized to rapidly changing images projected onto faceted screens. Between sets, dancers could move around a floor pulsing with colored lights. Jim and his colleagues shot hours of footage that included wooded landscapes, speeding traffic, falling water, and the crowds at Shea Stadium to be matched to gentle ballads or driving rock music. He scouted locations and designed furniture, but his vision remained unrealized as he moved on to other ventures.

❶ An annotated photo of a test ceiling for Cyclia. ❷ Jim's idea was to project images on both the faceted ceiling and on dancers dressed in white bodysuits. ❸ Jim's design for the faceted ceiling. ❹ Jim's design for the Cyclia dome exterior. ❺ Furniture designs for Cyclia.

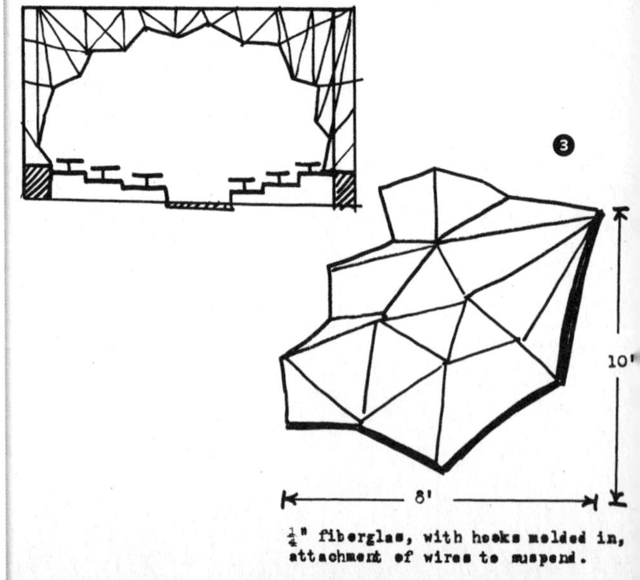

4

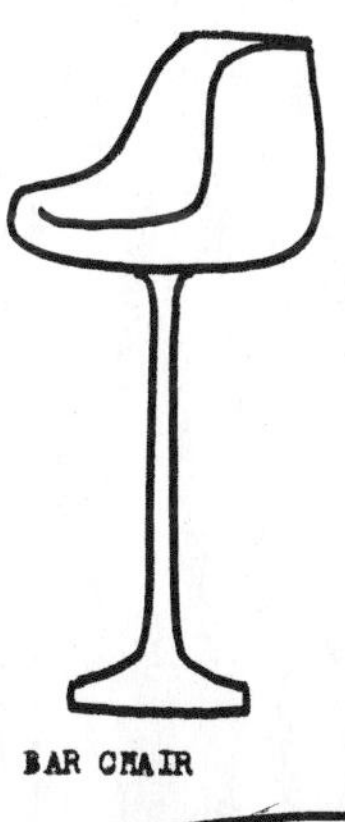

5

Oct 8 - Sullivan - "Monster eats Machine"

Oct - filming 2 La Choy's in N.Y. -
- also shooting IBM "Paperwork Explosion"
filming Bufferin commercial with
Johnny + Cheryl in Wash.

BAR CHAIR

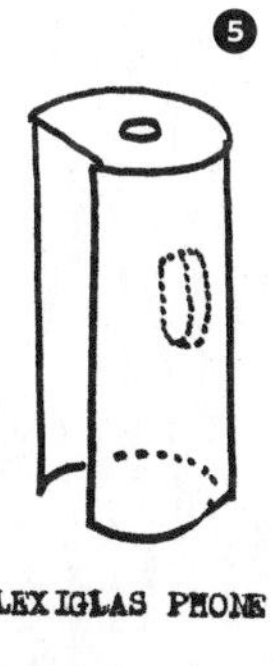

PLEXIGLAS PHONE BOOTH

MIRRORED*SURFACE TABLE

1968

Feb. 26 begin filming Youth 68 – in NYC travel to SanFrancisco – L.A. – Houston – Omaha + Miami – finish in NYC mid March

Feb 13+14 VTR Youth 68 in studio

Sun April 21 · 4:00 P.M AIR Youth 68

NBC's *Experiment in Television* series showcasing new talent and new ideas allowed Jim to pursue his interest in exploring youth culture in a unique format. Billed as "an exciting mixed-media portrait of youth today," his program, *Youth '68*, was a visual and sound collage interweaving interviews, literary quotations, popular music, and modern dance. The fast-paced documentary addressed such topics as drugs, religion, race relations, war, and the future, and featured appearances by a variety of rock groups. By interviewing people of all ages around the country, Jim, without editorializing, attempted to demonstrate the juxtaposition of different value systems within the context of a changing world, creating a portrait of society as a whole.

❶ Promotional photo for *Youth '68*. ❷ Jim's list of Los Angeles interviews with musicians for *Youth '68*. ❸ Young people interviewed for *Youth '68*. ❹ Interview transcripts cut up and pasted together to create Jim's editing script for *Youth '68*. ❺ Dance sequence from *Youth '68*.

3/1

ROLL
28 100' 7242 } The Happy Apples session
29 100' "
—
31 100' "
32 100' "
33 100' "
34 400' 7255 – Interviews – The Happy Apples
1. Jim De Marco – manager in control room
2. Jim Pitman – lead guitar w/coffee
3. Dick Russell – pianist – outside w/cas
35 400' 7255 } interview – Jefferson Airplane
36 400' "
37 400' "
38 400' 7242 } interviews The Free Clinic
39 400' 7242
40 400' 7242 } interviews – Tandyna Party
41 400' "
42 300' "
Tiny
Dale – bass
– drummer

❷

❸

May 20 VTR Sullivan Show-Java

2

question - exciting time to live?

oh I think any time you live is exciting

it's just yeah, it's exciting now

but it was exciting for the breakthroughs in the past for youth

109-7 P. U of Omaha red hair girl 1103 it's oh, youth is always an exciting time, A

1104. I mean W?

question

5-7 prof. type 87. she laughs, what questions? okay, think about it....

Wash Sq. P

Is this an exciting time to live right now?

No, I don't think of it in terms of being exciting. I think its more like a nightmare

Désirée 203-1 2018. Q.A. (Sound 3) (Girl) Well, it's certainly more exciting than it ever was before. Let's put it that way.

(someone else - than what?)

M+P Cass P 423. yeah, sure it's always more exciting than what? (laughs) what do ya mean?

question

35-5 Jefferson A P 267. I thin I really think ah you can do anything and make it exciting - any ah anything that you're free to do. In other words I don't

Generation Gap

5-4 angry hair Wash Sq. much hair Ext. P 78. Man

The reasons for the generation gap? That everything's constantly changing and attitudes are constantly changing, and people are always behind in catching up with these views.

6

film clip (2)

you know most people don't care like,

we've travelled around the United States and played millions of people and uh my one sentence for all that is uh there's so few people that really care, you know mmm and I think that all the young people I see are the only people that really care.. you know,, and there're

(+CREDIT)

36-7 Jefferson A. Marty P 289. B

CUT

MUSIC + QUOTE (5)

MUSIC 2 - (12:30). NEW FTG N.Y.

Man

2-6 ad man Columbus Circle 41. P B-0

the young people today. I think the great majority of our young people today are good and decent people..like they were many years ago. I think that if they're brought up in a proper environment with a feeling of responsibility and a feeling of love. I think that they'll come out all right. But they don't have that much today, they're lacking a lot of that.

question

94-7 Doral Great Lady 909. P B-D

uh insecurity nothing else nothing else

but they're not they're not being loved in the way they feel they should or they're not being children like to be disciplined whether people realize it or not they love discipline just like a puppy does, I mean they

98-3 P 4H father

telling them what they want to do youngsters

13 100-2 P 994-B

think we have that uh that outlook for sters that we as adults should have...thank that the big majority of young

Sound 24

Man

old bum

Causes of frustration of young people.

5-6 old bum Wash Sq. P 85.

The causes of frustration regarding young people is would have to come naturally from the older people. We as older people were young people,too, at one time. So

"On a personal level, there are many people who have meant a great deal to me. My father and mother were certainly most important, not only in themselves, but because they created a world for me to revolt against."

reader #2

p.XIX
Ingmar Bergman - 4 Screenplays
Simon & Schuster - 1960

older people, and the proper understanding. and if we don't receive from the older people setting examples for younger people, then we become old. We grow and we become old and

5-6 old bum Wash Sq. P 86.

friend of Kristin pretty back lit P

sound 32

the problems facing people today are pretty much the same actually as the problems that have been facing all generations --uh the problem being to find a valid reason for living and continuing in whatever social scene is happening, the complexity of today being the imminent destruction of the world in a nuclear war, the uh the idea that there are many different beliefs as to what's morally right and what's morally wrong I think more so probably than has ever ever been before in history.

44-3 Fern Del B-Lit Kristin friend 381. P B

44-3 Fern Del B-Lit Kristin friend 382. P. E-B.

question

the drug scene is kind of strange. uh I think eventually it will come down to the fact that marijuana will have to be legalized but uh the chemicals and hard drugs, LDS pills are bad things

MUSIC 4

4

5

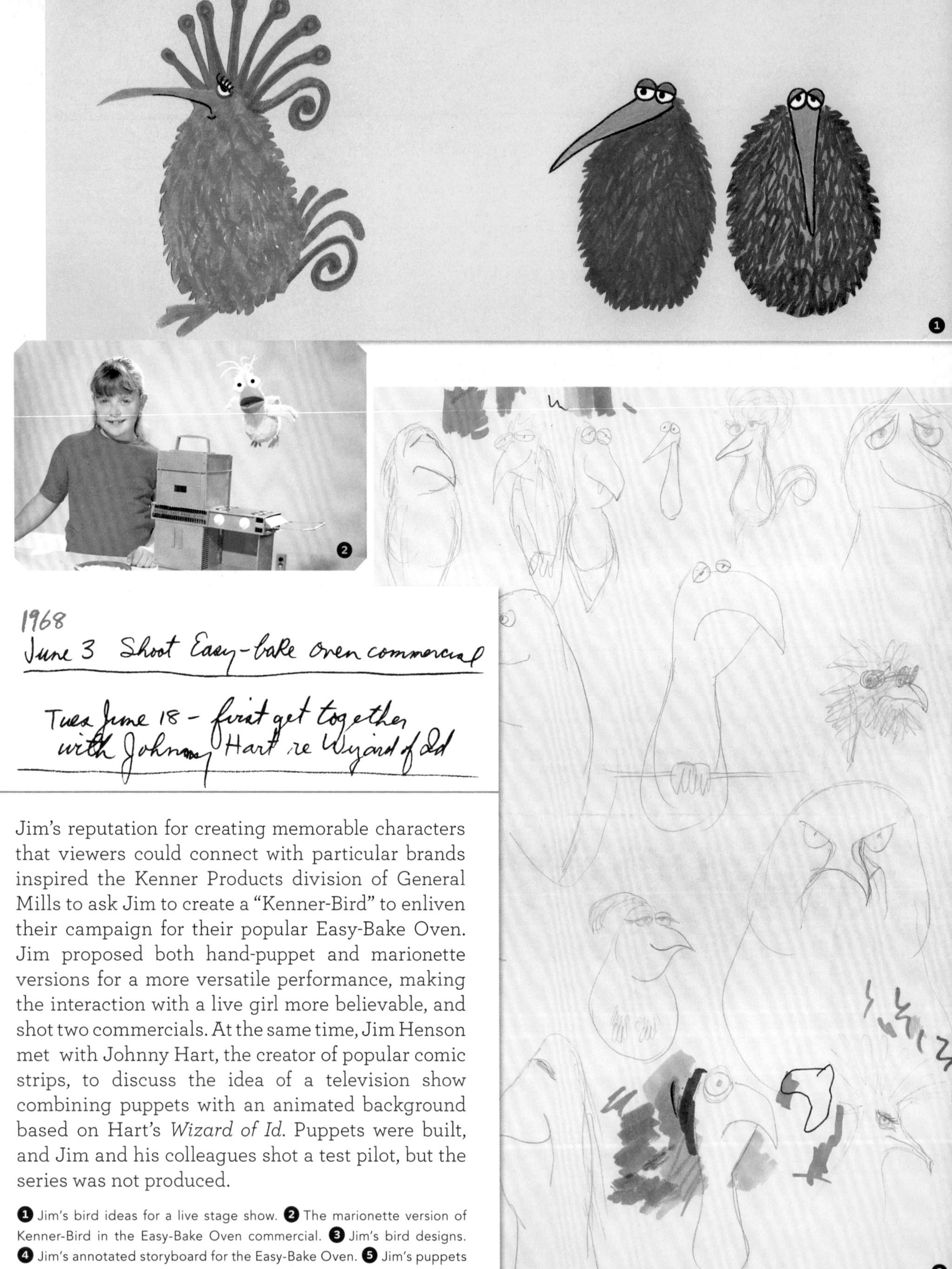

1968
June 3 Shoot Easy-bake Oven commercial

Tues June 18 – first get together with Johnny Hart re Wizard of Id

Jim's reputation for creating memorable characters that viewers could connect with particular brands inspired the Kenner Products division of General Mills to ask Jim to create a "Kenner-Bird" to enliven their campaign for their popular Easy-Bake Oven. Jim proposed both hand-puppet and marionette versions for a more versatile performance, making the interaction with a live girl more believable, and shot two commercials. At the same time, Jim Henson met with Johnny Hart, the creator of popular comic strips, to discuss the idea of a television show combining puppets with an animated background based on Hart's *Wizard of Id*. Puppets were built, and Jim and his colleagues shot a test pilot, but the series was not produced.

❶ Jim's bird ideas for a live stage show. ❷ The marionette version of Kenner-Bird in the Easy-Bake Oven commercial. ❸ Jim's bird designs. ❹ Jim's annotated storyboard for the Easy-Bake Oven. ❺ Jim's puppets based on *The Wizard of Id* by Johnny Hart and Brant Parker.

5

6

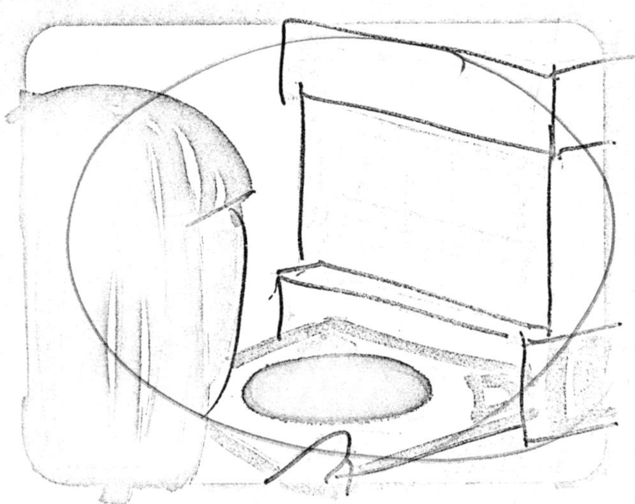

-CU

~~LITTLE GIRL:~~
~~I LOVE MINE.~~
I love my Easy bake oven 30-2
BIRD:
GOOD! YOU KNOW HOW TO WORK IT, AND ALL?

LITTLE GIRL:
OF COURSE, YOU JUST PUT THE EASY BAKE MIX IN HERE, LIKE THIS... 30-3

6-A- C.U. Barbara
6-AB- alt. wording

4

5

1968

July 25 + 26 attend seminar in Cambridge re Children's TV workshop

Jon Stone, television director and co-creator of *Sesame Street*, had worked with Jim on his fairytale parodies and as director of *Youth '68*. When he and Joan Ganz Cooney, founder of Children's Television Workshop, discussed puppets for their developing show, it was clear that Jim was the only choice. With four small children at home and an interest in TV's impact on kids, Jim was pleased to be invited by Stone to a series of curriculum seminars along with other artists, educators, and television people in New York and at Harvard University. These served as his introduction to the main ideas and goals of *Sesame Street* and the personalities behind it.

❶ Joan Ganz Cooney and her *Sesame Street* friends in the 1970s. ❷ Jim's designs for Ernie and Bert were developed in tandem as the characters were meant to play off one another from the beginning. ❸ Jim and Jon Stone's mutual admiration was key to their successful collaboration. ❹ Jim sketched numerous birds for *Sesame Street* before settling on the design for Big Bird. ❺ John, Brian, Lisa, and Cheryl Henson around 1969. The following year, Heather would join the family. ❻ Bert and Ernie finger puppets, produced in 1971. ❼ Jim's original sketch for Oscar the Grouch showed him in magenta fur. ❽ Jim's variations on the Anything Muppets, blank puppets that could be transformed into any type of character.

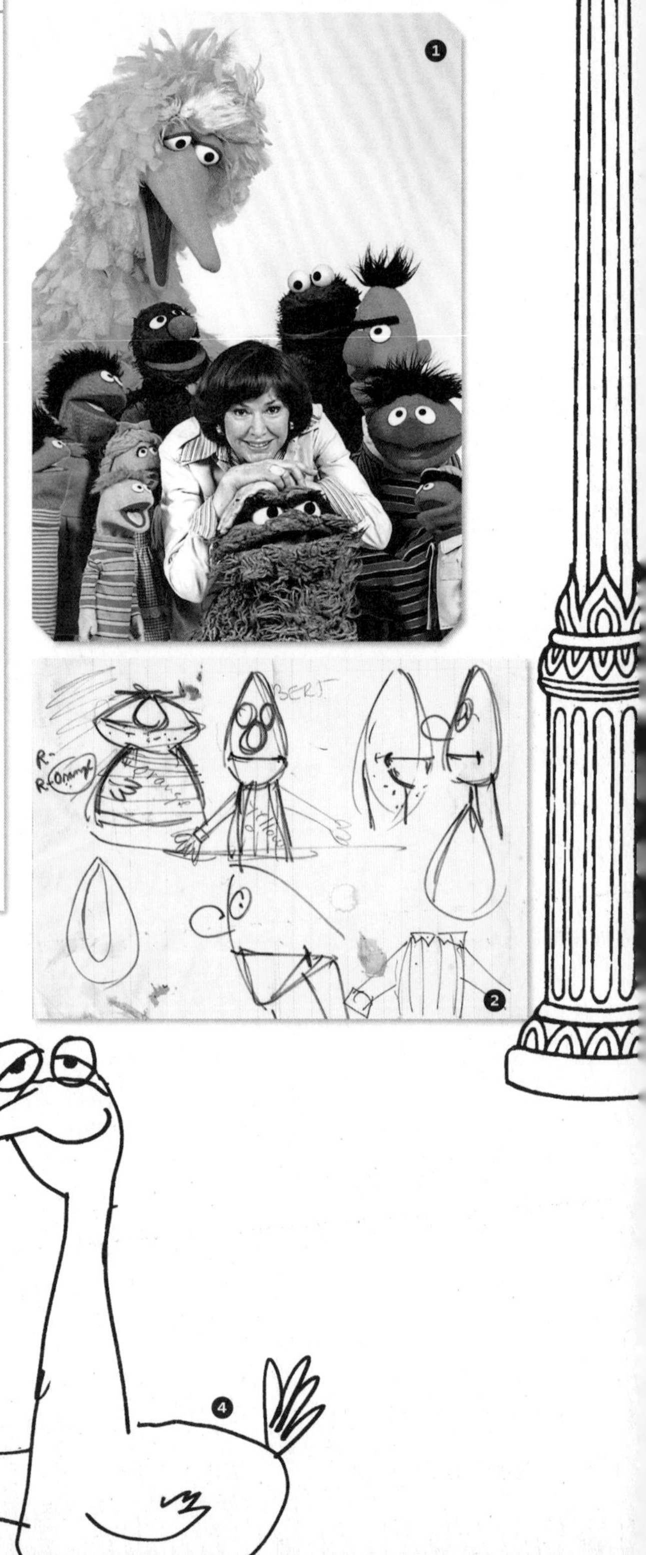

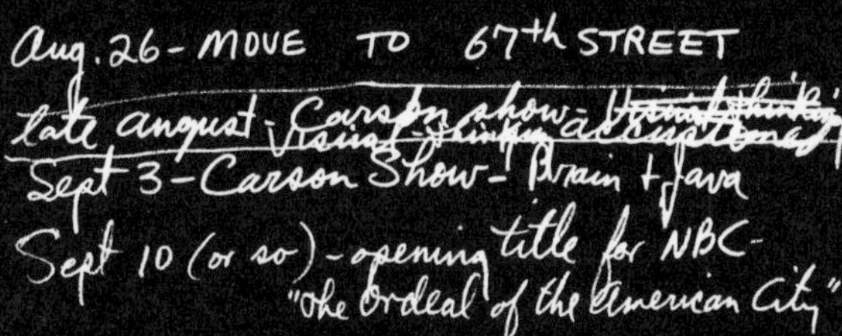

Aug. 26 - MOVE TO 67th STREET
~~late august - Carson show - Visual thinking~~
Sept 3 - Carson Show - Brain + Java
Sept 10 (or so) - opening title for NBC - "The Ordeal of the American City"

1968

Sept 22 - Oct 5 - 6:30 AM filming Cinderella in Toronto

In 1965, Jon Stone and Tom Whedon, familiar with Jim's variety show work, signed him to coproduce a series based on offbeat versions of fairy tales, taping a pilot that never aired. Resurrecting the idea, Jim and Stone managed to sell it as a one-hour special called *Hey Cinderella!*, which appeared on ABC in 1970. Joe Raposo wrote the music, making this the first collaboration between Raposo, Stone, and Henson, a trio who became the main creative team behind *Sesame Street*. With a cast of humans and Muppets, *Hey Cinderella!* updated the traditional story, adding humor and deliberate anachronisms. With sponsor R.J. Reynolds's help, the show was a hit, opening doors for more fairy-tale specials from Jim.

❶+❸+❹ Jim's designs for the 1965 unaired pilot version of *Cinderella*. ❷ Jim's design for his first fairy-tale king, King Goshposh, 1962. ❺ Jim and R.J. Reynolds executives consult with Splurge on their promotional plan for *Hey Cinderella!*, 1970. ❻ Jim's design for his first big monster Splurge, 1965. ❼ R.J. Reynolds booklet promoting their products and *Hey Cinderella!*, 1970. ❽ Promotional ticket reminding viewers about *Hey Cinderella!*

5

6

SPLURGE

Oct 29 – Tonight Show – Beautiful Day

Nov 30 – Dec 5 – in Houston VTR
Soupy Sales in Astroworld

Dec 22 – Sullivan – Reindeer Bit

HEY KIDS—

This ticket is from a very good friend of R. J. Reynolds Foods. So please fill him in about us when you watch our show together.

We'll also be introducing some new muppets to you and the whole family. Like Splurge, the hairy purple monster who ravishes radishes. And Mona and Lisa, Cinderella's somewhat out-of-step sisters. And others too humorous to mention. See you and the family April 10th.

KERMIT + RUFUS

FAMILY TELEVISION THEATRE

APRIL 10th 1970

FRIDAY EVE. AT 7:30 P.M. ABC-TV

"TALES FROM MUPPETLAND"
(FIRST TALE — "HEY CINDERELLA")

PRESENTED BY
R. J. REYNOLDS FOODS, INC.

RATED "DOUBLE F" (FAMILY FUN)

An "M.G.M." Production (Merchants Golden Muppetunity)

Please note show time. Latecomers will be seated, but management cannot be responsible for the laughs lost.

THE BEST SEAT IN THE HOUSE

8

1969

Feb 8 Go to Toronto - tape Feb 10 - 15
THE CUBE - Edit 16 + 17 show to
NBC Feb. 18

Sun Feb. 23 4:30 - AIR - THE CUBE

On the strength of the spirited response to *Youth '68*, NBC green-lit production of Jim's script for *The Cube*, written with Jerry Juhl back in 1966. Billed as a surrealistic comedy that "dramatizes the complex, baffling problems of reality versus illusion," *The Cube* featured a man, played by Richard Schaal, trapped in a doorless room and visited by a series of diverse guests. Unable to distinguish what is and isn't, he is confined as much by his own perception of reality as by the walls. Jim enjoyed these existential contemplations, and he was gratified to direct an hour-long live-action show with professional actors for the first time. Though mixed, reviews showed great appreciation for the unusual effort to use television to tackle philosophical questions.

❶ Puppeteer Jerry Nelson, who played the monk, with Jerry Juhl, who served as an extra. ❷ Jim directing on the set of *The Cube*. ❸ Jim's design for the logo for *The Cube*. ❹ A newspaper advertisement promoting the program. ❺ Production shots of Richard Schaal in *The Cube*. ❻ NBC's press release describing the program.

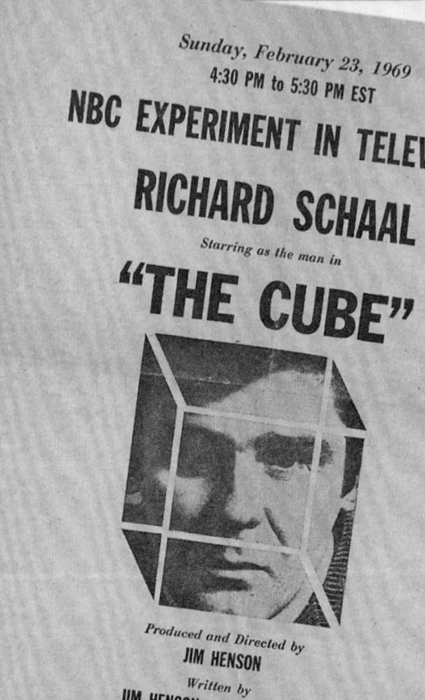

March 3 - Go to Hershey Pa to VTR
3 short shows on Puppetry
with Don, Danny + Frank

March 11 · shoot 2 commercials MUNCHOS

March 13 - 14 shoot Community Coffee

March 17 - deliver #5 storyboards

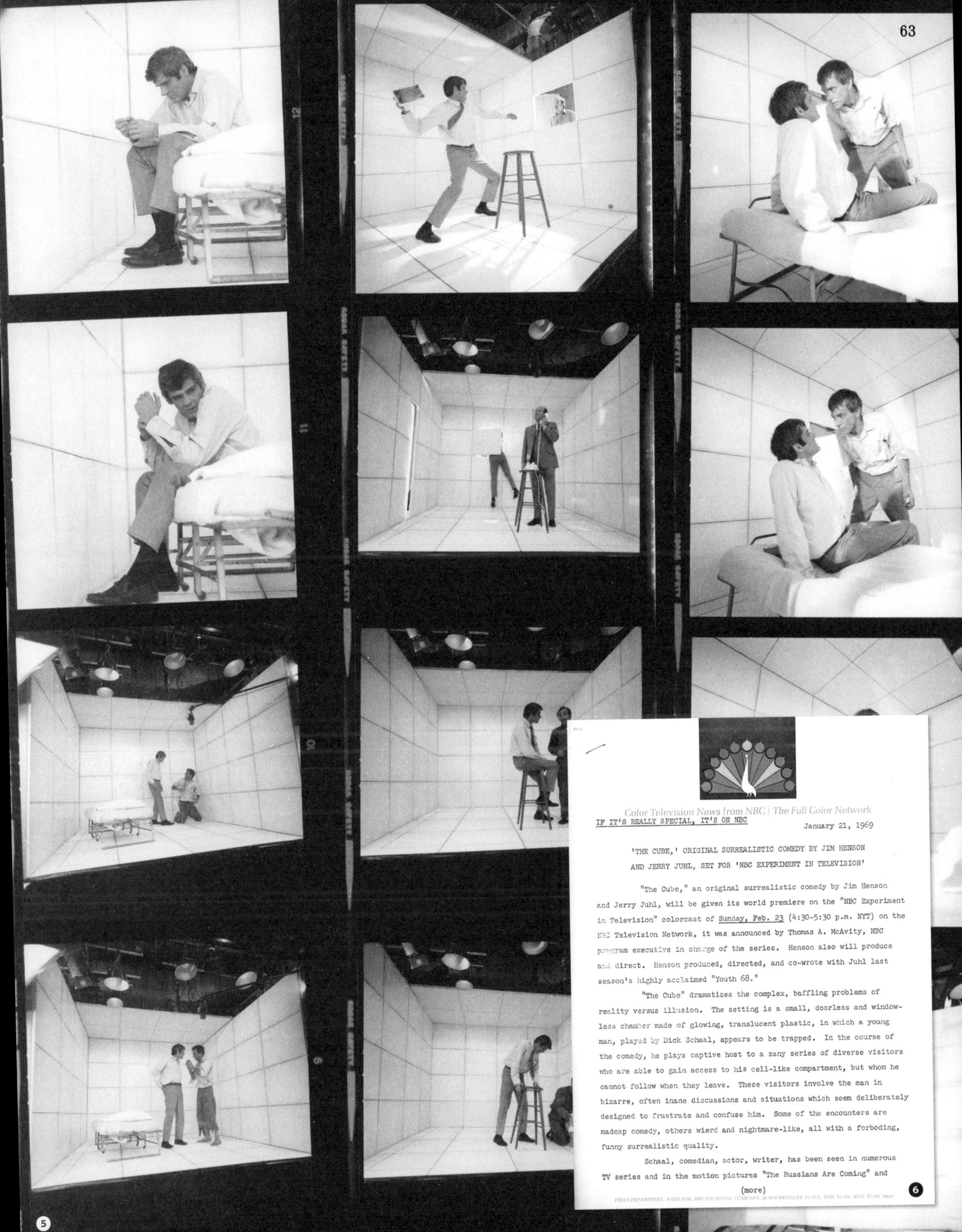

Color Television News from NBC | The Full Color Network

IF IT'S REALLY SPECIAL, IT'S ON NBC

January 21, 1969

'THE CUBE,' ORIGINAL SURREALISTIC COMEDY BY JIM HENSON AND JERRY JUHL, SET FOR 'NBC EXPERIMENT IN TELEVISION'

"The Cube," an original surrealistic comedy by Jim Henson and Jerry Juhl, will be given its world premiere on the "NBC Experiment in Television" colorcast of Sunday, Feb. 23 (4:30-5:30 p.m. NYT) on the NBC Television Network, it was announced by Thomas A. McAvity, NBC program executive in charge of the series. Henson also will produce and direct. Henson produced, directed, and co-wrote with Juhl last season's highly acclaimed "Youth 68."

"The Cube" dramatizes the complex, baffling problems of reality versus illusion. The setting is a small, doorless and windowless chamber made of glowing, translucent plastic, in which a young man, played by Dick Schaal, appears to be trapped. In the course of the comedy, he plays captive host to a zany series of diverse visitors who are able to gain access to his cell-like compartment, but whom he cannot follow when they leave. These visitors involve the man in bizarre, often inane discussions and situations which seem deliberately designed to frustrate and confuse him. Some of the encounters are madcap comedy, others wierd and nightmare-like, all with a forboding, funny surrealistic quality.

Schaal, comedian, actor, writer, has been seen in numerous TV series and in the motion pictures "The Russians Are Coming" and

(more)

PRESS DEPARTMENT, NATIONAL BROADCASTING COMPANY, 30 ROCKEFELLER PLAZA, NEW YORK, NEW YORK 10020

april 30, 1969 - shoot Select-a-Vision slide film for RCA w/ Chuck Olson

With his interest in new media technologies, Jim was enthusiastic about contributing to two consumer-electronics market-research projects for RCA. The first, exploring demand for Prerecorded Electronic Video Systems, precursors to home video players, involved creating a six-minute slide film to show focus groups. It featured still images representing the best of programming projected on a TV set while a narrator explained the concept. Additional photos showed people of all types and ages enjoying programs of their choice. The following year, Jim shot a host of musical performances, a stock car race, and a dramatic piece with intense sound effects. Edited together, these demonstrated the audio advantages of the new RCA stereo television.

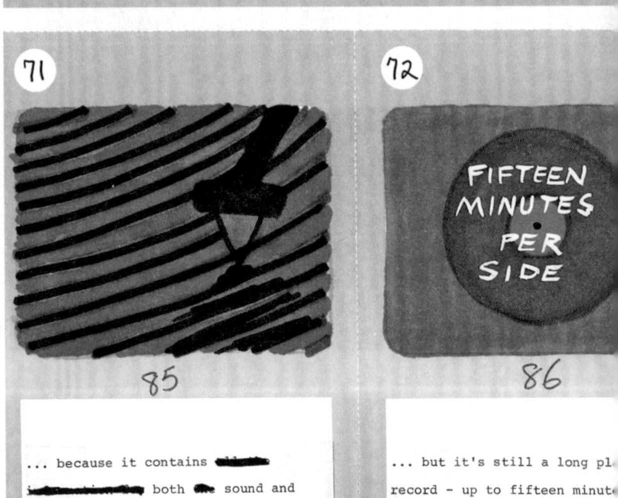

❶ Jim's storyboard panels from his *Select-A-Vision* slide film, 1969.

May 11 - Sullivan Show Beautiful Day again

May 24 - Do Puppet Show for North Street Elementary School - Childrens Fair
Frank - Eric - Bonny -

31

38

WOMAN #1

By the time I get my kids in bed and the dishes done, all the good shows are over.

32

39

TEEN-AGE BOY #1:

Yeah, I like to listen to Bobby Gentry but I'd rather watch her.

33

40

MAN #2:

Remember Ernie Kovacs? Boy, I'd give anything to see one of his classic routines again!

34

41

WOMAN #2:

I love television, but I do wish they'd put on more of my kind of show.

49 Pearl Bailey - Carol Channing Wonderful Town alternate

61

It's called Select-a-Vision, or S.V. for short, and it will open up a whole new world of viewing entertainment, designed specifically for you.

ELECTRONIC MUSIC: BOUNCY THEME.

50

62 63

MAN #3:

Hey Honey! What are we in the mood for watching tonight? How about a musical?

MUSIC :35 — 114-2-9

69

83

TEEN-AGE BOY#1:

What will the records be like?

70

84

NARRATOR: :24

Although a Select-a-Vision record looks like an ordinary phonograph record, it is actually quite different ...

108-1-4 — begin :38½ in

02

122

MAN #2:

Well, let's face it, once in a while, I like to see a good ballet.

103

123

MUSIC: "SWAN LAKE" COMES TO A DRAMATIC END.

104

124

NARRATOR:

So this is Select-a-Vision. Recordings that give you picture + sound

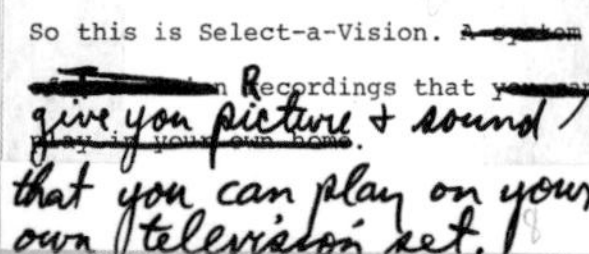
that you can play on your own television set.

105

125

MAN #3:

Well, it sounds like a good thing.

off white

1969
May 28-29 shoot #5
June 2, 4, 6 - " " (4th chef falls)

July 9-18 tape CTW - Sesame Street Pilot shows

As work began on *Sesame Street*, it was clear that miles of footage would be needed to fill 130 episodes of the one-hour daily show. Along with his Muppet inserts, Jim signed on to create short films to teach numbers, letters, and other concepts. The first batch of ten were all in the same style. They began with Jim's hand-drawn animations accompanied by children singing to a melody by Joe Raposo. Examples of the given number were revealed, ranging from body parts and shapes to toys and animals, and each film ended with the dramatic entrance of a baker, played by Alex Stevens, carrying the appropriate number of cakes, pies, or ice cream sundaes. In Jim's voice, he announced what he was carrying and immediately tumbled down the stairs.

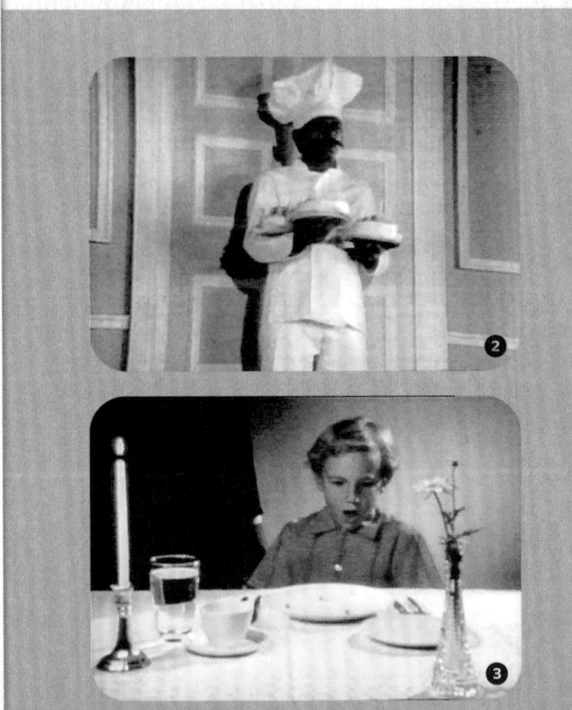

❶ Jim's storyboard panel for the *Number 8 Baker* film. ❷ Alex Stevens, with a fake mustache, as the clumsy Baker. ❸ Brian Henson in the *Number 3* film. ❹+❺ Jim's storyboard panels from the opening sequence for the Baker counting films. ❻+❼+❽+❾ Jim's storyboard panels for the *Number 3 Baker* film.

4
5
6
7
HA
PPY
BIRTHDAY
8
9

1969

August - P of A Festival Salt Lake City - met Carroll Spinney asked him to join us

Sept 29 began CTW inserts

Oct. 13 began 1st Sesame Street shows
Oct 31 1969 - Life Magazine picture Jim + Muppets SS

Dec 14 - Sullivan - used BIG BIRD in a Dance - choreographed by Pete Genero

Assuming that children would have difficulty separating fantasy from reality, the *Sesame Street* producers did not mix Muppets with human actors in the sample pilots. Test audiences didn't respond as expected, and Jim was asked to find a way to add more fantasy to the street. He designed a large, walk-around character, a big yellow bird, and asked builder Kermit Love to figure out how to make him. Jim also needed a performer, and during his annual trip to the Puppeteers of America festival, he watched Massachusetts puppeteer Caroll Spinney present a multimedia extravaganza. Jim was impressed and invited Caroll to join him in New York. Within a year, Big Bird was a star and on the cover of *Time* magazine.

❶ Kermit Love's drawing used to determine the construction of Big Bird. ❷ Jim's design for Big Bird showing a simplified look at how he is performed. ❸ An accomplished cartoonist, Caroll Spinney sent his friends this visual account of his life in New York with his holiday greetings. ❹ Kermit Love and Big Bird, and ❺ Caroll Spinney in Public Television's *IMAGE* magazine. ❻ Big Bird on the cover of *Time* magazine at the start of season two.

❶

❷

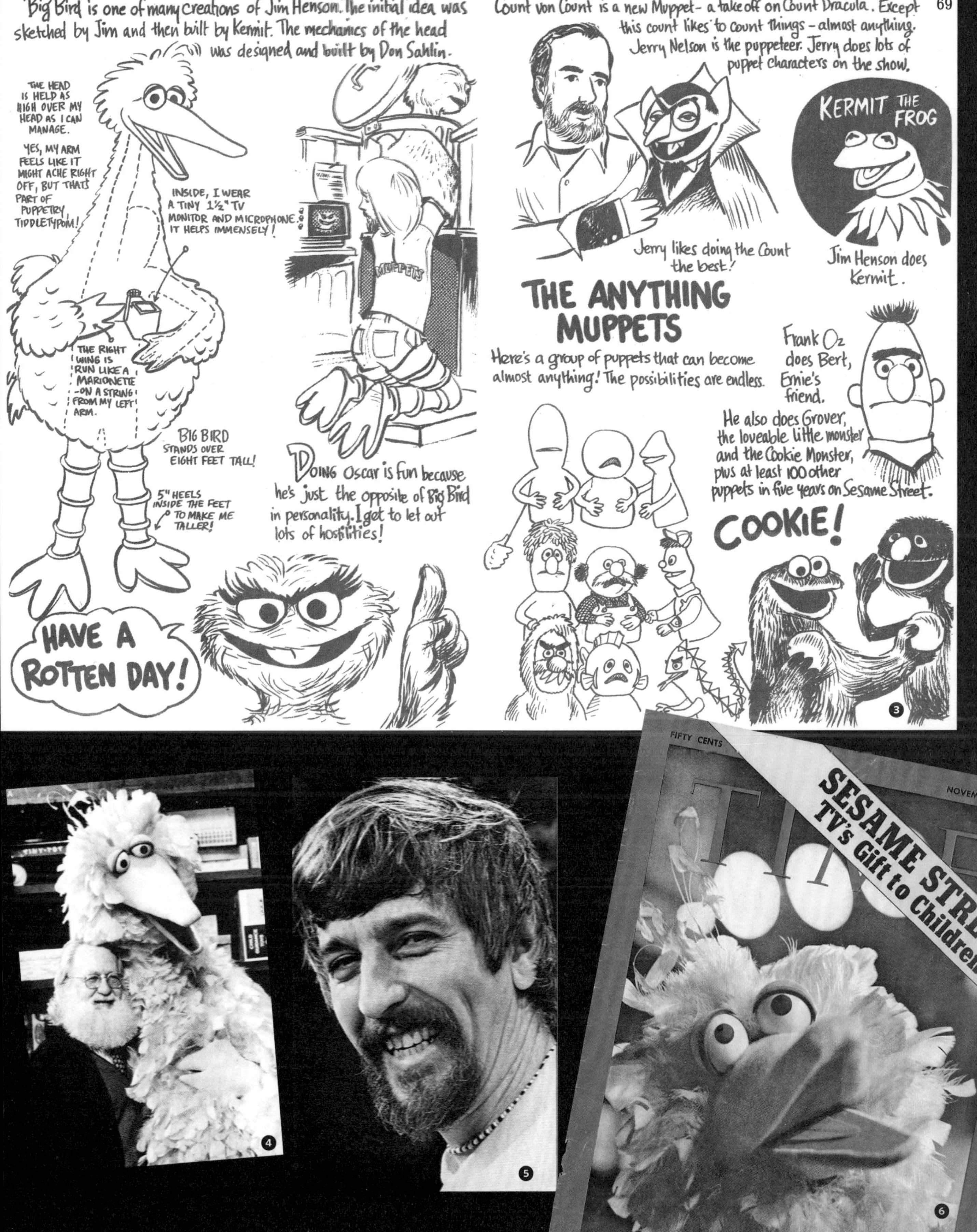
Big Bird is one of many creations of Jim Henson. The initial idea was sketched by Jim and then built by Kermit. The mechanics of the head was designed and built by Don Sahlin.
THE HEAD IS HELD AS HIGH OVER MY HEAD AS I CAN MANAGE.
YES, MY ARM FEELS LIKE IT MIGHT ACHE RIGHT OFF, BUT THAT'S PART OF PUPPETRY, TIDDLETYPOM!
INSIDE, I WEAR A TINY 1½" TV MONITOR AND MICROPHONE. IT HELPS IMMENSELY!
THE RIGHT WING IS RUN LIKE A MARIONETTE - ON A STRING FROM MY LEFT ARM.
BIG BIRD STANDS OVER EIGHT FEET TALL!
5" HEELS INSIDE THE FEET TO MAKE ME TALLER!
MUPPETS
Doing Oscar is fun because he's just the opposite of Big Bird in personality. I get to let out lots of hostilities!
HAVE A ROTTEN DAY!
Count von Count is a new Muppet - a take off on Count Dracula. Except this count likes to count things - almost anything. Jerry Nelson is the puppeteer. Jerry does lots of puppet characters on the show.
KERMIT THE FROG
Jerry likes doing the Count the best!
Jim Henson does Kermit.
THE ANYTHING MUPPETS
Here's a group of puppets that can become almost anything! The possibilities are endless.
Frank Oz does Bert, Ernie's friend.
He also does Grover, the loveable little monster and the Cookie Monster, plus at least 100 other puppets in five years on Sesame Street.
COOKIE!
FIFTY CENTS
NOVEMB
SESAME STRE
TV's Gift to Children

3

4

5

6

CHAPTER 3

THE WORLD TUNES IN

1970–1979

ALMOST AS SOON AS IT WENT ON THE AIR, *Sesame Street* was a hit and made instant celebrities of its Muppet stars. In 1970, Big Bird appeared on the cover of *Time* magazine and as a guest performer on network variety shows. Publications of all types sought interviews with Jim and his colleagues, and audiences clamored for books and toys and any access to their friends from the show. At the same time, Jim's popularity on *The Ed Sullivan Show* led to a Christmas special featuring new characters, and the offers for other appearances poured in.

While Jim relished his success on public television, he also pursued the possibility of a Muppet show on network TV and spent the early 1970s amassing ideas, developing characters, and pitching various formats to programming executives. A live appearance with Nancy Sinatra in Las Vegas infected him with interest in a stage show, and he gave his imagination a vigorous workout inventing characters that would work in that setting. And to avoid being pigeonholed as a children's entertainer, Jim embraced the opportunity to create original characters for the first season of *Saturday Night Live*. But a primetime Muppet series was the ultimate goal.

After creating two specials that would serve as pilots for *The Muppet Show*, Jim finally found a backer in London, moved his production team across the Atlantic, and taped the first episode in 1976. By this time, he had dozens of people working for him and had more than doubled his performer roster. The relationships he had developed in the variety show circuit and through *Sesame Street* provided a pool of guest stars, and soon celebrities were lining up to be on the show. Audience response was enthusiastic and affectionate, and characters that had started off on a local television channel in Washington, DC, were now beaming into living rooms around the world. The Muppets were dubbed and subtitled, making Jim's creations global citizens, licensing phenomena, and darlings of the press.

Jim's television triumph allowed him to pursue all types of projects and personal ambitions. By the end of the decade, he translated his vision to the big screen with *The Muppet Movie*, setting his characters on a road trip of discovery and proving that they could succeed in any medium. He began development of his first fantasy film, laying the groundwork for what would occupy much of the next ten years, and he gained personal recognition by way of awards, honors, and a spot in an American Express commercial. In his journal, Jim was right to note that 1979 was "A Very Major Big Year." It was the culmination of an extraordinary run of successes and set the stage for the creation of complete worlds, mind-boggling technical innovations, and communities of characters never before imagined.

❶ *Muppet Show* proposal cover, late 1960s. ❷ Jim and his *Muppet Show* stars, 1979.

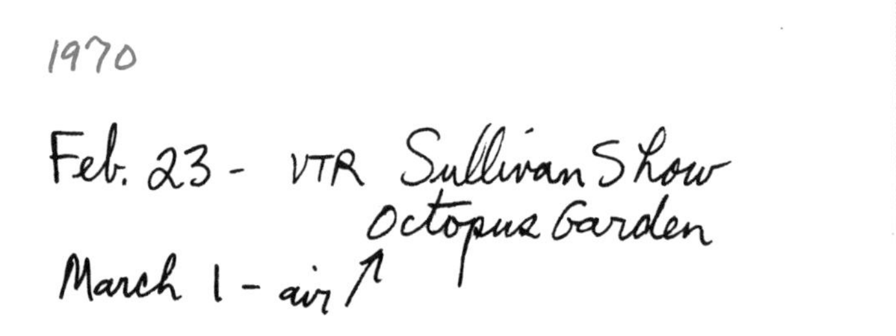

1970

Feb. 23 - VTR Sullivan Show
Octopus Garden
March 1 - air

When the Beatles' album *Abbey Road* was released, Jim got a copy and immediately found songs that would make great material for his characters. The album's fanciful track "Octopus's Garden" captured his imagination and inspired several Muppet versions. Jim first performed the song for the debut season of *Sesame Street*, using it as an opportunity to count to eight. For *Ed Sullivan*, it was pure entertainment. As Jim's swimmer and a clam sang, the smart-mouthed Octopus (performed by Frank Oz) made awful undersea puns. The bit ended in a typical Muppet way—the Octopus deservedly was eaten by a giant clam. Six weeks later, Jim used another track from *Abbey Road*, "Come Together," clearly tickled by the visual possibilities of the humorous lyrics.

❶+❷ Jim's ideas for puppets based on the Beatles. ❸ The Glutton, another *Sullivan Show* character. ❹ Jim's list of ideas for *Ed Sullivan Show* appearances. ❺ Jim on East 67th Street around 1970. ❻ Jim's design for the Flat Top character to use in his "Come Together" appearance on *Ed Sullivan*. ❼ Muppets sing "Come Together" on *The Ed Sullivan Show*.

SULLIVAN IDEAS

Grump as Hippy
Harry - Yorick
Splurge - Thog
Rowlf - Baskerville
Dripsnout
Men-People - Mr X - Munchos Man - Gleam
Tap Dance - Fred Astaire
Changing Piece - Fashion

Visual thinking
Java
Mahna Mahna

4

5

6

7

april - Record 1st Sesame St. cast album

April 10 - HEY CINDERELLA aires U.S.

May 4 VTR Sullivan for "What Kind of Fool am I" - Kermit + Grover

June 1-3 auditioning Puppeteers for Workshop

Aug 24-26 VTR Santa Switch at CFTO Toronto

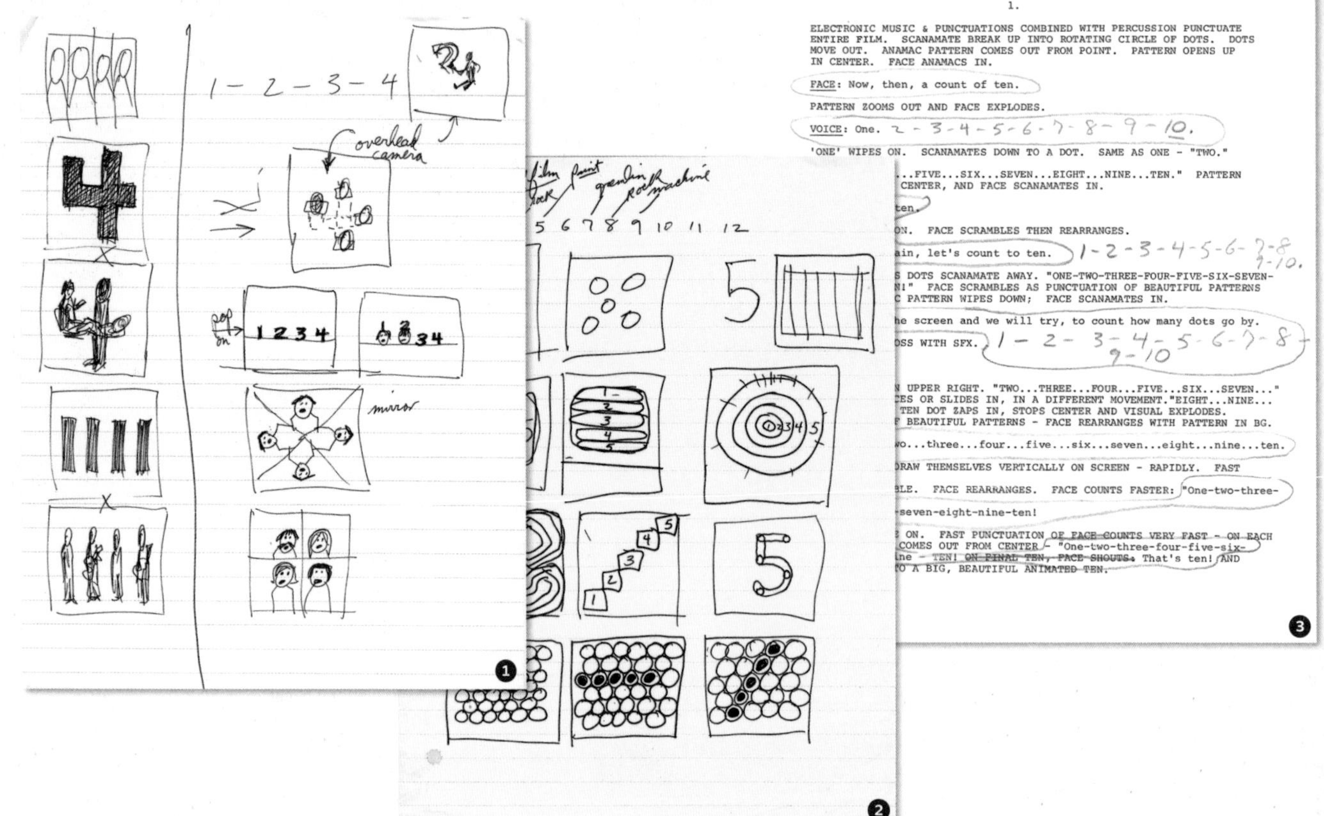

1970

Sept 10-12 in Denver doing Computer animation for Sesame #'s 10 + 4.

Sept 22. shoot Doll House Film – (#2)

Oct. 21-24 shoot #12 Rocks film

Oct 14+15 Shoot #8

Oct 29+30 shoot #6

For season two of *Sesame Street*, Jim made eleven more number films using a variety of styles and techniques. For numbers four and ten, Jim was eager to try a new analog computer system called Scanimate, invented by Lee Harrison III and built by the Computer Image Corporation in Denver. The process, involving backlit high-contrast artwork scanned by a progressive scan monochrome camera, created animation in real time, allowing Jim to finish the visuals in just three days. Back in New York, he took a more traditional approach and made a charming live-action film depicting two girls playing with two dolls and a dollhouse. While a departure from the manic mood of his other films, Jim's sense of humor surfaces when two cats wreak havoc at the end.

❶ Jim's notes and sketches for the *Number 4* film made using the Scanimate system. ❷ Jim's storyboard for his *Number 5* film, which he made by shooting still images of a painting as it progressed. ❸ The script for the *Number 10* Scanimate film with Jim's annotations. ❹ Jim's storyboard for the *Number 4* film. ❺+❻+❼ The Henson's Greenwich house (top) was the model for the dollhouse Jim built for his daughter Cheryl. ❽ Two girls, two dolls, Cheryl's dollhouse, and the cat as they appeared in Jim's *Number 2* film.

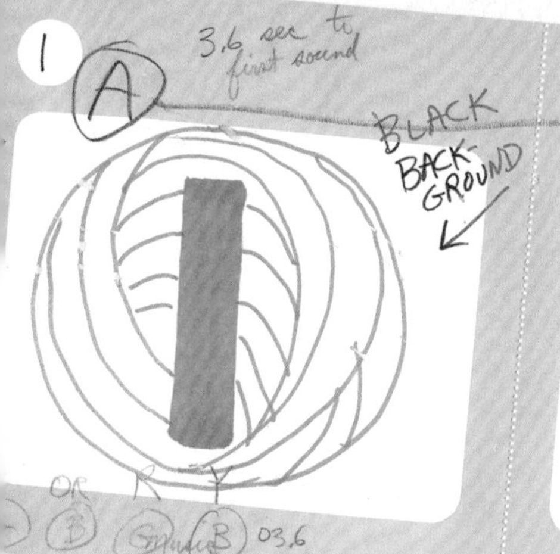

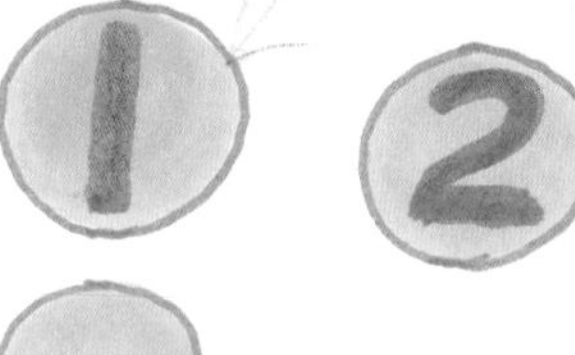

4

5

6

7

Nov. 16-20 in L.A. VTR Goldie Hawn Special
did "Green" some talk-
Nov 23-24 Visit Mom & Dad in Albuquerque
Nov 23 - Big Bird - Cover of Time Magazine

8

1970
Dec 19 – Heather arrives – during final mix of Santa Switch
Dec 20 – SANTA CLAUS SWITCH AIR

Throughout the 1960s, Jim and Jerry Juhl pitched an idea for a television special that mixed traditional Christmas characters with monsters and fairy-tale characters. Jim designed bird-like villains called Frackles and two giant monsters named Thig and Thog to populate Jerry's script. The resulting show, *The Great Santa Claus Switch,* told the story of magician Cosmo's failed plot to kidnap and impersonate Santa Claus (both played by Art Carney) in order to rob every home in the world. Produced and narrated by Ed Sullivan with music by Joe Raposo, *The Great Santa Claus Switch* served as a training ground for new talent, including performers Fran Brill and Richard Hunt, broadening the core group and allowing Jim to build toward more ambitious projects.

❶ Jim directing Thig on the set of *The Great Santa Claus Switch.* ❷ Jim's illustration for his show proposal, mid-1960s. ❸ List of potential villain names from 1963. ❹ An array of Frackles as imagined by Jim. ❺ Jim with his son John, Ernie, and Lothar from *The Great Santa Clause Switch.* ❻ Jim's Frackle sketches.

4

Pag 22

THE GREENWICH SOCIAL REVIEW

50¢

Vol. 23, No. 8

November, 1970

A Monthly Magazine Devoted to the Civic and Social Interests of the Greenwich Area

"Sesame Street" story on page 22

JULIET NEWMAN

5

6

1971

Feb 4–15 in London for Tom Jones Show
Jane over for a couple days

Feb 15 - Goldie Hawn Special AIR

Feb 18 N.Y. Puppetry Guild honor J.H.

1971

March – to + from Toronto re Frog Prince

March 22 – April 1 VTR FROG PRINCE in Toronto

Early April editing VTR in Toronto for first screening April 26

May 2 – Kermit reviews 11 Frog book in N.Y. Times BR

MAY 11 – FROG PRINCE AIRS

Having acquired flippers in 1968 for *Hey Cinderella!*, Kermit truly embraced his frog identity and began introducing himself on camera as Kermit the Frog. In *The Frog Prince*, Jim's second R.J. Reynolds sponsored television special, Kermit led the local amphibian community and narrated the story of Robin, a young frog performed by Jerry Nelson. The show also featured Taminella (the witch performed by the show's writer Jerry Juhl), and the cigar-smoking King Rupert II (performed with glee by a gravel-voiced Jim Henson), originally created for their early 1960s *Tinkerdee* projects. A new monster, the charismatic Sweetums, rounded out the cast, stealing the show from the human actors and starting a long career with the Muppets.

❶ Kermit and other frogs with Princess Melora (played by Trudy Young) and the human Sir Robin the Brave (played by Gordon Thomson). ❷ Jim's press kit artwork for *The Frog Prince*. ❸ Jim's sketches of his ogre-like monster, Sweetums. ❹ Promotional stickers for *The Frog Prince*. ❺ Jim, Sweetums, and Robin pose on *The Frog Prince* set. ❻ The Henson family in 1971: (left to right) Jane, Heather, Jim's dad Paul, Lisa, Cheryl, Jim, Brian, John. ❼ Jim's rough designs for Taminella Grinderfall, his fairy-tale witch.

May 10-11 in Boston for Sesame Street and the Boston Pops - with Lisa

1971
June 8-24 in Las Vegas for Nancy S.
JUNE 16- opening Night Nancy Sinatra
Hilton International - thru July 18

With the almost overnight success of *Sesame Street,* audiences began to think of the Muppets as just something for children. Recognizing an opportunity to perform for adults and remind them of his characters' wide appeal, Jim jumped at the chance to join Nancy Sinatra in her Las Vegas casino show. The live performance also allowed Jim to experiment with puppetry techniques for the stage, creating new characters and reusing his full-body characters and other comic bits that had originally been performed in other settings. While the ultimate goal of *Sesame Street* was education, Jim said of this show, "There is that whole feeling of brotherhood and kindness and gentleness beneath it all, but the idea here is basically to entertain."

❶+❸ Nancy Sinatra and the oversized Thog sing Richard and Robert Sherman's "Fortuosity" from *The Happiest Millionaire.* ❷ Jim testing out Big Bossman on the roof of his 67th Street office. ❹+❺ After performing his giant feather creatures called Bossmen to Carole King's "I Feel the Earth Move" with Nancy Sinatra, Jim sketched these ideas to translate them to a Broadway show. ❻ Jim designed an oversized version of his Mahna Mahna character for the live stage, performing him with Nancy Sinatra instead of the Snowths.

Associated Press Photo

Nancy and Muppet

Sinatra clowns with Thog, on of the Muppet char-
Street to the Las Vegas

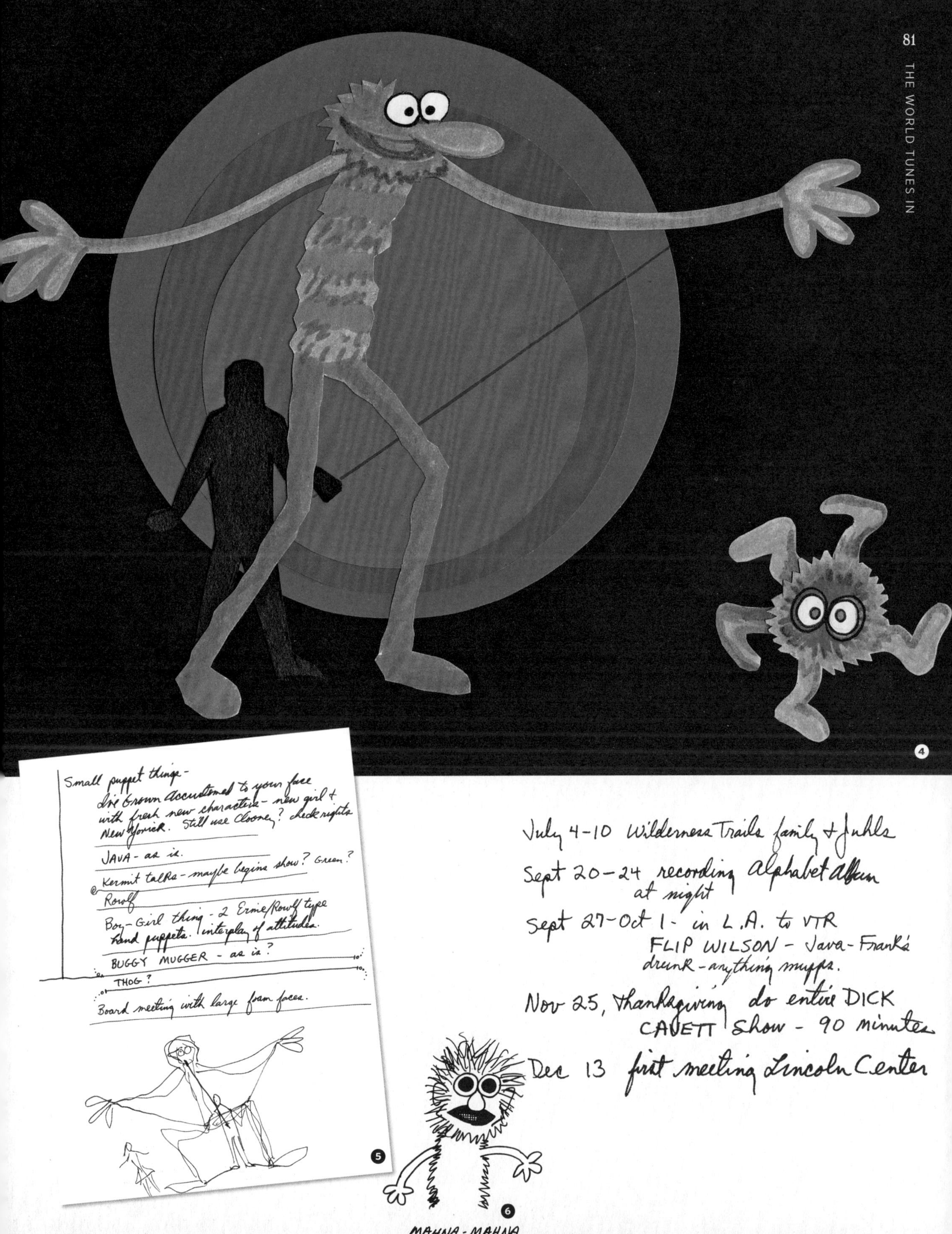
Small puppet things -
I've Grown Accustomed to your face
with fresh new characters - new girl +
New Yorick. Still use Clooney? check rights
JAVA - as is.
Kermit talks - maybe begins show? Green?
Rowlf
Boy - Girl thing - 2 Ernie/Rowlf type
hand puppets. interplay of attitudes.
BUGGY MUGGER - as is?
THOG?
Board meeting with large foam faces.
July 4-10 Wilderness Trails family + Juhls
Sept 20-24 recording Alphabet Album
at night
Sept 27-Oct 1 - in L.A. to VTR
FLIP WILSON - Java - Frank's
drunk - anything muppet.
Nov 25, Thanksgiving do entire DICK
CAVETT show - 90 minutes
Dec 13 first meeting Lincoln Center
MAHNA - MAHNA

1972

Jan - several trips to Toronto - casting voices Bremen

Feb 2-5 prerecording Bremen in Toronto

Feb 14 - March 2 - shoot Bremen

April 26 - AIR - MUPPET MUSICIANS OF BREMEN

In a departure from the European setting of his other Muppet fairy-tale projects, *The Muppet Musicians of Bremen* was set in the swamps of Louisiana, reflecting Jim's memories of his Delta boyhood. Puppet builders Bonnie Erickson and Caroly Wilcox joined the team, and Jim incorporated their design ideas into the look of the show. The production utilized dual versions of the barnyard animals: hand puppets for close-ups, and marionettes for distance shots, while the human characters were played by actors wearing oversized foam heads and hands, turning them into life-sized puppets. Earlier projects had featured more abstract characters, but the animals in *Bremen* were more recognizable and set the design standard for future Muppet animals, particularly the chorus of chickens dancing to the Dixieland soundtrack.

1 Jim on set with Kermit, Caleb Siles, Farmer Lardpork, Mean Floyd, and Mordecai Sledge. 2 Bonnie Erickson's design for Caleb's face, to be worn over an actor's face. 3 The barnyard animals created for *The Muppet Musicians of Bremen*. 4 Jim's directing script indicates whether a character would be performed as a hand puppet or a marionette. 5 When designer Michael Frith started working with Jim in the early 1970s, his characters, like this sketch of Rover Joe, had a slightly more realistic feel to them. 6 The chicken chorus in *Bremen*.

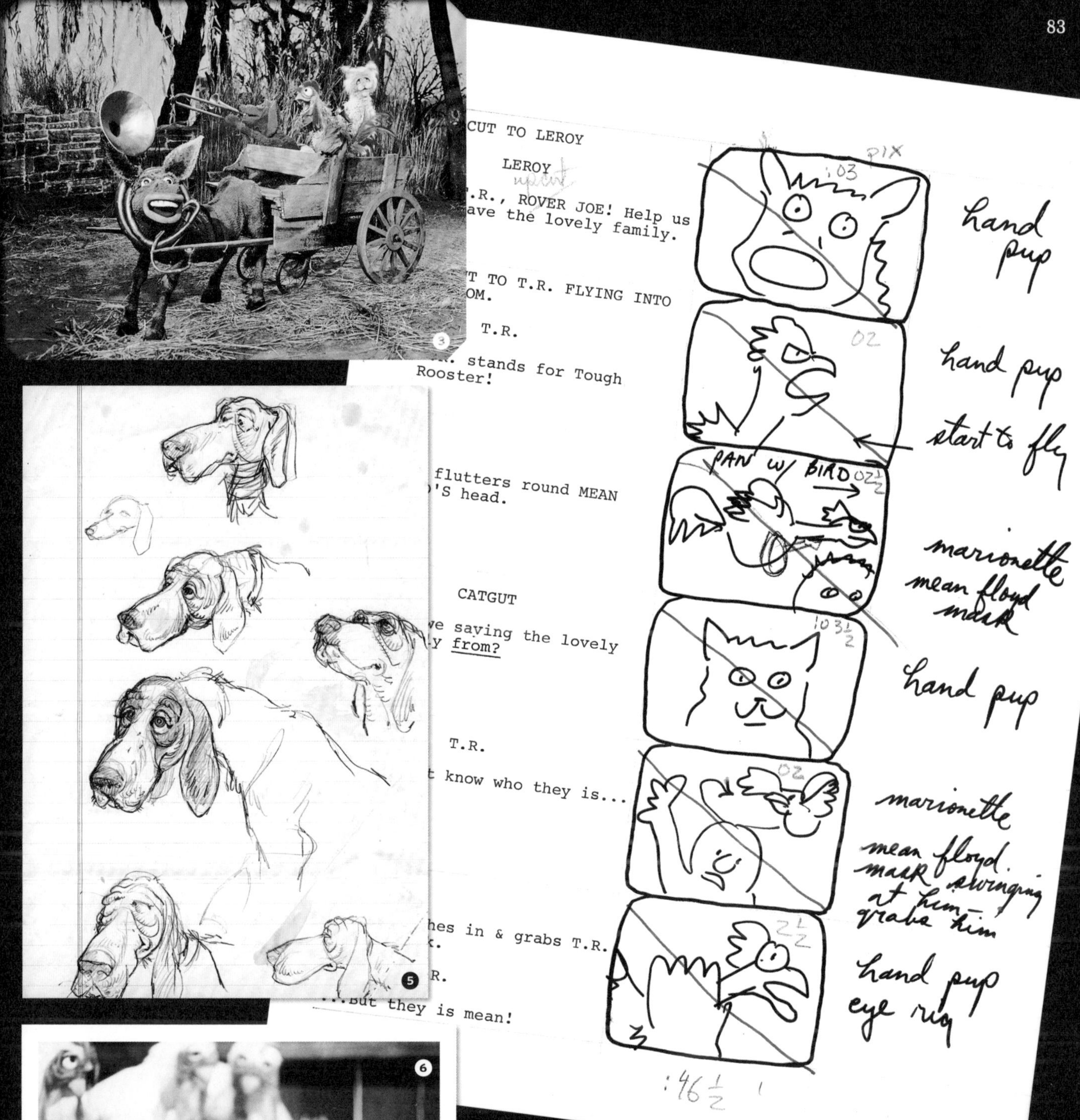

April 29-May 1 Family drives to Cape Cod- fly Kites

July 6 meeting w/ Ideal Toys- games etc.

July 25-28 record ERNIE + BERT album

aug 7-11 in LA Flip Wilson Show
dancing Frogs- Ballroom + Clink Clank

1972

Aug 31 - ROBOT due on Sesame Street

As the popularity of *Sesame Street* grew, the producers and writers became more ambitious, expanding their storyline possibilities in the fourth season with a new character: SAM the Robot. SAM was an acronym for Super-Automated Machine and, as an automated machine, he was supposed to be infallible but, of course, was constantly confused. Jim enjoyed creating SAM, having spent time over the years doodling scores of robot-like characters, and writing numerous scenarios involving man's conflicted feelings toward machines with Jerry Juhl. Performer Jerry Nelson took on SAM with relish. While SAM did not catch on, Nelson was, at the same time, developing his signature character, Count von Count.

❶ Jim's robot designs for a trade show and corporate meetings, early 1960s. ❷+❸ Jim's initial designs for SAM the Robot for *Sesame Street*. ❹ SAM the Robot. ❺+❼ Jim worked with Jerry Juhl in creating his first robot puppet. ❻ Jim's machine puppet created for IBM in the late 1960s.

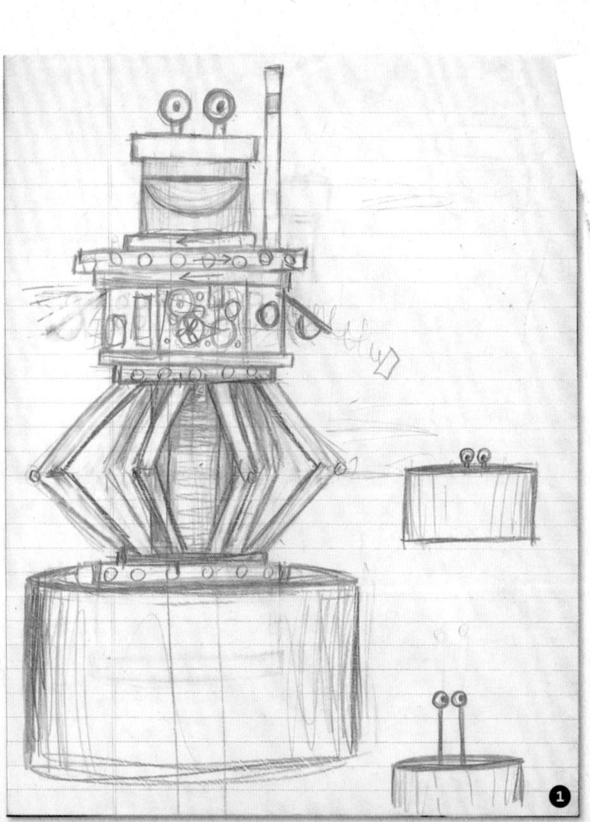

Oct 16 - go to LA with Diana meet with Networks - specials - Billy Goldenberg + Larry Gelbart Oct 20 - 20th cent. Fox about BBC specials

Oct 22 - in LA - VTR Como Christmas Show trio - "Don't mess around with Jim" Jane joins me.

TOP OF HEAD

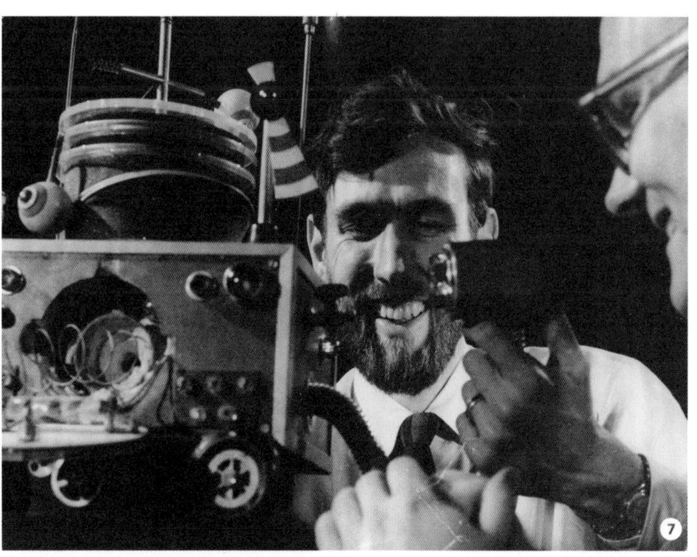

3 4 5 6 7

1972
Dec – set deal.
– Lincoln Center – with Larry Gelbart

After his appearance in Las Vegas, Jim was intrigued by the challenges of live performance; unlike for television, characters had to be visible and expressive to audiences both in the front row and far away in the balconies. Larry Gelbart, then known for both his television and stage writing, met with Jim, and they made a deal to do a live show at New York's Lincoln Center. The Gelbart deal fell through, but Jim continued with the project, amassing an accordion file labeled "Broadway Show" bulging with drawings, scripts, concepts for unique puppet construction, and polished presentation artwork. *The Muppet Show* interrupted Jim's plans, but his ideas did not go to waste—many of the concepts for large or abstract puppets were used on the television show.

1 + 4 + 6 Jim's artwork created to pitch his Broadway show idea. 2 Performer Dave Goelz was originally hired by Jim as a puppet designer and builder. These designs for the Broadway show project were some of his earliest efforts. 3 + 5 Jim's rough ideas for his live Broadway style review.

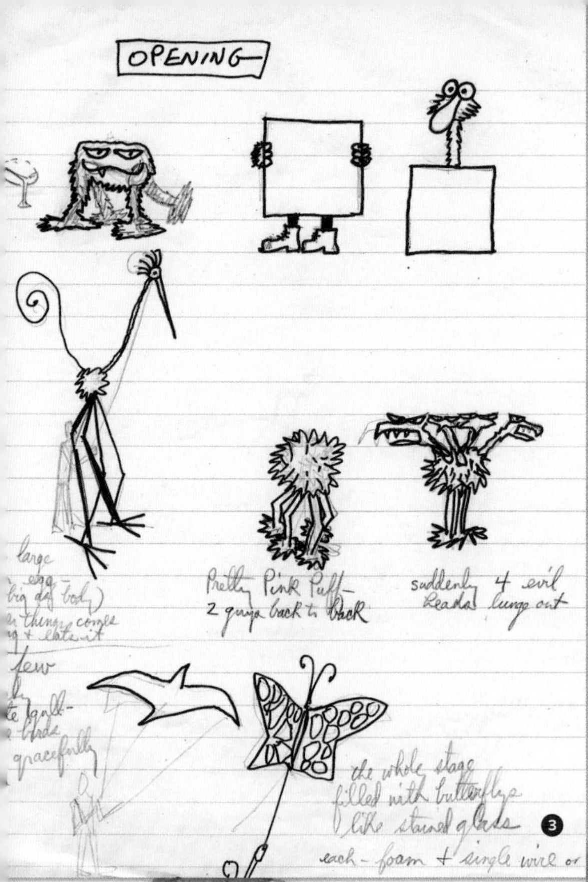
OPENING
large
Pretty Pink Puff–
2 guys back to back
suddenly 4 evil
heads lunge out
few
gracefully
the whole stage
filled with butterflys
like stained glass
each– foam + single wire or
3

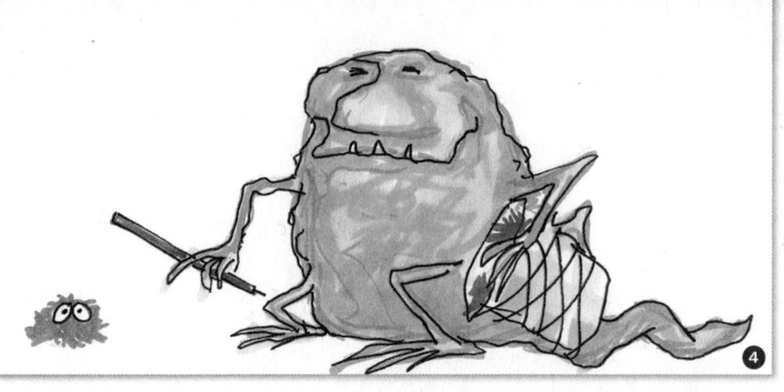

4

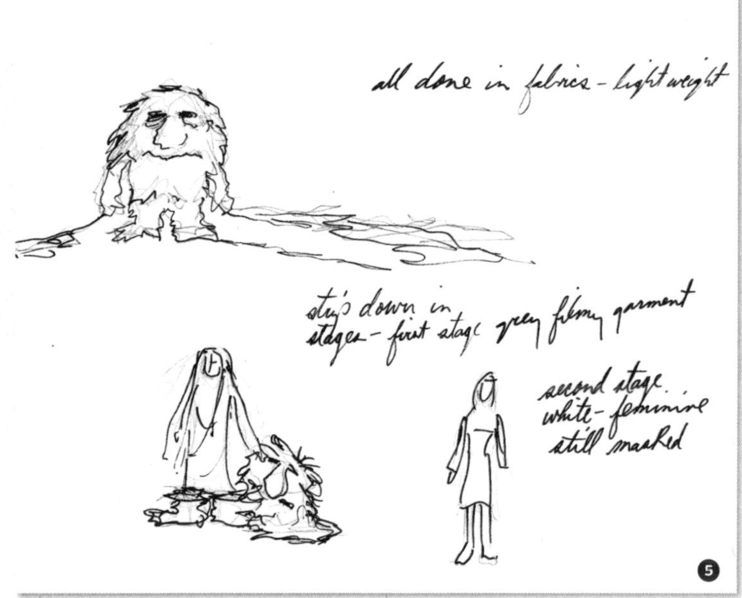

all done in fabrics – light weight
strips down in
stages – first stage grey filmy garment
second stage
white – feminine
still masked
5

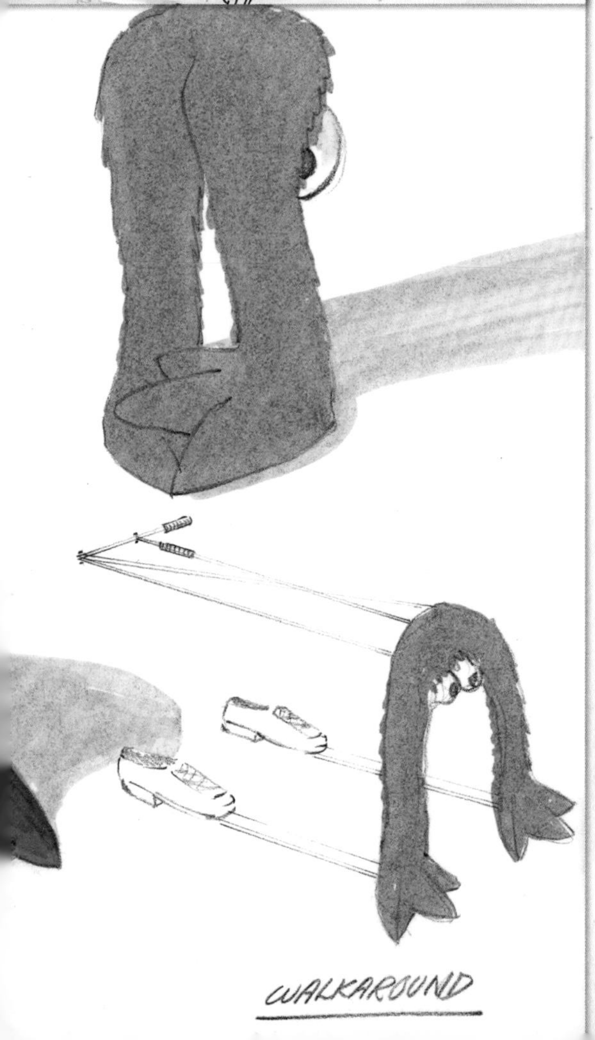
WALKAROUND

1973

Jan 13-15 ski at Stratton

March 27 Ecology Special - "Keep US Beautiful" airs

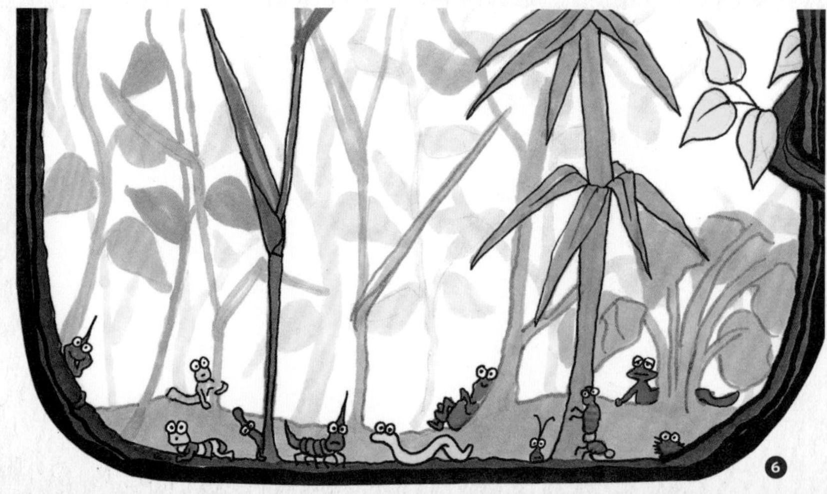

6

1973
april 17 do CAVETT Show - Rock Trio
"Mama don't 'Low"

On Thanksgiving in 1971, Dick Cavett's entire ninety-minute show was devoted to Jim and his team performing just about everything in their repertoire. A family-friendly way to end the holiday, audiences tuned in at 11:30 p.m. to see Kermit, Big Bird, Mahna Mahna, clips from *Time Piece* and *Youth '68*, Big Bossman, the changing faces of the Southern Colonel, and animated counting films. When Jim was invited back in 1973, he needed something new. Bonnie Erickson had designed three caricature puppets resembling Jim Henson, Frank Oz, and Jerry Nelson that Jim decided to use for the show. Channeling his country roots, the trio performed the traditional song "Mama Don't 'Low" with a rock 'n' roll beat, hinting at The Electric Mayhem and other Muppet bands to come.

❶ Jim and Bonnie Erickson with puppets she created. ❷+❸ Bonnie Erickson's ideas for caricature puppets based on Jim Henson, Frank Oz, and Jerry Nelson. ❹ Press coverage of the Muppets' 1973 appearance on *The Dick Cavett Show*. ❺ Puppet builder Caroly Wilcox's ideas for the changing faces of the Southern Colonel performed on an earlier *Cavett Show* appearance. ❻ Jim's script for "Mama Don't 'Low."

❶

❷

❸

The Muppet rock group, Jim, Frank and Jerry
and Kermit the Frog (lower left) join "The Di
Tuesday, after Channel 4's 11:30 p. m. movie.

May 12 + 13 Judging Emmy awards
May 20 do EMMY AWARDS show with
Kermit + Cookie Monster w/ Jane + Frank
May 22 in Albuquerque
May 23 - in LA for Affiliates + see Eisner
May 26 - fly to London with Lisa + Cheryl
Grovesnor House
June 8 - return from Copenhagen

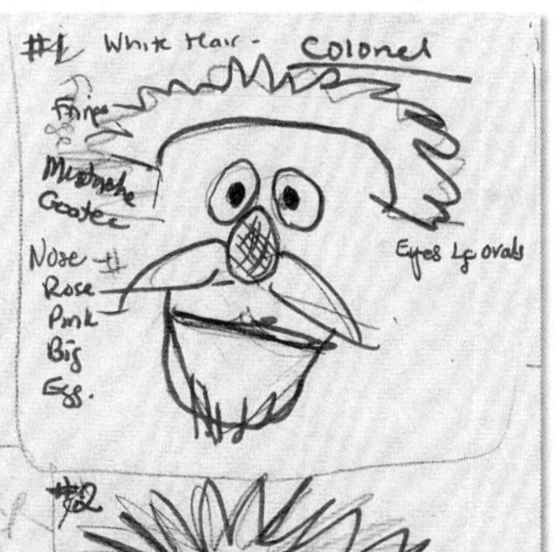

Dick Cavett Show April 17, 1973

Mama don't 'low no bass playin' in here
what do you mean?
Mama don't 'low no bass playin' in here
well I don't care what low, gonna play
this bass anyhow
But Mama don't 'low no bass playin' in here.

Now what are you doin'?

strummin' my guitar

You can't do that!
Mama don't low no guitar strummin' in here
aw she don't care
Mama don't low no guitar strummin' in here
Well let me tell you somethin
I don't care what mama don't low
gonna strum my guitar anyhow
But mama don't low no guitar strummin' in here

O. Pick that Banjo

H. You mean like this?

O. yeah.

6

June 11 - Dave Goelz begins with us
July 23, 1st meeting w writers Valentine Show
27 Will Glickman Jerry Ross + Jull

1973

May - order Jag XJ6

Success on television meant that Jim, who enjoyed the road, could drive whatever he wanted. Each new car brought real pleasure, meriting a mention in his journal and a photo in the album. With his first earnings from *Sam and Friends*, Jim bought a white Thunderbird and posed in it with Sam. In 1960, he drove a used Rolls-Royce Silver Cloud to his graduation at the University of Maryland and then with Jane and baby Lisa to the Puppeteers of America festival in Detroit. Subsequent cars included station wagons for family trips, a Porsche, a BMW, a VW, and a Mercedes. But Jim's 1978 Lotus Éclat, customized in Kermit green with headlights detailed to look like Kermit's eyes, was, in his daughter Cheryl's words, "the best."

❶+❻+❼ Jim's fantasy car doodles, late 1960s. ❷ Jim and Sam in his Thunderbird near his home in University Park, Maryland, 1956. ❸ Jim, ready to graduate from the University of Maryland in 1960, stands by his Rolls-Royce. ❹ Kermit takes the wheel of Jim's 1978 Lotus. ❺ Jim poses in his Porsche Speedster around 1961.

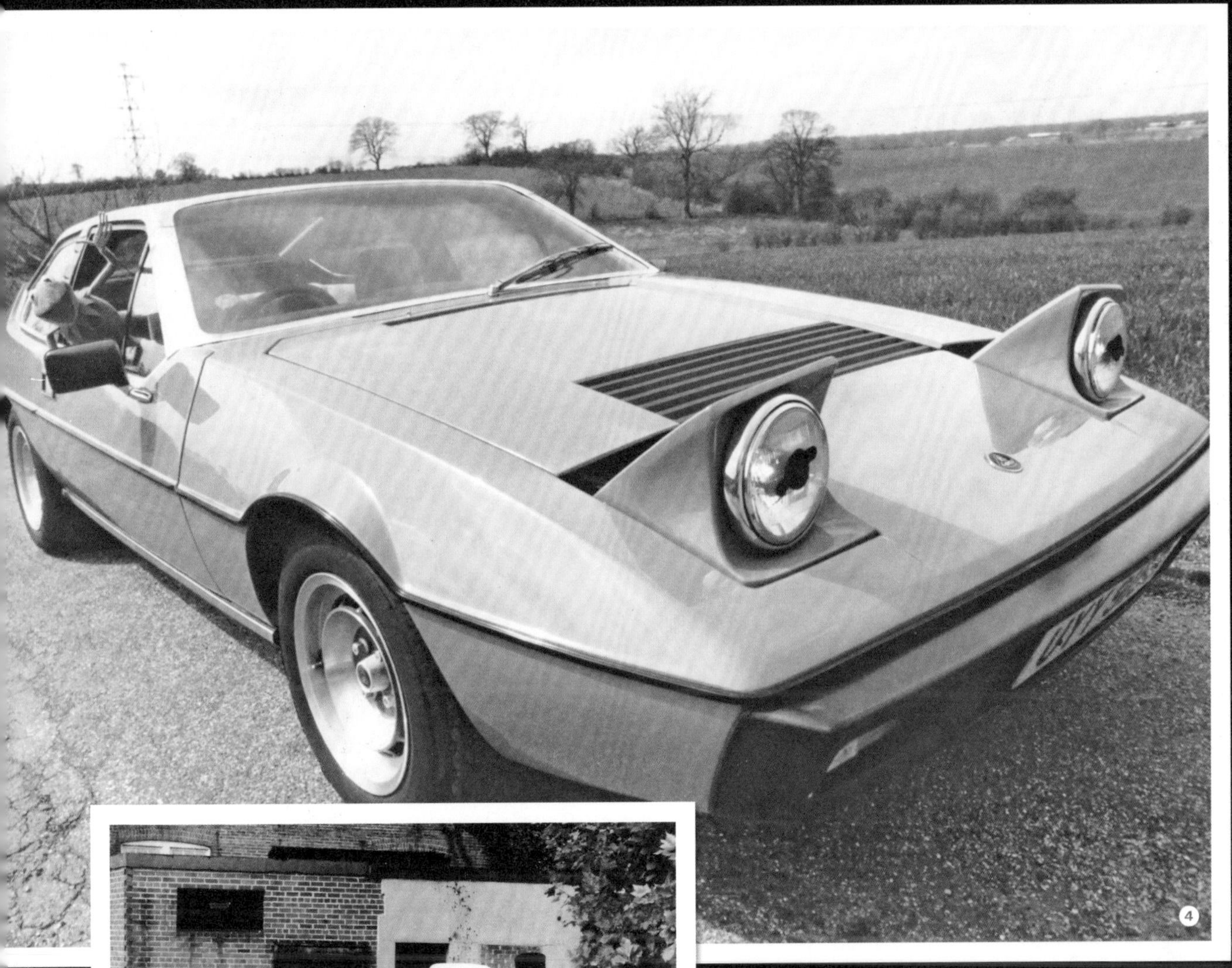

4

5

7

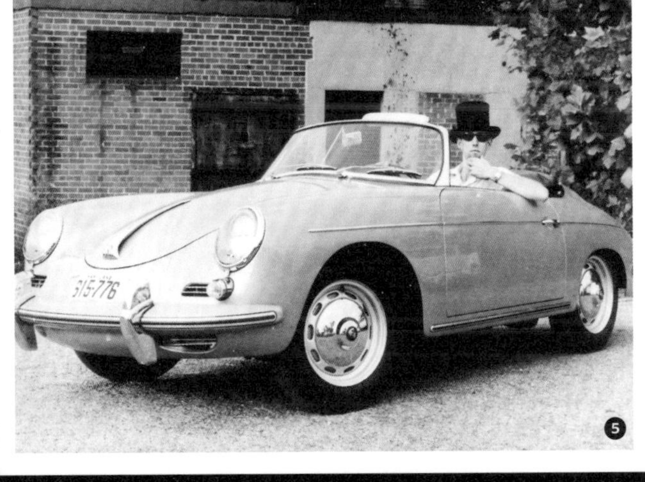

Aug. 10 get JAGUAR XJ6

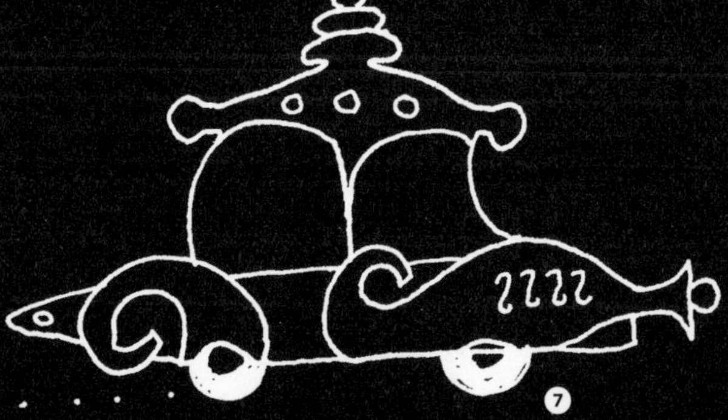

Oct 20 fly to London
dinner Joe R at Dorchester
VTR Oct. 27-29 "Julie on Sesame Street"
Oct 30 Jane arrives B'way Medley
VTR Nov 3-5

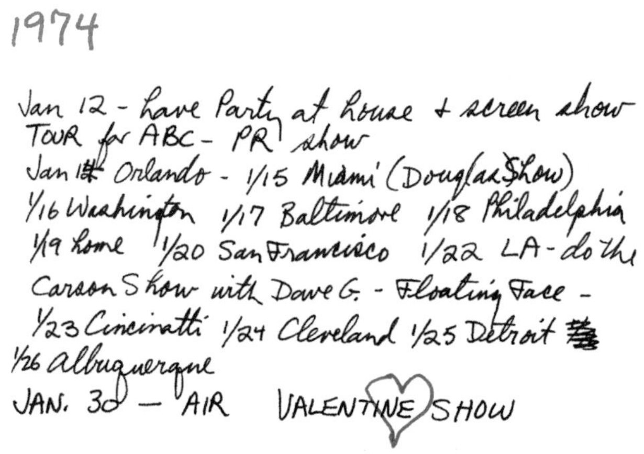

1974

Jan 12 - have Party at house + screen show
TOUR for ABC - PR show
Jan 14 Orlando - 1/15 Miami (Douglas Show)
1/16 Washington 1/17 Baltimore 1/18 Philadelphia
1/19 home 1/20 San Francisco 1/22 LA - do the
Carson Show with Dave G. - Floating Face -
1/23 Cincinatti 1/24 Cleveland 1/25 Detroit
1/26 Albuquerque
JAN. 30 — AIR VALENTINE SHOW

At an April 6, 1973, meeting with then–senior network programming executive (and future Disney CEO) Michael Eisner, Jim got the green light for *The Muppets Valentine Show*, a pilot of sorts for a possible series. The special starred Mia Farrow, demonstrating how celebrities would eventually work with the characters on *The Muppet Show*, and the living room set provided a home base for the action. The sketches and songs all related to love and romance, and the obviously pregnant Farrow further underlined the theme. A report from the Planet Koozebane helped explore the meaning of love in that alien world, and a soulful duet united Farrow with the oversized Thog. Kermit courted a giant mouse, and the entire show was syncopated by gleeful explosions.

❶+❺ Jim's creatures from the Planet Koozebane whose romantic antics were chronicled by Kermit. ❷ Promotional poster for *The Muppets Valentine Show* with artwork by Ted CoConis. ❸ Thog and Mia Farrow. ❹ Thog in his Valentine sweater. ❻ Jim and Mia Farrow on the set of *The Muppets Valentine Show*. ❼ Jim's designs for a giant mouse, Kermit's competition when he went a-courtin'.

1

T. CoConis

A Valentine Poem from Thog-ROSES ARE RED AND VIOLETS ARE...DELICIOUS
Watch The Muppets Valentine Special with special guest star, Miss Mia Farrow
Wednesday, January 30 on your local ABC-TV station.

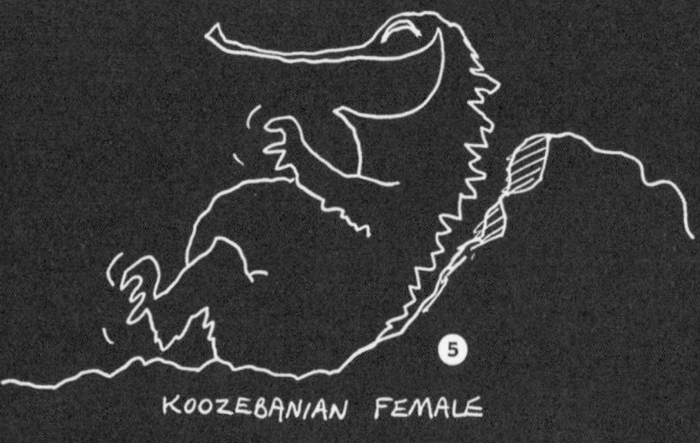

april 3 - TODAY SHOW - Bert as Gene Shalit

april 27 - Jane + I go to Kent State conference
TV and Young Children

May 9 - see Frank in off B'way play

May 19-22 in albuquerque with Jane, Lisa + Cheryl

aug 2 - Film Heather for end of Ball Film

1

1974
Aug 13 - get final OK from ABC regarding deal - pilot - afterschool - consultant + film development

The positive response to *The Muppets Valentine Show* allowed Jim to negotiate an extensive agreement with ABC that included two television specials, a prime-time movie treatment, and ABC's exclusive use of the Muppets. Up first was a special aimed at school-age audiences called *Out to Lunch* with the casts of *Sesame Street* and *The Electric Company* and Elliott Gould, Carol Burnett, and Barbara Eden. According to Jim, the idea was to parody commercial television by having "all these wild people" take over the ABC-TV studio. Jim also began work on the other special which he wanted to call *Sex and Violence with The Muppets*, but the network insisted on the less controversial *The Muppet Show*. The anarchy remained, and numerous characters were introduced that would make the subsequent series a hit.

3

❶ Jack Davis's illustration made for ABC's promotion of *Out to Lunch*. ❷ Jim's sketch of Nigel, Floyd, and Sam the Eagle as seen in *The Muppet Show* pilot. ❸ Jim's sketch of Animal, The Electric Mayhem's drummer. ❹ Michael Frith's detailed drawing of Dr. Teeth. ❺ Michael Frith's idea for Animal. ❻ Jim's sketches of Dr. Teeth, leader of The Electric Mayhem. ❼ Around 1973, Jim asked *Sesame Street* artist B.K. Taylor to create some monster designs. Among them was his drawing of "The Boogie Man," which inspired Dr. Teeth's design.

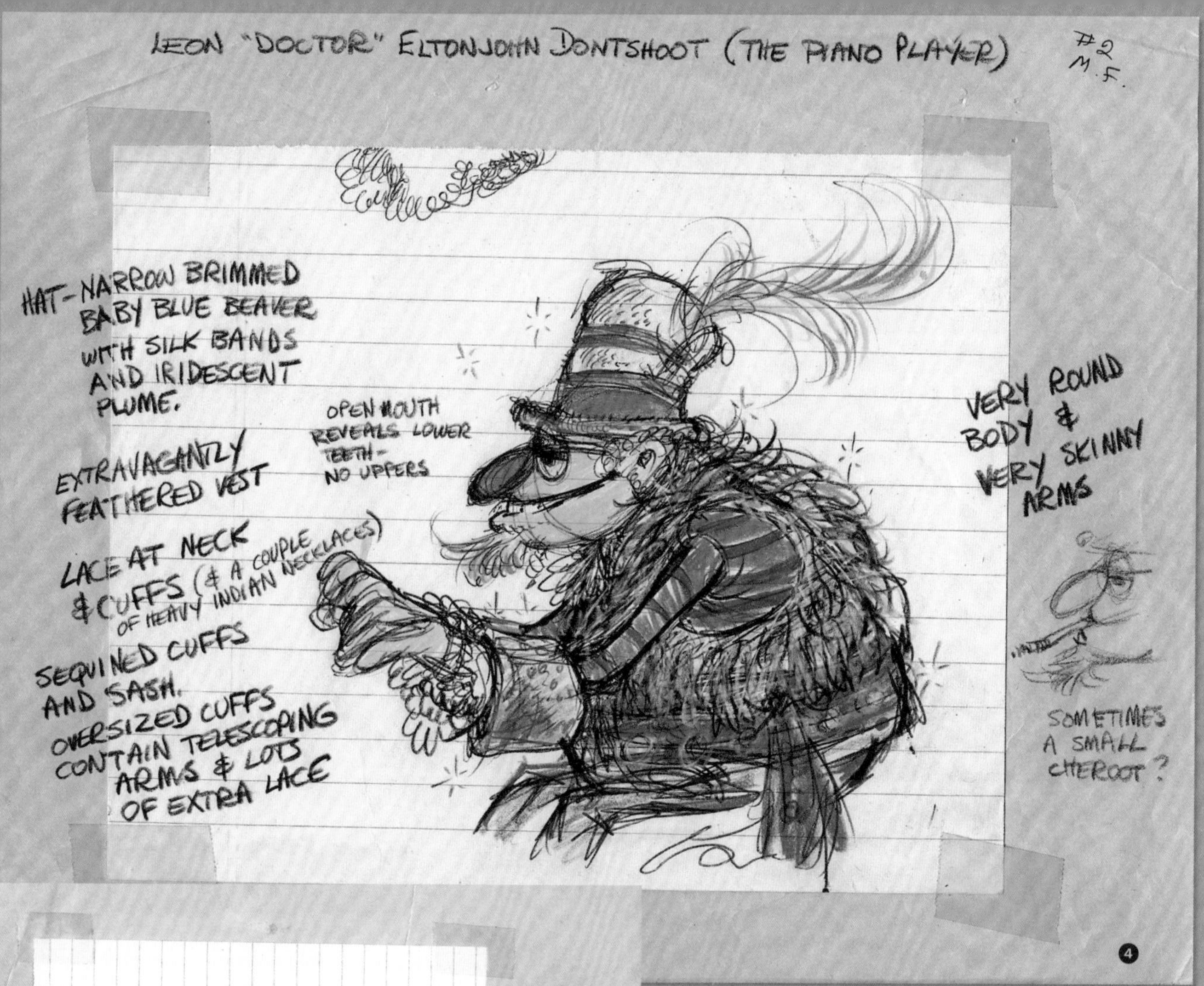

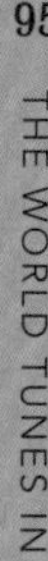

LEON "DOCTOR" ELTONJOHN DONTSHOOT (THE PIANO PLAYER)
#2 M.F.
HAT- NARROW BRIMMED BABY BLUE BEAVER WITH SILK BANDS AND IRIDESCENT PLUME.
OPEN MOUTH REVEALS LOWER TEETH - NO UPPERS
EXTRAVAGANTLY FEATHERED VEST
LACE AT NECK & CUFFS (& A COUPLE OF HEAVY INDIAN NECKLACES)
SEQUINED CUFFS AND SASH.
OVERSIZED CUFFS CONTAIN TELESCOPING ARMS & LOTS OF EXTRA LACE
VERY ROUND BODY & VERY SKINNY ARMS
SOMETIMES A SMALL CHEROOT?
4

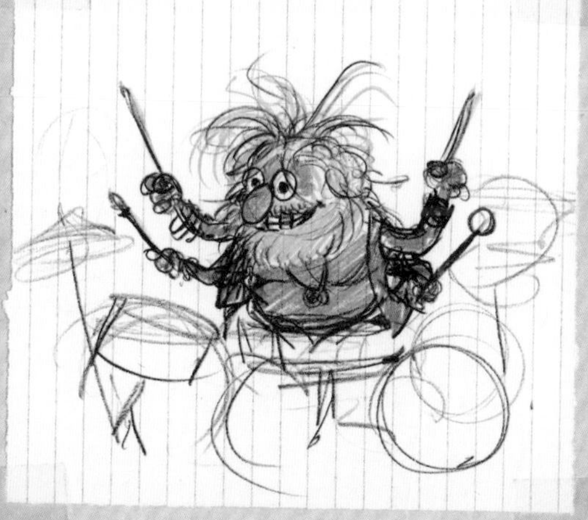

WILDLY FLYING HAIR - AT REST MIGHT COVER FACE COMPLETELY
GOLD TOOTH
FOUR ARMS
IT WOULD BE NICE IF HE COULD PERSPIRE
5

Sept 15- Henson Family Show in North Salem Hammond Museum
Sept 16- film Public Service Nutrition Commercial with Cookie M in Staten Is.

Sept 4- EMMY SHOW- Muppets win outstanding achievement in Childrens Programs- Big Bird talks to Cavett

TEETH #1 - JIM
6

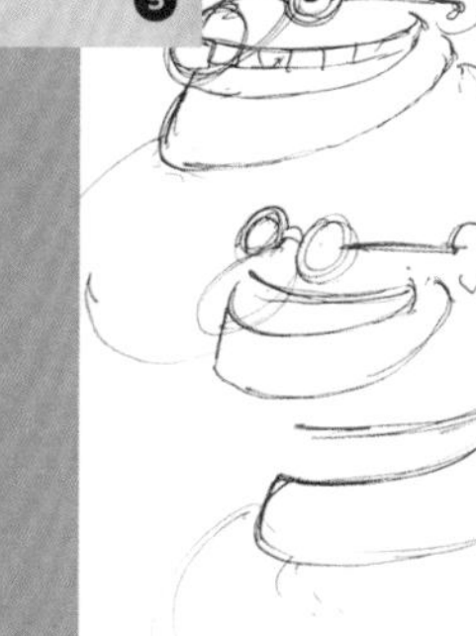

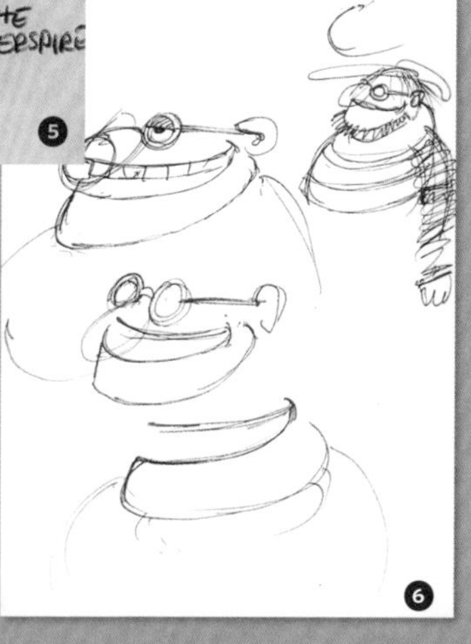

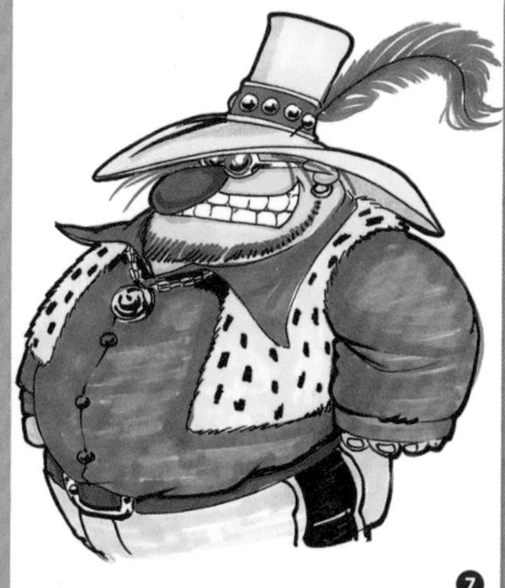

7

1974

Sept 22-Oct 3 in London VTR Herb Alpert Show - stayed at Inn on the Park - did Boss Men

Oct 13 - AIR - HERB ALPERT SHOW-ABC

While planning for both his *Out to Lunch* special and *The Muppet Show* pilot, Jim and his team flew to London to tape the Herb Alpert and the Tijuana Brass special. Along with some Snerfs and Big Bossmen puppets, they packed a couple of pigs that had been made for a "Return to the Planet of the Pigs" sketch planned for the pilot. On his show, Alpert is accosted by a pushy pig talent agent, performed by Jim, and his protégée, a glamorous lady pig called "Piggy Lee," performed first by Jerry Nelson. This proto–Miss Piggy had instant charisma and didn't leave the stage without a contract. Her star quality was obvious, and when she reappeared on the series as an attractive glee club member, she was a hit.

❶ Bonnie Erickson's drawings of a pig and a chicken for a glee club sketch planned for the first episode of *The Muppet Show*. The pig drawing, based on Erickson's "Piggy Lee" character, has hooves rather than Miss Piggy's signature gloves. ❷ Jim's choreography for the Big Bossmen puppets' dance to Alpert's "Spanish Flea." ❸ John Lovelady's design for Rex. ❹ Newspaper promotion for ABC's Herb Alpert special. ❺ Jim tests out a Snerf during rehearsals for the "Spanish Town" song on the Herb Alpert show. ❻ Astronaut Rex in the "Return to the Planet of the Pigs" sketch from *The Muppet Show* pilot. ❼ Set design plans for the operating scene in "Return to the Planet of the Pigs" showing the stage elevated to accommodate standing puppeteers.

Nov 14 - VTR What's My Line as Mystery Guest
Thanksgiving - Parade - on float Sesame Characters + John Pane
Dec 10-16 - VTR The Muppet Show (Sex + Violence) for ABC

SPANISH FLEA

— VAMP
:06 JERRY ENTERS
:17 FRANK ENTERS
:29 LEAN OVER/HEAD TURNS
:35 CROSS
:44 TUMMY DRUMS
:48 HI + LOW
:57 STOP GRIN
:59 FOOT TAPS

SPANISH FLEA

VAMP
:05 TRUMPET MELODY 4 8
:17 2nd PART - MELODY ⑧ 8
:29 VAMP (12½) 4 — LEAN-OVER HEAD TURNS — GRIN
:34 SWINGIN' (14½) 8 WINDMILL — 5 line up - SEMAPHORE
:43 STOPS (18½) V V V v v v v v v v TUMMY DRUMS
:48 MELODY (20½) { JERRY DOWN 4 / FRANK UP 4 } HI-LOS
STOPS (23)
:57 HIGH STOP (24½) BACK + FORTH - PULSES
VAMP (25½) FOOT TAP STOP-GRIN
SWINGIN'

❷

❸

HERB ALPERT & THE TJB

OCTOBER 13. The king of brass is back with his unique style. Special guests The Muppets.

❹

October VTR- Out to Lunch - Special with CTW for ABC

❺ ❻

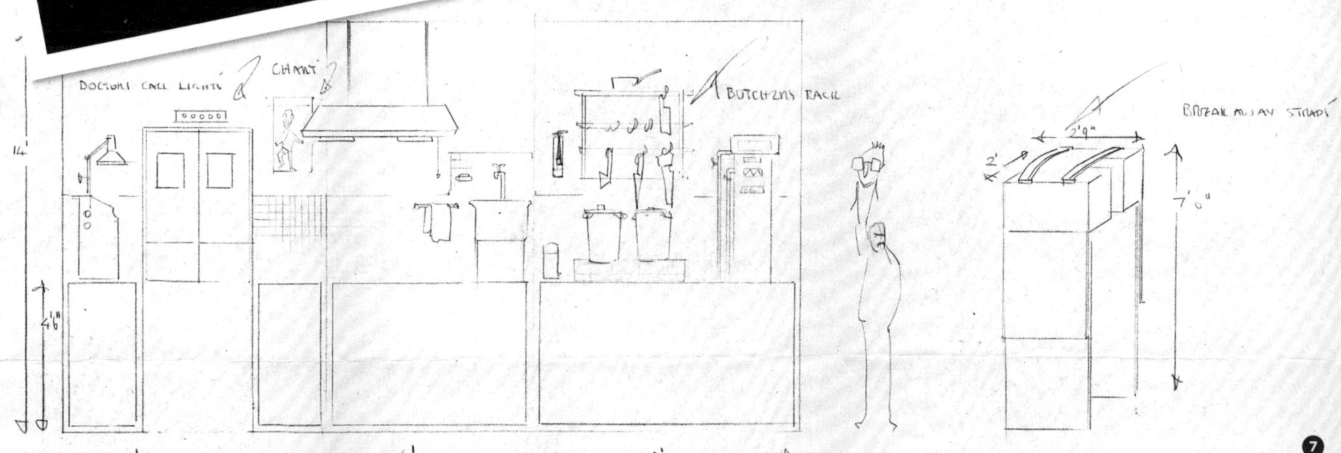

❼

1975

Jan 2–7 1st edit – the Muppet Show
Jan 11 – 1st assemble

March 19 AIR THE MUPPET SHOW ABC
watch it with Dad + Bob in Albuquerque

When Jim sat down at his dad's house to watch *The Muppet Show* pilot, it marked a major step in a long effort to create a musical variety series in prime time. Back in 1960, Jim had made notes and sketches for a hypothetical show called *The Zoocus,* which was to include many recognizable elements and, of course, a repertory company of puppets led by Kermit. After fifteen years of pitching, Jim's ABC deal gave him the chance to start building his cast of characters, creating a community of distinct personalities. Joining the existing troupe were several new pigs and the members of the house band, The Electric Mayhem. The two old men, Statler and Waldorf, started their heckling, and the Swedish Chef took charge of the kitchen.

❶ Announcement card for *The Muppet Show* pilot designed by Michael Frith. ❷ Jim's concept for *The Zoocus*, a musical variety show featuring the Muppets, c. 1960. ❸ *New York Newsday* TV guide, March 16, 1975, featuring the Seven Deadly Sins Pageant from *The Muppet Show* pilot. ❹ Caroly Wilcox's design sketch for the two old men, Statler and Waldorf, based on Bonnie Erickson's design. ❺ Jim's sketch of The Swedish Chef with annotations from puppet builder Caroly Wilcox. ❻ Sam shows his displeasure on the set of *The Muppet Show* pilot.

THE MUPPETS' DEADLY SINS PAGEANT AND IT ISN'T RATED X. SEE JIM HENSON'S STORY ON PAGE 4.

May 31 Ernie + Bert open at the Smithsonian in exhibit "We the People"

July 16-20 take family to DISNEY World

Aug 30 in LA shooting Kermit for CBS presentation tape

1975

Oct 11 - SAT NIGHT LIVE! first show
#2 - Oct 18 #3 Oct 25

When superagent Bernie Brillstein sold the idea for *Saturday Night Live* to NBC, he made sure that there was a place on the show for Jim, one of his oldest clients. The talent on *SNL* was young, creative, and mildly subversive—a seemingly perfect fit for the Muppets. The first season included a segment each week called "The Land of Gorch," which featured new Henson characters designed by Michael Frith. They had a more naturalistic look, with glass eyes, and the segments' themes were edgier and adult. For Jim, it was a return to late-night television and an opportunity to remind people that his work was not just for kids. When the Muppets left *SNL* the following year for *The Muppet Show*, they took the experience of creating a weekly show and many celebrity connections with them.

❶ Richard Hunt performing Wisss. ❷ Collaborative design by Jim and Michael Frith of the Mighty Favog. ❸ Advertisement for the premiere of *Saturday Night Live*, 1975. ❹ Michael Frith's Ploobis design. ❺ Jerry Nelson performing Scred with guest host Ron Nessen. ❻ Scred as imagined by Michael Frith.

❷

❸

"NBC SATURDA
NIGHT–LIVE"

This is a big one! Don't miss the exciting premiere of a new series that's a whole new dimension for TV! It's **live from New York** spotlighting the comedy and music stars of today—and tomorrow!

Tonight's host:
GEORGE CARLIN

A comedy film by
ALBERT BROOKS

Jim Henson and the
MUPPETS

Special musical guests
JANIS IAN
BILLY PRESTON

Plus two brilliant, new comedy finds:
BILLY CRYSTAL
ANDY KAUFMAN

Next week: Paul Simon, host, with special guest star Art Garfunkel!

11:30 PM
NBC 4,20

Oct 18 - sat meeting ITC - ATV
Oct 22 - Press Conference "21" announce "The Muppet Show"
Oct 22 do Dinah Shore Show

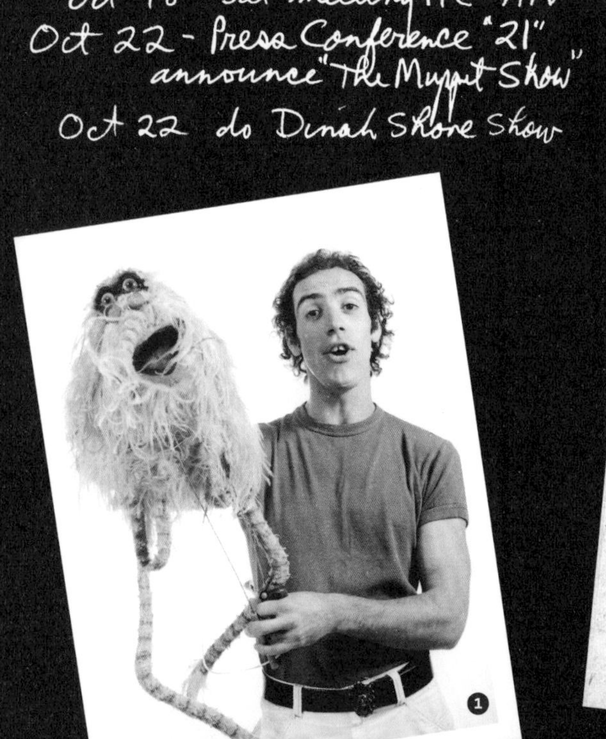

❶

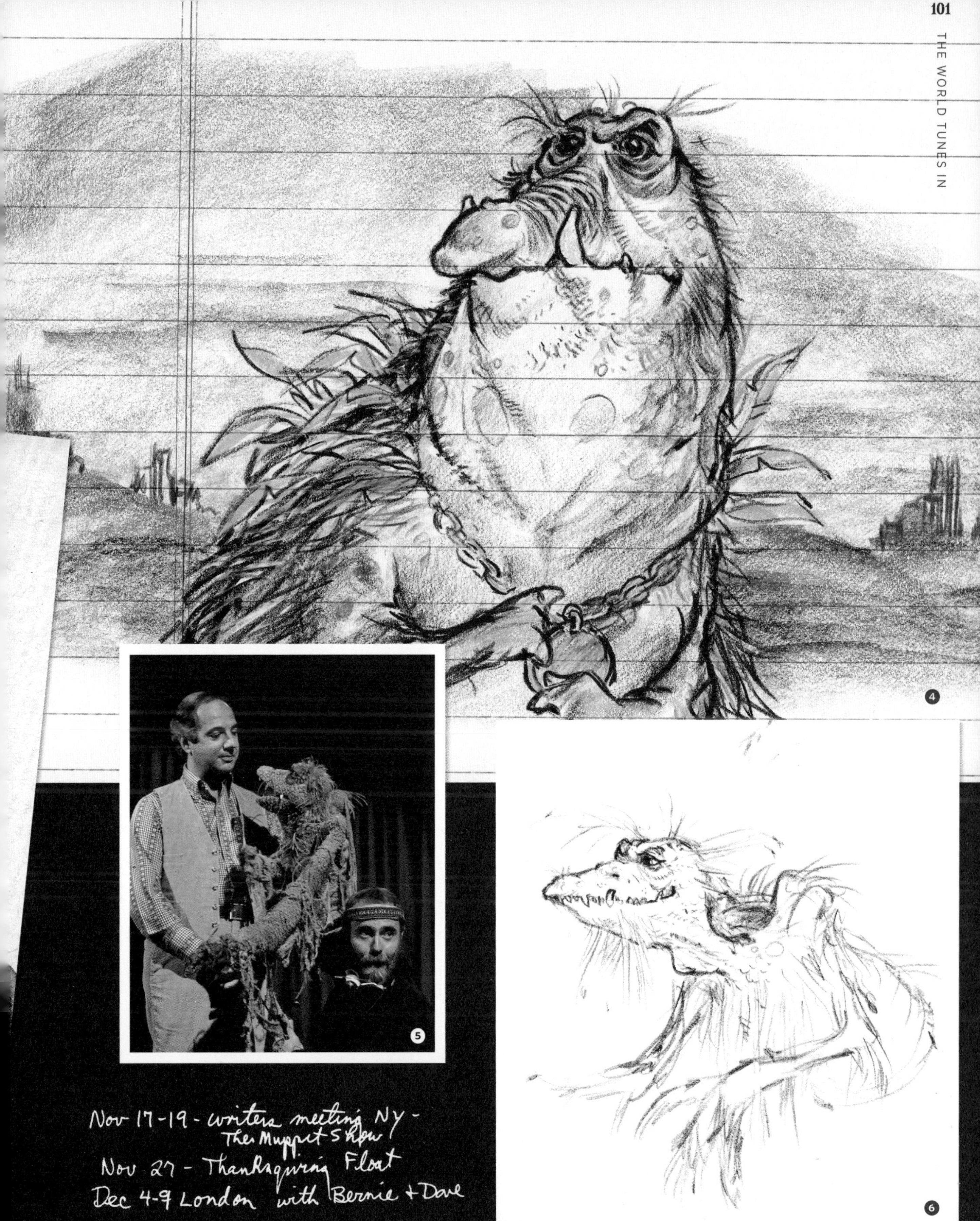
4
5
6
Nov 17-19 - writers meeting NY -
The Muppet Show
Nov 27 - Thanksgiving Float
Dec 4-9 London with Bernie + Dave

1976

Jan 11 - travel to LONDON to do
2 pilot shows - Connie S +
Juliet P.
VTR 19-20-21, 29 - Feb 1
return Feb. 14

April 24 - Sat Night Live - I write

May 5 take QE2 to London
with Jane + Jack
THE MUPPET SHOW

The Muppet Show

Sept 20th - The [...] w
airs in NYC/+ Mondays + 7:30
Rita M. first

After airing two Muppet specials as part of a bigger production deal, ABC ultimately passed on *The Muppet Show*. Jim aggressively pitched the series to CBS to no avail. He really wanted a network deal, but was eventually persuaded to produce a syndicated show for Lew Grade at his ATV studio outside London. On hiatus from *Saturday Night Live*, Jim and his team shipped their entire puppet inventory to London and taped the first two episodes, featuring Juliet Prowse and Connie Stevens, as prototypes for the series. Taping resumed in May, and in September 1976, *The Muppet Show* premiered with the Rita Moreno episode in both the U.K. and the U.S. Thanks to Grade's distribution company's international reach, Jim's show was airing in dozens of countries within a year.

❶ Season one performers (left to right) Dave Goelz, John Lovelady, Eren Ozker, Jim Henson, Jerry Nelson, Frank Oz, and Richard Hunt. ❷ Juliet Prowse chats with Kermit on *The Muppet Show*. ❸ Connie Stevens on *The Muppet Show*. ❹ Jim's storyboard for *The Muppet Show* opening. ❺ Michael Frith's design for Connie Stevens's dance partners, the Mutations. ❻ *The Muppet Show* logo designed by Michael Frith. ❼ John Lovelady's ideas for Beaker.

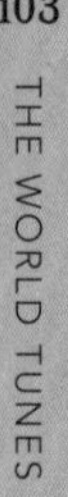

WIPE FROM GUEST STAR TO THIS SHOT
Kermit: BUT NOW LET'S GET THINGS STARTED
Red tabs behind Kermit open - reveal big group against limbo - black?
OUP: ON THE MOST SENSATIONAL
PULLING BACK
INSPIRATIONAL CELEBRATIONAL
MUPPETATIONAL THIS IS WHAT
WE CALL
HE MUPPET
OW!
any OTHER LANGUAGE VERSIONS
MANY DIFFERENT GONZOS

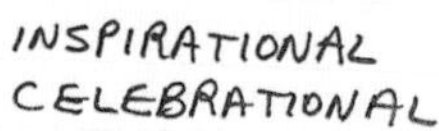
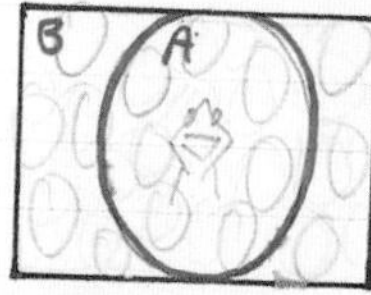
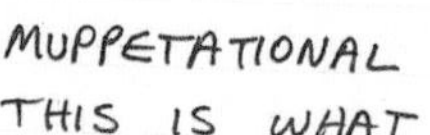
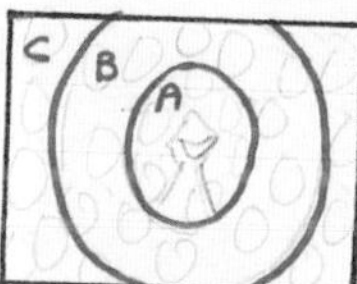
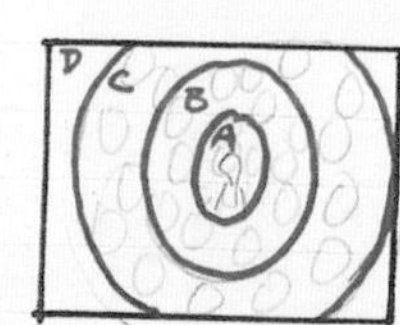
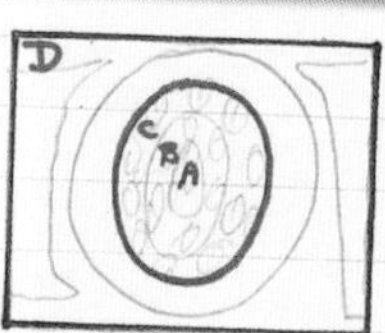
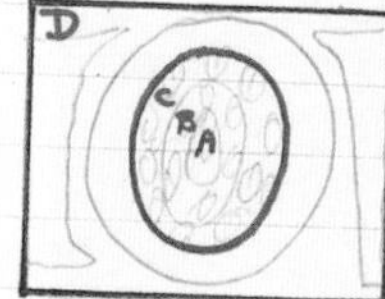
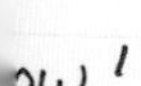

Die
MUPPET
SHOW

The
MUPPET
SHOW

Hi-Ho!
It's...
The
MUPPET
SHOW

1977

Jan 3-5 in LA - Paul W. - Emmet O.

As a *Muppet Show* guest star, Paul Williams seemed particularly in tune with Jim's musical sensibility. Williams's performance on songs like "Just an Old Fashioned Love Song" (with his Muppet doppelganger) made him seem like part of the troupe. Within a year, Jim asked Williams to compose music for the television project *Emmet Otter's Jug-Band Christmas*, based on the book by Russell and Lillian Hoban. He wrote ballads and hoedowns, and working closely with Jim, Williams enhanced the visuals with evocative musical elements. The banjo pickin' chosen for Kermit's entrance laid the groundwork for perhaps the most satisfying collaboration between the two men. In 1978, Williams, with Kenneth Ascher, wrote the music for *The Muppet Movie*, including Kermit's banjo-accompanied song, "The Rainbow Connection."

❶ Paul Williams on *The Muppet Show*. ❷ Faz Fazakas working on Emmet and his boat. ❸ Michael Frith's map of the setting for *Emmet Otter's Jug-Band Christmas*. ❹ Scenes from *Emmet Otter*. ❺ Janet Lerman's Doc Bullfrog sketch. ❻ Squirrel mechanical plan by John Lovelady for *Emmet Otter*. ❼ John and Heather Henson visiting the *Emmet Otter* set.

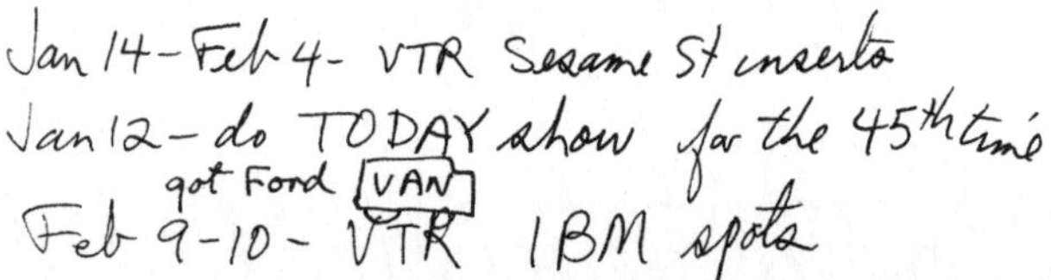
Jan 14 - Feb 4 - VTR Sesame St inserts
Jan 12 - do TODAY show for the 45th time
got Ford VAN
Feb 9-10 - VTR IBM spots

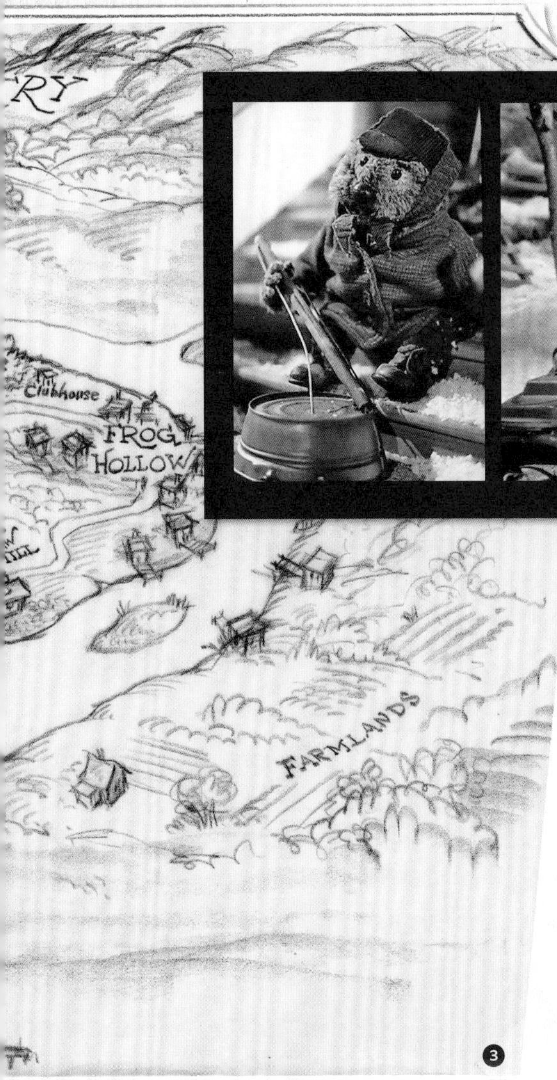

'RY
Clubhouse
FROG HOLLOW
FARMLANDS

3

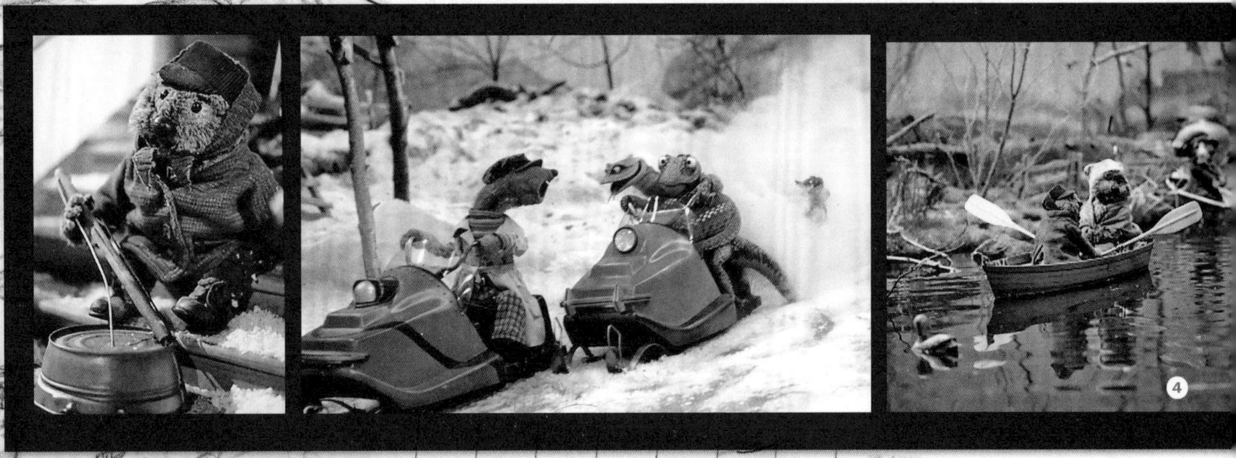

4

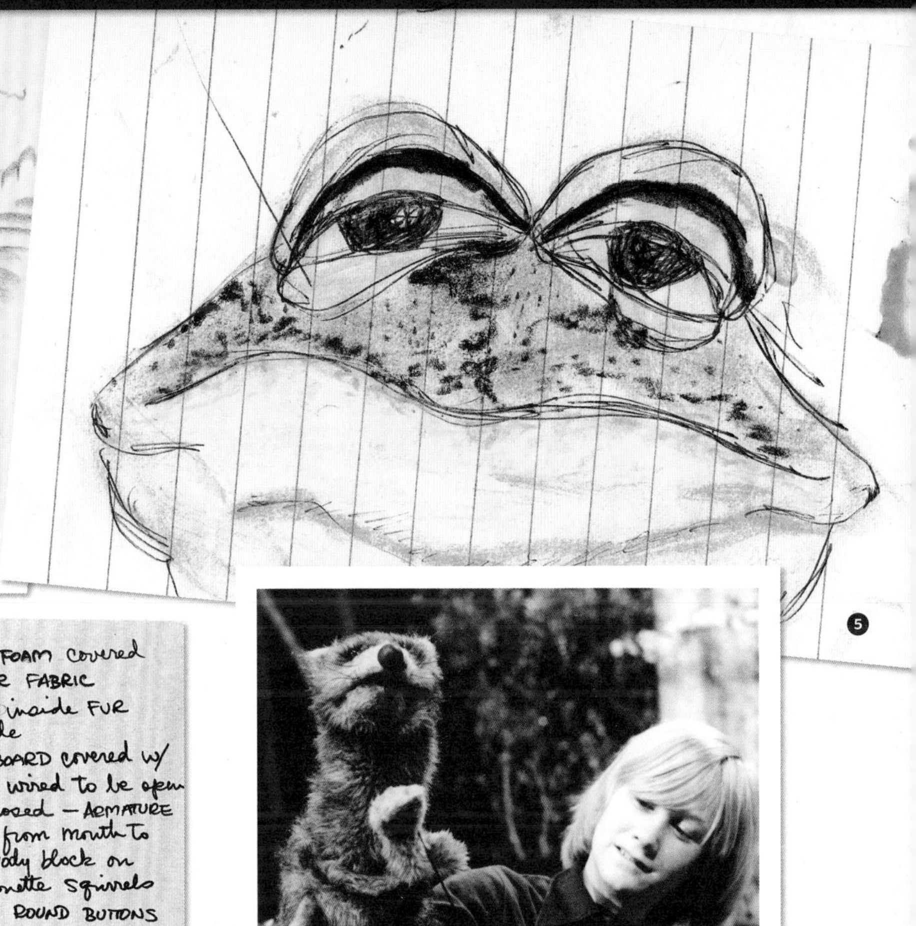

5

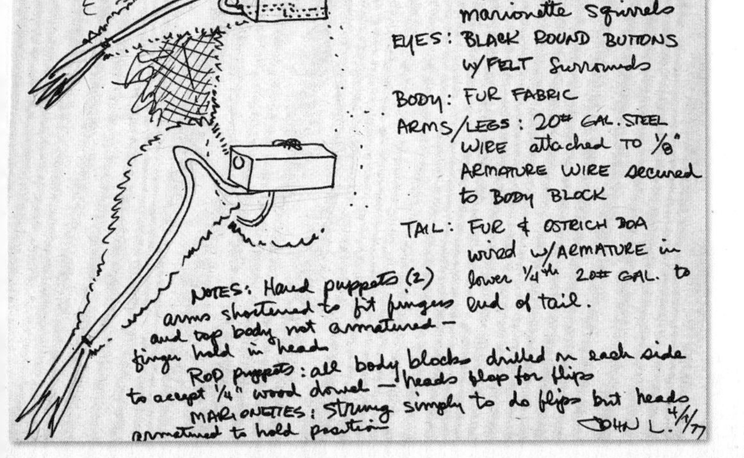

SQUIRRELS: E.O.
HEAD: 3/8" SCOTT FOAM covered by FUR FABRIC
EARS: FELT inside FUR outside
MOUTH: CARDBOARD covered w/ FELT wired to be open or closed — ARMATURE WIRE from mouth to top body block on marionette squirrels
EYES: BLACK ROUND BUTTONS w/FELT Surrounds
BODY: FUR FABRIC
ARMS/LEGS: 20# GAL. STEEL WIRE attached to 1/8" ARMATURE WIRE secured to BODY BLOCK
TAIL: FUR & OSTRICH BOA wired w/ARMATURE in lower 1/4th 20# GAL. to end of tail.
NOTES: Hand puppets (2) arms shortened to fit fingers and top body not armatured — finger hold in head
ROD puppets: all body blocks drilled on each side to accept 1/4" wood dowel — heads flop for flips
MARIONETTES: Strung simply to do flips but heads armatured to hold position
JOHN L. 4/1/77

6

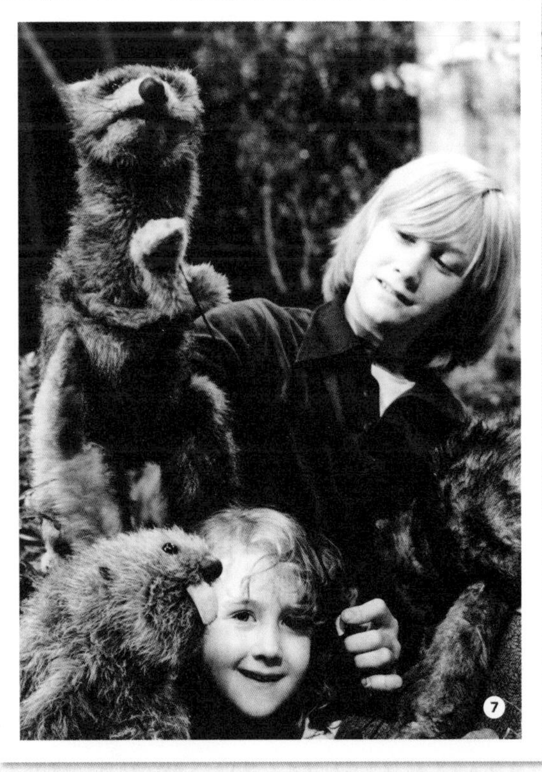

7

1977

Feb 11 shoot AMERICAN EXPRESS commercial - began running next summer

By 1977, the Muppets were gaining global recognition, but the man behind them was rarely seen. An occasional talk show appearance put Jim before the camera, but it would be more than a decade before he hosted his own show and developed a visible public persona. He was a perfect celebrity for the American Express "Do You Know Me?" advertising campaign orchestrated by the Ogilvy & Mather agency. After being heckled by Floyd, Scooter, and some others, Jim promised that he wouldn't leave home without his American Express card. It was fun for Jim and gratifying to be in the same limelight as other "Do you know me?" celebrities. Jim's commercial—and celebrity—was clearly enduring. When AmEx revived these spots in 2008, Jim's was included.

❶ American Express print advertisement featuring Jim, 1977. ❷ Print advertisement for 2008 campaign using Jim's image. ❸ Storyboard for Jim's American Express commercial. ❹ Jim and Jane Henson at their Bedford, NY, home.

Ogilvy & Mather, Inc.

COMMERCIAL NO.

AMERICAN EXPRESS/Card — February 4, 19

CLIENT PRODUCT — RTO

"Jim Henson" (Studio)

TITLE — LENGTH — TIMED B

PROMISE — NUMB

IS MINORITY TALENT APPROPRIATE? IF NOT, WHY NOT? — APPROVED FOR

VIDEO

OPEN ON JIM HENSON IN HIS STUDIO WHERE THE MUPPETS ARE MADE. HE CARRIES A RAINCOAT OVER HIS ARM.

HENSON: Do you know m I created the muppets,

MUPPETS: ~~Hey. Hi, How ya. Hi there.~~ So what? Big Deal?

HENSON: and everybody them, but not me.

FRAME TIME — TOTAL

HENSON WALKS ACROSS STUDIO. WE SEE SOME MUPPETS IN THE BKG.

So when I travel, I ca the American Express C It's backed by over 60 travel offices around world, to make my trav easier.

FRAME TIME — TOTAL

HENSON STOPS, PICKS UP HIS SUITCASE.

Each one is ~~like my~~ a home away from home... except the muppets aren't there

CUT TO CU OF GROUP OF MUPPETS WITH TINY SUITCASES.

MUPPETS: Wait up, Jim!

FRAME TIME — TOTAL

CUT TO CARD, AS JIM HENSON IS TYPED ON CARD.

4 044 533
JIM HENSON

SFX: TYPEWRITER SOUNDS

FORM 8-22 (REV 11-7 3

4

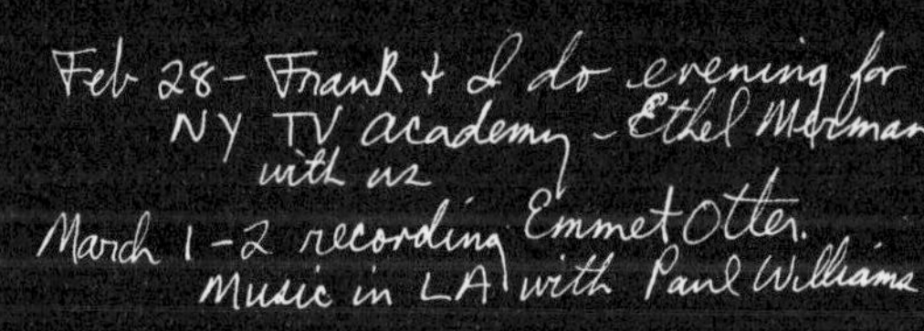

Feb 28 - Frank + I do evening for NY TV academy - Ethel Merman with us

March 1-2 recording Emmet Otter. Music in LA with Paul Williams

April 12 in LA -
13 Kermit's 21st birthday party on "Dinah" show - Berphie's party afterwards

Mather, Inc. — 2. — PAGE NO.

AN EXPRESS/Card — November 15, 1976 — DATE

enson" (Studio) — RTO

TITLE — LENGTH — TIMED BY PRODUCER

PROMISE — NUMBER OF WORDS

IS MINORITY TALENT APPROPRIATE? IF NOT, WHY NOT? — APPROVED FOR PRODUCTION

VIDEO — AUDIO

AMERICAN EXPRESS
4 044 533 500X
JIM HENSON
800 528 8000

ANNCR(VO): Apply for a card now. Call 800-528-6000.

FRAME TIME — TOTAL

CUT BACK TO HENSON WITH THE MUPPETS.

HENSON: The American Express Card.
MUPPETS: Don't leave home without it.

FRAME TIME — TOTAL

1977

august we make deal with BRIAN FROUD to do great film

With *The Muppet Show* well underway, Jim pursued other projects that were occupying his thoughts. Imagining a society governed by malevolent reptiles, inspired in part by the characters from *Saturday Night Live*, Jim envisioned an ambitious feature film set in an unknown world. Acknowledging the far-ranging talents of his creative team and evolving animatronic technology, he unleashed his boundless imagination and began to invent an entire world, picturing singing mountains, animal-like plants, and an array of mysterious species. Impressed with the images he encountered in a book, *The Land of Froud*, Jim sought out British illustrator Brian Froud as a collaborator. Jim hoped to sketch out his fantastic universe before plotting a story, and Froud signed on to design the world of *The Dark Crystal*.

❶ Brian Froud's book *The Land of Froud*. ❷ Froud working on the Gelfling Jen. ❸ Early Froud sketch of a Pod person. ❹ Brian Froud's self-portrait from *The Land of Froud*. ❺ Froud's sketches of Mystic heads.

❶

❷

❸

Sept 10 fly to LA for EMMY AWARDS on Sun. 11th - up for 3 - only Rita won - sigh.

Sept 16 - dinner at Joe Raposo's - met Ted Geisel + Abe Burrows

Sept 19 2nd Season of MUPPET SHOW goes on the air in NYC

Oct 8 - working with Jack Burns - story outline - The Muppet Movie

MARVIN KITMAN SHOW

nd now, let's go back to

Hip Parade" (tomorrow night on
3 at 8:30 PM; re-run Thursday morning
AM) is a behind-the scenes look at the
al Macy's Thanksgiving Day Parade
presents an
nt develop-
TV journal-
arks the de-
Kermit the
a reporter.
ear as a pa-
mentator is
first in jour-

nay be it—
step in hap-
journalism.
ppets replac-
puppet people
n't go from
ght on the set without directions being
nto their ears from the control rooms.
t about such great reporting teams of
as Lorne Greene and Phyllis George.
Kermit and Fozzie is a charming idea
ks brilliantly. "Hip Hip Parade," pro-
Isabella Dane of WNET/13, is a terrific
lf-hour show. It's innovative, informa-
fun. It's also historic.
pet News and Public Affairs, one has the
is beginning tomorrow. Maybe we can
mit the Frog to replace Marilyn Berger
ET/13's "Special Edition" news. Or how
The Miss Piggy/Grover Report?"
key to any parade on television is the list
stars who join the commentators in the
They usually are from television series
e the mind levels of coconuts. Who will
get Bonnie Franklin's discussions of last
Rose Bowl Parade, which won the coco-
ne year award? Keep your ears on Valer-
elli ("One Day at a Time") and Lyle Wag-
of "Wonder Woman") for honors in "The
l-American Thanksgiving Parade" show
Thursday at 9 AM) for rhetorical honors.
things about "Hip Hip Pa-

Executive Producer

Kermit the Frog

wearing his old wrinkled trenchcoat and crushed
fedora with press card. Sartorially, his style is
your basic Joel McCrea (in "Foreign Correspon-
dent"). He is as sober as a church mouse. One
looks forward to comparing his remarks to the
commentary on Thursday morning's traditiona
Macy's Parade TV coverage on WNBC/4, deliv
ered this year by that wild and crazy guy, E
McMahon.

"Hip Hip Parade" is not as good as "T
Muppet Show." It only has the reality of the
rade itself to work with; "The Muppet Show
based on show business, which is a much fun
reality to deal with than any passing para

"Hip Hip Parade" asks such questions, as

1977

THANKSGIVING – KERMIT BALLOON IN
Macy's Parade in NYC

Nov 29 – Jaye P. Morgan
★– NOV. 30 – BOUGHT BUILDING ON 69th STREE
Dec 6 – Peter Sellers
Dec 13 – Petula Clark
Dec 7 – Cloris Leachman
Dec 16 return to NY

Jim loved a parade and was delighted to hear the roars of recognition when his characters appeared with marching bands and musical floats. The Macy's Thanksgiving Day Parade, perhaps the most visible in the country, hosted the *Sesame Street* characters on a float as early as 1974. With Kermit's international celebrity and commercial appeal, he was an obvious candidate for transformation into an oversized balloon, making his debut in 1977 and appearing regularly for a decade. In 1978, Kermit reported on the parade preparations for a television special *Hip Hip Parade!*, and in 1979, it was Miss Piggy's turn—in celebration of *The Muppet Movie*, she appeared riding in a Hollywood star-appropriate Rolls-Royce, followed by the Henson family in The Electric Mayhem's bus.

1982 OFFICIAL PARADE SOUVENIR PROGRAM

Friends and Neighbors

HENSON ASSOCIATES

The 93rd Tournament of Roses

$2.00
tax included

❶ Review of *Hip Hip Parade!*, a PBS special about the Macy's Parade featuring Kermit the Frog and Fozzie Bear from *Newsday*, November 21, 1978. ❷ The Kermit balloon on Broadway. ❸ The Muppets have appeared in numerous parades, including the Tournament of Roses parade. ❹ Kermit celebrates the launch of his balloon for the Macy's Thanksgiving Day Parade.

ERMIT THE FROG serves as newscaster at e launching of his aerial alter ego: the 3-feet-high, 24-feet-wide helium-filled ermit balloon which will be introduced in acy's forthcoming Thanksgiving Day Parade.

1978

Feb 6 — try to fly to London —
SNOWED in with Cheryl at
Howard Johnsons at Kennedy Airport -
did outline for Dark Crystal - just
called The Crystal - concept of Skeksis/
oo-urs etc. MUPPET SHOW

As he began to build his team for *The Dark Crystal*, Jim received an intriguing gift: an exquisite Japanese-style marionette made by a young artist, Wendy Midener. Jim immediately saw the potential in combining her talent for sculpting dolls with Froud's designs and, after meeting in New York, Midener signed on. Jim headed back to London with his daughter Cheryl only to be delayed by a blizzard. Unable to depart, the two holed up at an airport hotel. As Cheryl remembered, "The world appeared to be one enormous blank white slate. Before cell phones and laptop computers, being stranded by a snowstorm meant quiet time, time to imagine new worlds and their inhabitants." Jim filled pages with musings and ideas, outlining *The Dark Crystal*.

❶ Wendy Midener building Kira. ❷ Jim and his daughter Cheryl on the set of *The Muppet Show* (with Tony Randall). ❸ The beginning of Jim's initial *Dark Crystal* outline. ❹+❺+❻ Jim's notes about the world of *The Dark Crystal*.

STORY OUTLINE ①

The story begins at the death bed of Oo-ur-zay, the eldest of the thirteen ancient remaining creatures called the Oo-urs. These are gentle hermit-like ~~woodland~~ beings who live in caves and ~~hoods~~ huts in a remote area of their world. They deal in magic and mystical things, ~~and don't~~ tend to know things by precognition, and communicate in phrases ~~pud~~ punctuated with many of their own words. →

to page 1-A

3

generosity
passiveness
brotherly love
love beauty/culture
diligent - worker
kind animals - nature lover
spiritual
meek - humble
wisdom - judgement - fair

4

6-29-8888
PL 3-2472

OO-URS
~~OOOR OOR-THEM~~
~~OOOR-THEM~~
OOOR-CLEA
→ OOOR-KLEEH
→ OOOR-ZAY
OOOR-KLIEH
OOOR-NEE
OOOR-NEH
→ ZEE

OO-URS

88888888 mmm

~~Nith~~ SKEK-NIK
Kaght
SK-CK
TK
SKOK

SKEKSA
KARACKT
SKEK-SIS
SK

Habeetahat

GAR-THEM
GAR-HE

the Crystal Fire

GELFLING
GELF-LING

JUN - HAHN - JEN

→ MARA DEE-ARI-GUENESTA-SI
SHE ~~DEEZool-iguestra-si~~
DE ~~Deeni~~

5

HISTORY of SPLIT

ceremony - central crystal
12-15 of each originally
crystal set to catch + combine the rays from 3 sources - sun + 2 moons?
3 ~~suns~~ suns? - suns come through forks in trees or carved stones set in branch - Stonehenge-like

present ceremony -
wizards circle around where the crystal used to be - set in such a way to catch reflected rays - piles of bones, sticks on ground to represent reptus.

Reptus baccanal around green pulsing blob incased for protection in some kind of cage - blob encloses the original crystal + controls the warriors. -
ancient carved wooden versions of the wizards are barely identifiable -
fire from below is power for crystal - slaves all around - tend fumes - play drums - warriors stand guard in balconys lit by rays from blob

6

1978

Jan/Feb Barclay - the Dog is being developed for Sesame Street - with Toby Towson

In anticipation of *Sesame Street*'s tenth season, ideas were solicited for new characters to expand the lessons and storylines. Jim was intrigued by the potential for a character that could not speak, leading to the concept for a large, shaggy dog as a pet for a human character who could not hear, Linda. Consulting with Michael Frith on design, and Toby Towson, a dancer and gymnast, on performance, Barkley emerged. Inside, the performer rested his hands on short stilts to equalize the leg lengths, using large dog-like movements to communicate. An extremely physical role, Barkley was doubly challenging as the performer's vision was severely limited. His complete reliance on physical communication (unlike Big Bird and Snuffleupagus, who speak) makes his believability that much more impressive.

❶ Jim working with his workshop team to develop Barkley. ❷ Jim's meeting notes with *Sesame* season ten ideas. ❸+❹+❺ Michael Frith's Barkley designs. ❻ Barkley. ❼ Caroly Wilcox's idea for a baby Snuffleupagus.

non-words - (Cecil Bill)
invisible man - Harvey the Rabbit
Snuffle - small or 2-legged?
Rocks - w/ hands -
NO Same characters as relatives -
Personality of Live - Boring
Jerry - Mask
abstract anythings - non realistic
Bella Abzug
Crazy - like Street Crazy - interesting old lady
landlady of E+B character of E or B
Little Bird - Marionette w/ tape stops
2 headed - cooperation - push me/pull you
CONTESTS

use of children
Space - Martian SAM
Costume making w/ E+B
Puppet Show by E+B
Puppet worked by live

❷

3

4

5

6

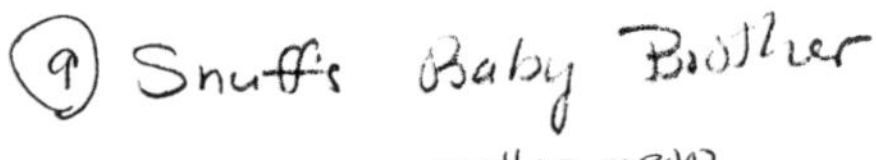

March 3-4 - go to Paris - Unima meeting
March 24 - begin very full on Muppet Movie w/ Brian
March 31 fly to NY for one night - staff meeting (concord)

April - Sesame Street begins talking about theme Park

7

1978

May 19 – University of Maryland honorary doctorate – dinner at Maria's

Sat – Sept 23 – fly to Atlanta to open Puppet Center

Despite being fully occupied with his nascent television career by the end of his freshman year, Jim continued his studies and graduated from the University of Maryland in 1960. He moved from Washington in 1963, but his ties to his alma mater remained strong, and he was awarded an honorary Doctor of Fine Arts degree. Jim continued to support the university as a member of their foundation board, arranging for Kermit to serve as a Maryland spokesfrog. At the same time, Jim began an important relationship with a new organization, The Center for Puppetry Arts in Atlanta. He traveled there with Jane and his daughter Heather to cut the ribbon at its opening, signaling his appreciation for the puppetry community and the importance of a national center for performance, education, and exhibitions.

July 5th – CAMERA ROLLS ON MUPPET MOVIE

❶ Jim, Jane, and Kermit at the opening of The Center for Puppetry Arts. ❷ Jim's sketch of a college graduation in the late 1950s. ❸ The University of Maryland's *Terp* magazine featuring the Jim Henson statue, 2004. ❹ Jim's honorary Doctor of Fine Arts Diploma from the University of Maryland. ❺ Jim took great pride in taking his daughter Lisa to Harvard to start her college education.

TERP

CONNECTING THE UNIVERSITY OF MARYLAND COMMUNITY

VOL. 1, NO. 2 WINTER 2004

Jim Henson and Kermit Come Home

3

5

The Board of Regents of the

University of Maryland

In recognition of scholarly attainments and distinguished service and on nomination of the Faculty of the University by virtue of authority granted by charter of the State of Maryland hereby confers upon

Jim Henson

the degree of

Doctor of Fine Arts

with all the honors, rights and privileges thereunto appertaining.

In witness whereof this Diploma, signed by the authorized officers of the University and sealed with the corporate seal of the University, is granted. Given at College Park on the nineteenth day of May in the year nineteen hundred seventy eight.

Chairman, Board of Regents

President

Chancellor

4

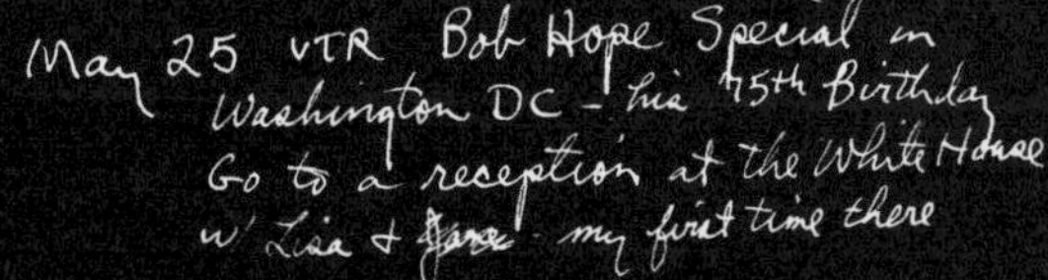

May 25 VTR Bob Hope Special in Washington DC - his 75th Birthday
Go to a reception at the White House w/ Lisa + Jane - my first time there

Sept 10 - drive Lisa up to begin at HARVARD

Nov - working with STAR WARS on YODA
Muppet Shows

The Muppet Show

SHOW #	VTR DATES	GUEST STAR	WORK PERMIT	FARE & EXPENSES	WARDROBE	MUSIC/CHORED.	AGREE'M
1	JAN 19.20-21	JULIET PROWSE					
2	JAN 30-31-FEB 1	CONNIE STEVENS					
3	MAY 18.19.20	JOEL GREY (19)					
4	25.26.27	RUTH BUZZI (15) HARVEY KORMAN (21)					
5	JUNE 2.3	RITA MORENO (5)					
6	8.9.10	JIM NABORS (10)					
7	15.16	FLORENCE HENDERSON (13)					
8	22.23.24	PAUL WILLIAMS (23)					
9	JUNE 29.30.JUL 1	CHARLES AZNAVOUR (4)					
10		([illegible])					
11	JULY 13.14.15	LENA HORNE					
12	20.21.22	PETER USTINOV (20)					
13	27.28	BRUCE FORSYTHE					
14	AUG 3.4.5	SANDY DUNCAN (3)					
15	10.11	CANDY BERGEN (10)					
16	SEP 28.29.30	AVERY SCHREIBER (22)					
17	OCT 5.6	BEN VEREEN (6)					
18	12.13.14	PHYLLIS DILLER (14)					
19	19.20	VINCENT PRICE (19)					
20	26.27.28	VALERIE HARPER					
21	NOV 9.10	TWIGGY					
	17.18	ETHEL MERMAN					

1979! (A VERY MAJOR BIG YEAR)

April 2 - The TONIGHT SHOW - hosted by the Muppets - guests Vincent Price - Bernadette Peters - Leo Sayer & a Vet

April 6 - VTR Party "The MUPPETS GO HOLLYWOOD"

Looking back through his calendars, Jim was well aware that 1979 was an extraordinary year. His *Muppet Show* was airing in over a hundred countries, *The Muppet Movie* had unparalleled ticket sales, and, for the first time, a nonhuman, i.e., Kermit, was invited to host *The Tonight Show*. Being asked to sit behind Johnny Carson's desk was a testament to the believability and humanity of Jim's characters and their popularity with television audiences. Showcasing the variety of *Muppet Show* guest stars, Kermit chatted with Vincent Price, Bernadette Peters (who performed with the young frog Robin), and Leo Sayer (who sang with Miss Piggy). A veterinarian, Dr. Charles Fox, rounded out the guest list. Favorable reviews suggested that if Carson's ongoing contract negotiations failed to work out, Kermit could replace him permanently.

HENSON ASSOCIATES, INC.
227 EAST 67 ST.
NEW YORK, N.Y. 10021
(212) 628-3804
ha!
PRODUCERS OF THE MUPPETS

May 12, 1976.

Dear

Welcome to London and "The Muppet Show" - we're delighted to be working with you!

As well as a brief schedule for the next few days, this envelope contains various bits of information on London which we hope will help you enjoy your stay here.

On Tuesday May 23 Dave Lazer will be at your hotel at 11:00am to talk down the show with you and discuss any details regarding your script, wardrobe, etc.

On the following three days, May 24, 25 and 26, your car will pick you up at 8:30am to take you to ATV's Studios in Elstree, for your rehearsals and VTR, and bring you back to your hotel each day. It will also be available for your return to the Airport at the end of your stay. Regrettably, we cannot make a car available to you permanently, but should you need transport for shopping, sightseeing, to the theatre or out for dinner, etc., please let our office know and we shall be happy to arrange for you to hire your own car for these journeys.

We are looking forward to you joining us here at the Studios and please do not hesitate to contact us if we can be of any further assistance.

April 19 - FLY TO LONDON - 4th Season of The MUPPET SHOW

May 1 - Purchase DOWNSHIRE HILL HOUSE

❶ Production chart of *The Muppet Show* guest stars for season one. ❷ Vincent Price on *The Muppet Show*. ❸ Bernadette Peters on *The Muppet Show*. ❹ Welcome letter for *Muppet Show* guest stars. ❺ Michael Frith's design for the "I've Got You Under My Skin" song from the Vincent Price episode.

Scot or foam carved

5

1

1979!
A VERY MAJOR BIG YEAR

May 31 - ROYAL PREMIER -
THE MUPPET MOVIE
Leichester Square Theatre - w/ Princess Anne
Jane / John & Bobbie all go - great evening

When *The Muppet Movie* was released in the June of 1979, it was a critical and box office hit, catapulting Kermit and Miss Piggy into the realm of superstardom. With a script from *Muppet Show* writers Jack Burns and Jerry Juhl, the film combined the show's wacky humor with the passions and decency of the characters, imbuing the film with heart. Entertainment was the paramount goal, and the movie was filled with celebrity cameos, terrible puns, and musical numbers set to Paul Williams's and Kenny Ascher's songs. But along with the laughter, audiences gained insight into the journey that Jim and his team had taken as they came together over twenty-five years, building on the strength of their talents and the depth of their relationships.

❶ The movie finale. ❷ Kermit's musical performances are lauded by an LA film-processing company. ❸ Michael Frith's design for Gonzo's plumbing truck decoration for the film. ❹ Orson Welles gave Jim this drawing after his cameo as movie mogul Lew Lord in the film. ❺ The fan club newsletter highlighted the royal premiere and Miss Piggy's pursuit of an Academy Award.

959 Seward Street, Hollywood, CA 90038 (213) 462-3161

2

3

4

June 3 – Jane + I + John to NY for P.R.

June 5 – LINCOLN CENTER LIBRARY – Party
exhibit of The Art of the Muppets
(runs thru aug.)

June 22 – MUPPET MOVIE opens NY + LA – Great!
June 29 – begin recording Christmas album
with John Denver

Aug 31 – We – Jane Cheryl John Heather + group
all go to BLACKPOOL to turn on their
ILLUMINATIONS
Sept 3 – PIGGY COVER – PEOPLE
Sept – Brian begins at Phillips Academy – ANDOVER
Sept 7 – fly to LA for the Emmys – we don't
win but Frank + I do a very successful
Piggy + Kermit Bit introducing rules.

5

The MUPPET SHOW FAN CLUB NEWS

VOLUME TWO

NUMBER

© Henson Ass

Another myth for MUPPET MOVIE

Jim Henson being presented to Princess Anne at THE MUPPET MOVIE Premiere.

At the end of May the world premiere of THE MUPPET MOVIE was held in London, England, in the presence of Her Royal Highness Princess Anne. However, the fairy tale was not put to the test when the P... and the F...

Theatre. Luckily for Kermit fans, discretion was the order of the day – the Princess did **not** kiss the Frog. Kermit was not turned into a prince and will...

AN OSCAR F... MISS PIG...

A group has recently been fo... the Oscar for Miss Piggy in 1980. "CAMPO" (Committee to Award... the Oscar) this movement was ... James Hall and Bruce Collin in Cin... is apparently spreading rapidly. Th... a group called "Cadets for CAMPO... Point, and similar groups in Car... Australia. "The response has bee... hog," said James Hall. Meanwhile M... Cooper, a vice president of the ... Picture Academy's public relations f... reported as saying, "While the Acade... not participate in the pork-barrel can... which are an unfortunate part of th... Oscar...

Nov 8 - fly to LA & VTR JOHN DENVER CHRISTMAS SPECIAL - thru Nov 16

Singer and songwriter John Denver shared Jim's gentle approach to life and desire to make the world a better place. After Denver's *Muppet Show* appearance, the two began planning a Christmas special and related record album. *John Denver and the Muppets: A Christmas Together* captured the joy and beauty of the holiday while also including the silliness expected of the Muppets. Original songs by Denver were interspersed with traditional carols, celebrating diverse groups coming together at the holidays—as Kermit said, "You know what the really nice thing about Christmas is? It's the one time of year when everyone seems to be part of everyone's family." In 1983, they produced an ecology-themed special together and later met up in Moscow and performed for children at the U.S. embassy.

❶ *John Denver and the Muppets: A Christmas Together* record album cover. ❸ John Denver's note to Jim regarding music choices for the TV special. ❷+❹ Jim's handmade Christmas cards with his message of peace. ❺ Michael Frith's illustration of the Muppet versions of "The Twelve Days of Christmas." ❻ John Denver with Miss Piggy in a *Muppet Show* promotional still.

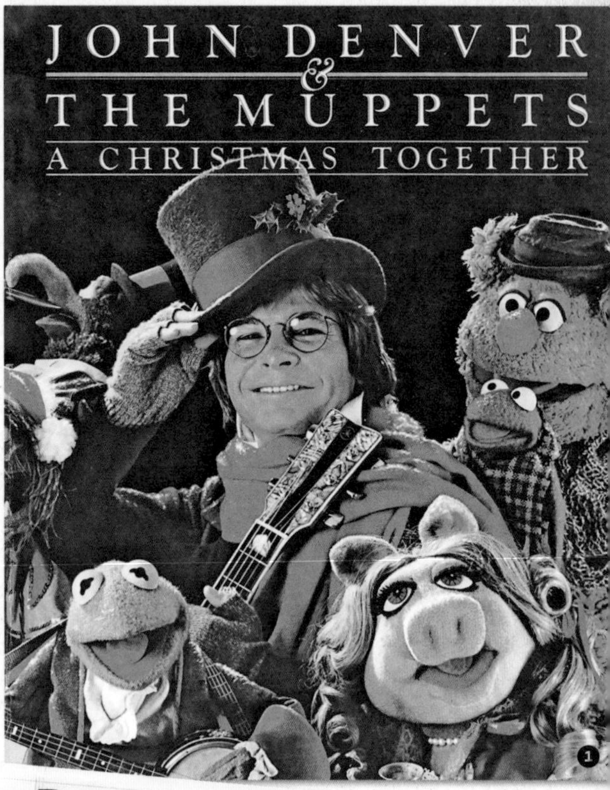

JOHN DENVER & THE MUPPETS
A CHRISTMAS TOGETHER

❶

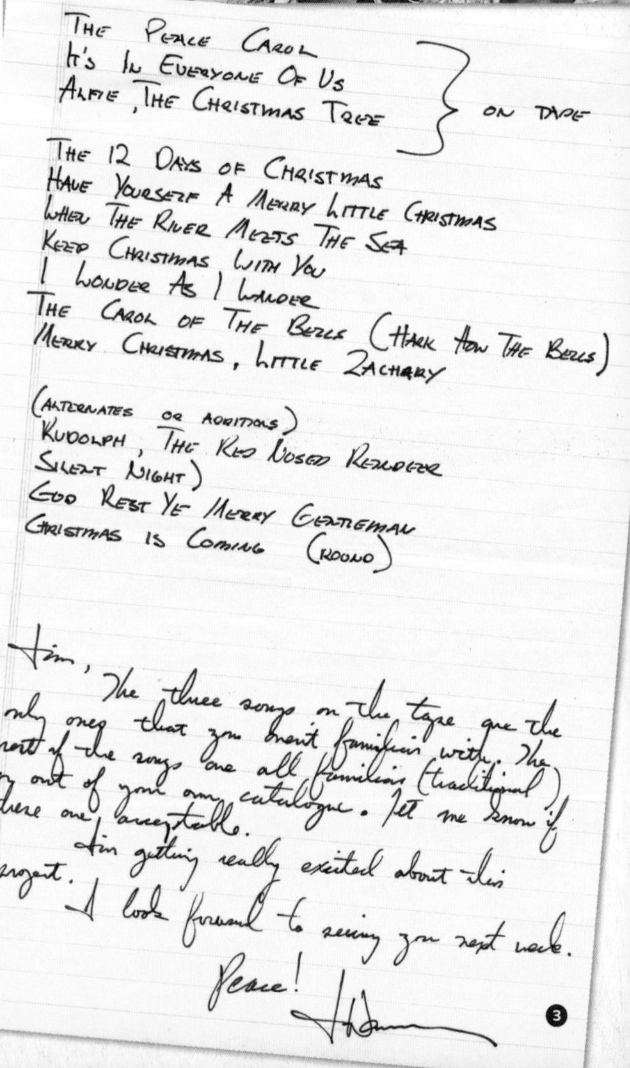

THE PEACE CAROL
IT'S IN EVERYONE OF US
ALFIE, THE CHRISTMAS TREE
} ON TAPE

THE 12 DAYS OF CHRISTMAS
HAVE YOURSELF A MERRY LITTLE CHRISTMAS
WHEN THE RIVER MEETS THE SEA
KEEP CHRISTMAS WITH YOU
I WONDER AS I WANDER
THE CAROL OF THE BELLS (HARK HOW THE BELLS)
MERRY CHRISTMAS, LITTLE ZACHARY

(ALTERNATES OR ADDITIONS)
RUDOLPH, THE RED NOSED REINDEER
SILENT NIGHT)
GOD REST YE MERRY GENTLEMAN
CHRISTMAS IS COMING (ROUND)

Jim,
The three songs on the tape are the only ones that you aren't familiar with. The rest of the songs are all familiar (traditional) or out of your own catalogue. Let me know if these are acceptable.
I'm getting really excited about this project. I look forward to seeing you next week.
Peace!

❸

❷

Nov 11 - in LA movie meeting with Jack Rose, Jerry Juhl - Frank Oz - Joe Raposo

Nov 19 - Dec 12 - taping SS inserts and pieces for Sesame Place - many evening sessions

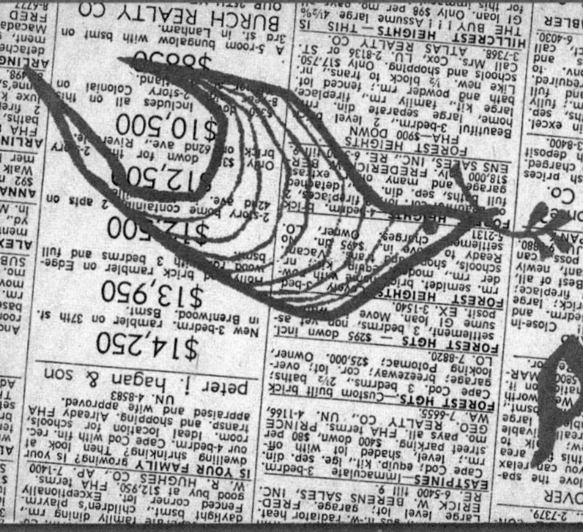

4

THE 12 DAYS of CHRISTMAS

John and the Cast

5

Nov 22 - Thanksgiving Parade - Macy's with Lisa Cheryl & Brian - Miss Piggy in Rolls - we in Mayhem Bus - new Sesame St float.

Pop superstar, JOHN DENVER, meets the devine MISS PIGGY on "The Muppet Show."

Printed in U.S.A.

6

Dec 7 - meet Ken Phillips - start him designing stained glass for bldg.
Dec 12 - Christmas Party for Friends - at Bldg.

Purchasing a double townhouse on Manhattan's East Side to house his growing business, Jim decorated it with the extra care of a visual artist. The centerpiece was a large spiral staircase that wound up from the lobby to Jim's third-floor office. Furnished with unique handmade pieces, the crowning elements were exquisitely designed stained glass expanses in the entryway and as a skylight above the stairwell. Designed by George W. Morris of the K.M. Phillips Studio with input from Henson art director Michael Frith, the skylight featured a view of the sky as seen from Kermit's lily pad, and the fanlight featured Kermit himself plucking his banjo. In this imaginative setting, Jim brought his colleagues and friends together for annual holiday parties and celebrations of their shared accomplishments.

❶ "The View from the Lily Pad" stained glass skylight. ❷ The invitation to the 1979 Christmas party. ❸ Kermit stained glass fanlight window used as the Henson Christmas card, 1980. ❹ Jim and his colleagues (clockwise from bottom left) Frank Oz, Dave Goelz, Richard Hunt, Steve Whitmire, and Jerry Nelson on the grand staircase. ❺ Jim's 1956 silk-screened holiday greeting. ❻ Michael Dixon's drawing of the facade of Jim's Manhattan headquarters.

1

Dec 17-19 - VTR test in London - Dark Crystal —

2

Christmas Day in LONDON - lovely

OTHER 1979 stuff - The Muppet Movie has grossed around 75 million - I think
The Muppet Movie album - with Atlantic - went gold just before Christmas

3

The Fisher Price Miss Piggy Doll (sigh) is selling fantastic

4

A JOYFUL YULETIDE

5

6

CHAPTER 4

FANTASY, FRAGGLES, AND FEARLESS IMAGINATION

1980–1988

THE SHEER VOLUME AND VARIETY of projects that Jim pursued during the 1980s is breathtaking. With the success of *The Muppet Movie*, audiences were eager for new evidence of Jim's ingenuity. He set the bar higher, challenging his growing team to perform increasingly complicated feats of puppetry while delving deeper into the psyches of his characters. *The Muppet Show* ended after five riotous seasons, but the characters kept up the act in two more Muppet feature films, riffing on Hollywood classics and Broadway traditions. Kermit, Miss Piggy, and their friends starred in several television specials, were interviewed on talk shows, appeared on all types of products, sang on record albums, and were portrayed as baby versions of themselves in an Emmy Award–winning animated series.

Meanwhile, Jim wasn't satisfied with the limits of the known world—his creative vision included all the details of another land complete with a unique ecosystem, diverse species, and an ordering of the universe that mimicked ancient accounts of our cosmology. Working with designer Brian Froud and a host of artists and inventors eager to stretch the possibilities of new materials and animatronic puppetry, Jim created the astounding world of *The Dark Crystal*. Building on the style and innovation of that film and the establishment of his Creature Shop, Jim enveloped audiences in the mysteries of *Labyrinth* and the involving tales of *The StoryTeller*. Jim's team helped realize his artistic ambitions but also gained a reputation for inventive work on outside projects.

With a much-stamped passport, Jim traveled between the continents with his colleagues, friends, and family. He was developing new work, promoting what was on the screen, and making connections with other puppeteers and creators around the world. The American puppetry community had been important to him from the beginning, and in the 1980s, Jim connected with international performers in meaningful ways—producing a documentary series, hosting and attending festivals, and teaching the next generation.

The international audiences that were captivated by *The Muppet Show* and *Sesame Street* were on Jim's mind as he contemplated the impact of his work and the importance of the messages that went out on the airwaves. For the most part, entertainment was the primary goal of his work, but in the early 1980s, he decided to focus on the children around the world who were watching his productions and create a show with a distinct philosophical message. Premiering in 1983, *Fraggle Rock* was designed to have multicultural appeal and was imbued with themes of tolerance, environmental responsibility, and awareness of the interconnectivity of all living things. With this joyful, musical gift to children, Jim hoped they would internalize these ideas and integrate them into their adult lives. As each generation of fans comes of age, Jim's vision for a more peaceful world is a continuing work in progress.

1 Jim directing on the set of *Labyrinth*, 1985.

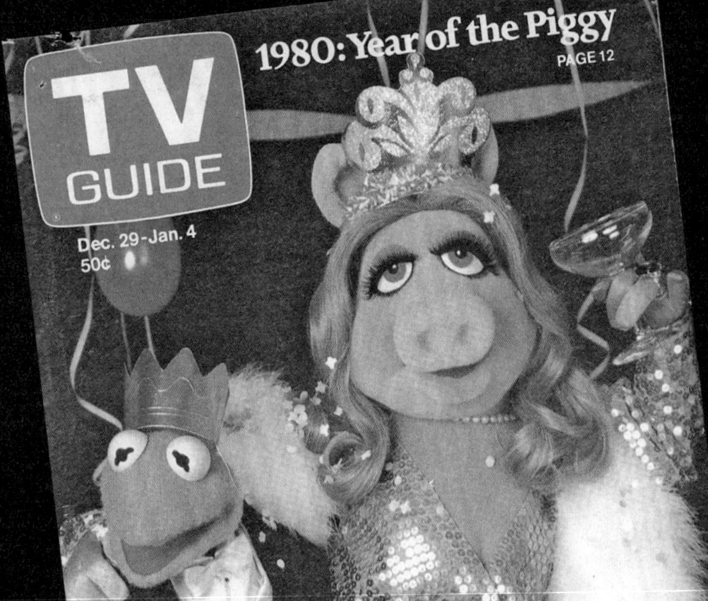

1

2

1980

Feb - continue on with MUPPET SHOW - Season IV - previously planned to start season V at this time - this compacts the schedule later on

April 11 fly to LA for ACADEMY AWARDS Live on April 14 Lisa comes out & goes with me. Kerm + Piggy do the rules - Kerm sings "Rainbow Connection" but we don't win the Oscar.
- MEET JAY + TOM IN LA -

With the experience of three seasons and *The Muppet Movie* under their belts, the *Muppet Show* team made season four the best yet. The intense taping schedule, completing one episode each week, gave the performers ample opportunity to fully develop their characters, creating deep backstories and involved complex personalities. New favorites emerged as younger puppeteers, like Richard Hunt, and newer members of the troupe, like Steve Whitmire, were allowed to showcase lesser-known characters, making stars of the rightfully nervous Beaker and the sarcastic Rizzo the Rat. An extraordinary roster of guest stars clamored to be invited on the show, and audiences in more than one hundred countries were tuning in. For Jim, *The Muppet Show* was now hugely satisfying in all respects.

ZERO MOSTEL
~~JIM HENSON~~

Mr. ~~Zero Mostel,~~ JIM HENSON
~~146 Central Park West,~~
~~New York~~, BOREHAM WOOD
~~10023~~ HERTS WD 1JF

15th ~~9th~~ June, 1977

Dear ~~Zero,~~ JIM

On behalf of myself, ~~David~~ KATE and all ~~the Muppet~~ STRANGE people, we thank you for ~~joining us on~~ LETTING US the Muppet Show.

It's such a joy to work with you, ~~Zero~~ JIM. You gave completely of your time, your energy, and your very great talent. ~~Un~~fortunately, a half hour show ~~can barely~~ scratches your ~~un~~limited resources.

Again, we thank you, and love you. DO YOU KISS MEN, DEAR?

~~Sincerely~~ yours IN HERS

Zero

~~JIM HENSON~~ ZERO MOSTEL

C/O 1. SOCIETY OF HERNIATED HEBREWS OF LATVIA.
2. FULTON ST. FISH MARKET
3. FBI.

P.S. WHERE DID YOU GET THE IMPRESSION THAT I WAS CHEAP AND HOSTILE? PLEASE ADVISE.

ZERO MOSTEL 146 CENTRAL PARK WEST. N.Y.C. 10023

~~THE MUPPET SHOW, P.O. BOX 78, ELDON AVENUE, BOREHAM WOOD, HERTS WD6 1JF~~

3

1+2 By 1980, the Muppets were superstars and Miss Piggy had captured the popular imagination as well as that of art director Michael Frith. His designs placed Miss Piggy in all types of glamorous situations. 3 Jim wrote each guest star a thank-you letter. Zero Mostel responded by annotating the one he received and sending it back. 4 Steve Whitmire with Rizzo the Rat. 5 During season one, (left to right) choreographer Gillian Lynne and performers Eren Ozker, John Lovelady, Jim Henson, Frank Oz, Dave Goelz, and Richard Hunt watch the playback. 6 Dave Goelz takes a break from performing Timmy Monster backstage at the Muppet theater. 7 Jim and guest star Carol Burnett on *The Muppet Show* set. 8 Longtime Henson producer Martin Baker on *The Muppet Show* set.

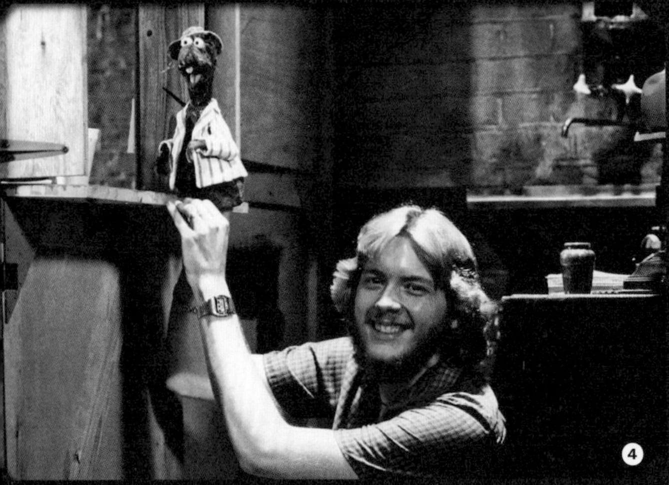

4

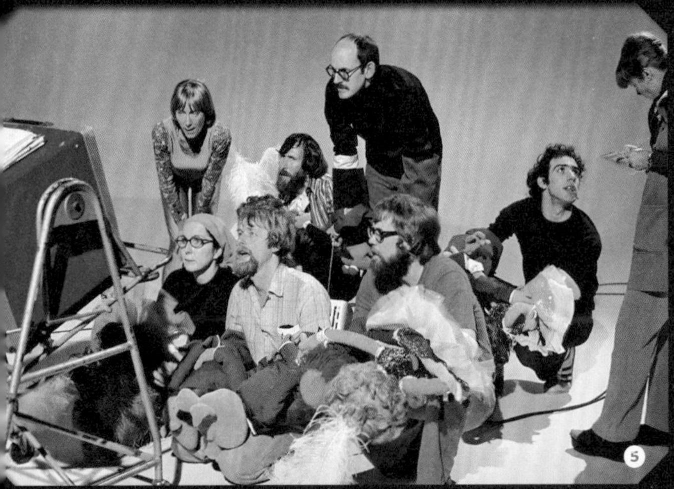

5

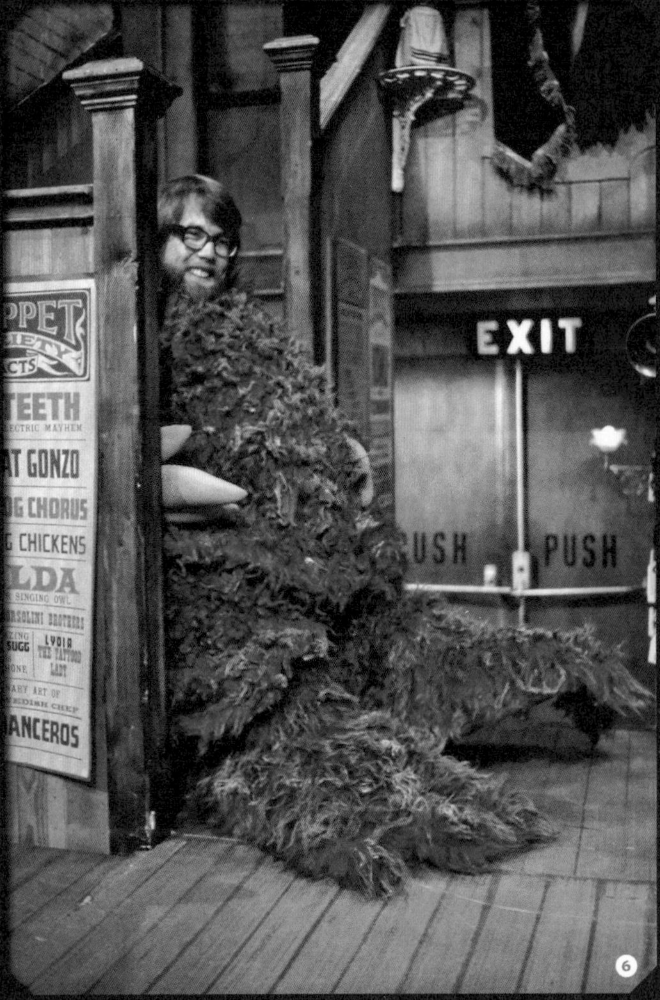

6

7

May 4 - drive in the country w/ Jane - Cheryl
John + Heather - lovely

May 20 Empire Strikes Back opens in London
YODA a big hit

8

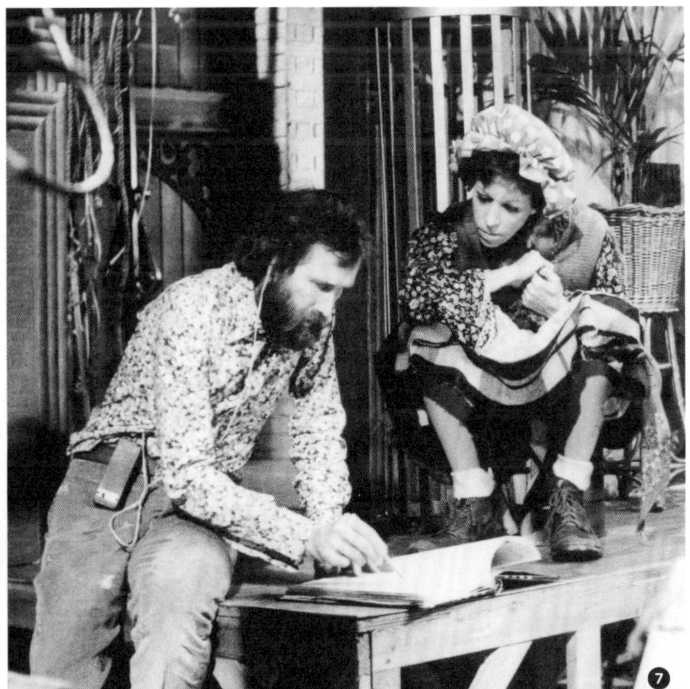

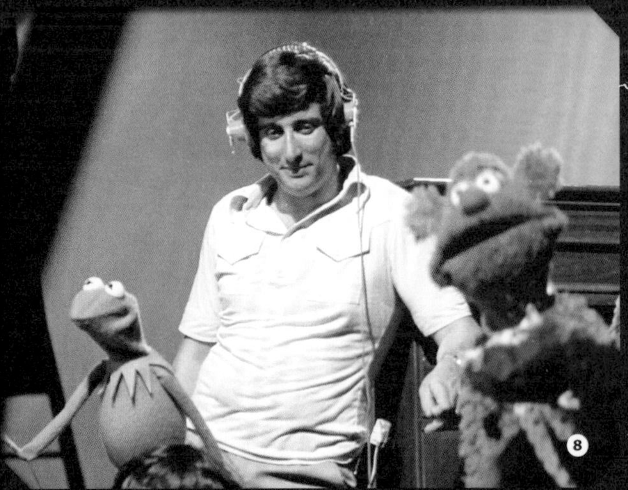

PLOTS

Kermit - reporter/detective - chasing a story
runs into characters in each place - come
together somewhere

foreign intrigue

Piggy a glamorous heiress
a fashion trend setter -
head of a cosmetic company - beauty aids

Piggy: Isn't this a wonderful part for me?
I wrote most of my own lines.

Some very good looking dashing leading man
type to be Kermit's rival - Robt Redford?
Chris Reeve?

He's totally in love with Piggy - she
treats him like dirt

Piggy works for older woman she worships -
turns out to be big criminal

Film should have

happy - a joyful - fun film - positive attitude towar[d] ...

funny - have several hilarious sequences -
big laughs -

Substance - some real emotions/relationships -
heart - showing inner good of characters
family - ties - brotherhood - caring - tender
touching - lump in throat scene

Adventure/Danger - excitement - real threat -
suspense - someone in real trouble

Music - of course - not to stop for song -
music to move the story along - tell
something new - show new side of
someone

Effects - something new - something to talk about
how did they do that. Puppet effects -
not normal special effects

1980

Sept 4 - begin shooting THE GREAT MUPPET CAPER! begin in Battersea Park - bicycle sequence - Brian operates marionettes -

Sept 23 meet Trevor Jones - loved him

Oct 6 - shooting Lady Holiday Interior
" 13 Fashion Show
" 17 Dubonnet Club
" 21 Mallory Gallery Exterior
" 27 Dubonnet Club
Nov 3 - Corridor - Treasure Room
" 10 Mallory Gallery Roof
20 Ext. Happiness Hotel - stunts
24 Happiness Hotel Int.
Dec 8 - Street Scenes for opening

Shortly after the premiere of *The Muppet Movie*, Jim began planning for his next feature film. He now knew what worked on the big screen and was excited to add directing to his other responsibilities. He compiled notes for a story that would have the cinematic range of the first film but with the feel of a 1930s movie musical, the intrigue of an international heist story, the pace of an action adventure, and the hilarity of a big comedy romance. All would be set in an atmospheric, European location and use state-of-the-art effects to achieve mind-boggling puppetry. A year of development followed, and just two weeks after taping the final *Muppet Show* episode, Jim yelled, "Action!" on the set of his most ambitious project yet, *The Great Muppet Caper*.

❶ Tad Krzanowski, Jim, and Franz "Faz" Fazakas in Battersea Park shooting the bicycle scene for *The Great Muppet Caper*. ❷+❸ Jim's notes and plot ideas for his second Muppet feature film, 1979. ❹ Storyboard for the bicycle scene in *The Great Muppet Caper*. ❺ Map plan for the bicycle scene in *The Great Muppet Caper*. ❻ After discovering marionette skills on *The Great Muppet Caper*, Brian Henson used them on various shoots including *The Muppets Take Manhattan*. ❼ Kermit and Miss Piggy on bicycles in Battersea Park.

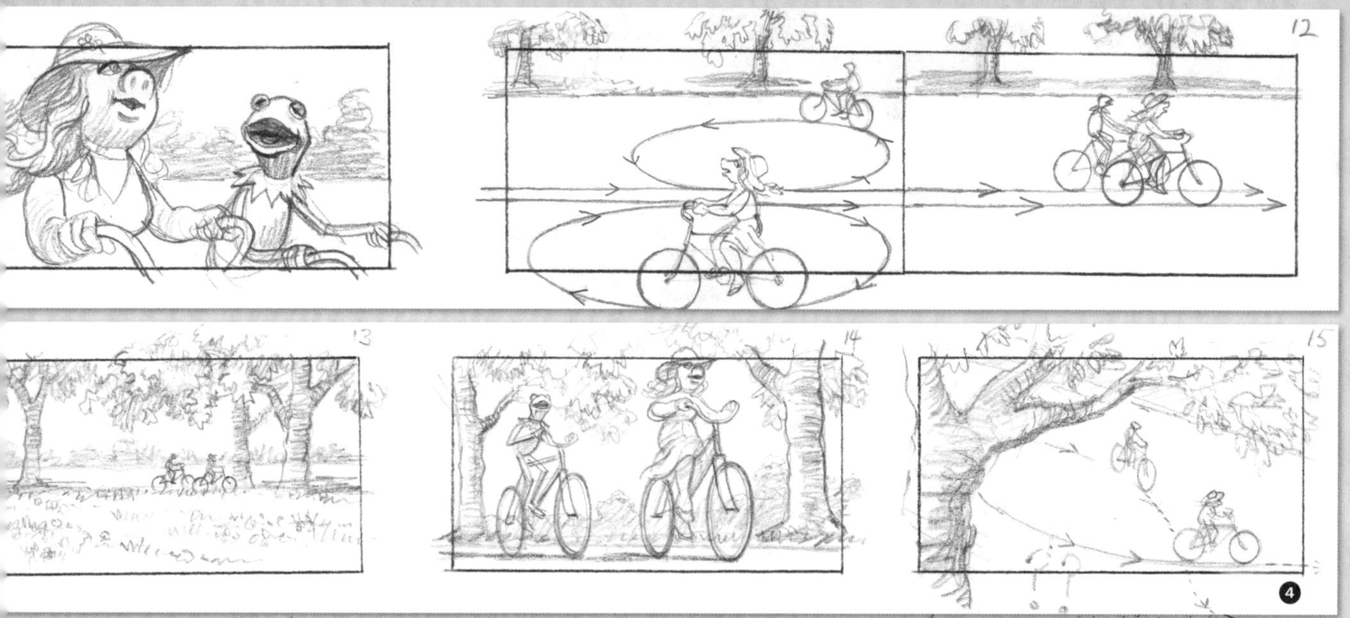

4

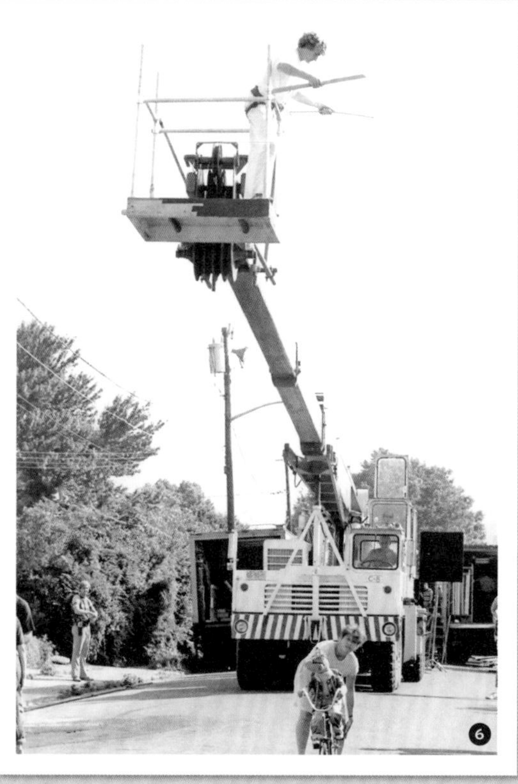

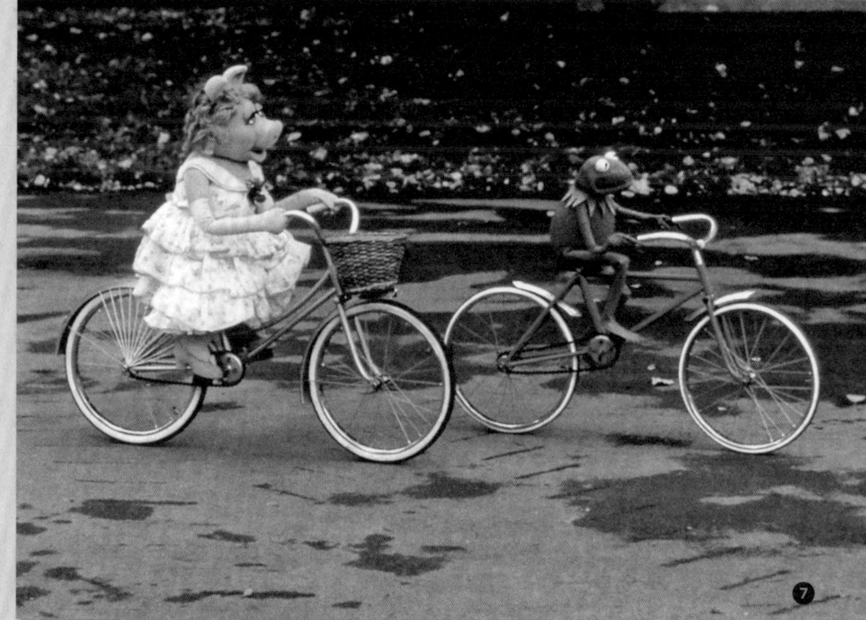

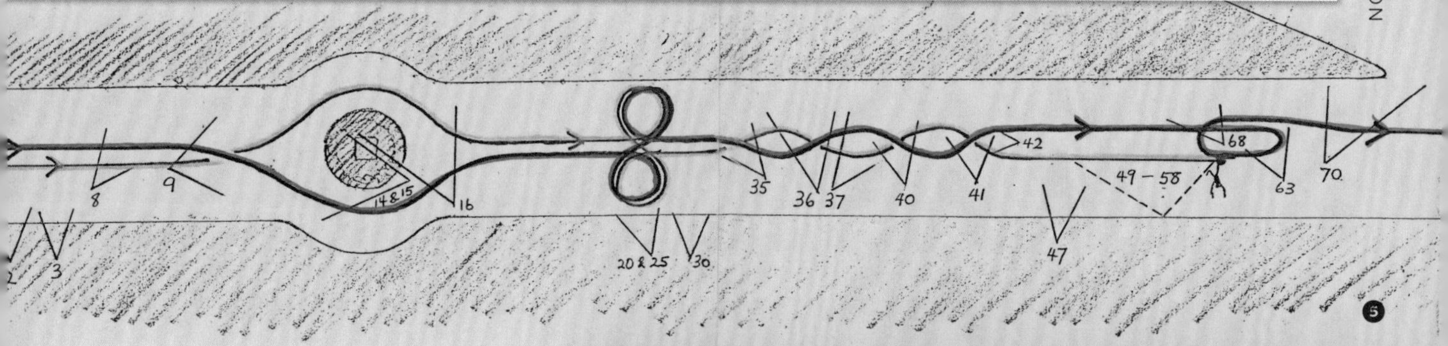

5

6

7

Oct – I get glasses for the first time
Oct 29 – dinner at Keatz – Peter Orten, Dave L
Jocelyn & Duncan to discuss
Childrens International Show
(becomes Fraggle Rock)

1981

Jan - Cheryl + John in London - w/ John Landis on boat
1st week - Jack Warden scene
2nd " Peter Ustinov -
Jan 8 begin Piggy Pool sequence
Jan 21 - " Parachute "
Jan 27 - end London shoot

While Kermit was the focal point in the first Muppet movie, *The Great Muppet Caper* showcased Miss Piggy's extraordinary talents. She sang, she danced, she rode a bike, and in her most spectacular scene, she performed a monumental water ballet in the spirit of Esther Williams. Tremendous imagination went into each of these technically demanding scenes. The aqua ballet involved extensive testing of materials, a specially rigged system for puppeteering underwater, and a child-sized pig costume. In the bicycle scene, frames of marionetted characters performing intricate maneuvers were intercut with close-ups of hand puppets, and combined with long shots of the group being towed by an unseen cyclist. For the final parachute scene, Jim chose the most obvious solution—he threw his characters out of a plane.

❶ Costume design for Miss Piggy's fantasy conceived by Calista Hendrickson and sketched by Michael Frith. ❷ Publicity still of Miss Piggy and her fellow water ballerinas. ❸ Memo from choreographer Anita Mann listing requirements for shooting Miss Piggy's fantasy sequence. ❹ Caroly Wilcox's memo outlining ways to shoot the parachute sequence. ❺ Storyboard panels drawn by Bill Stallion from the parachute credit sequence from the end of the film.

MARTIN BAKER

MEMORANDUM

To: All Heads of Departments

From: Anita Mann

Date: 2nd December, 1980

SUBJECT: "THE GREAT MUPPET CAPER" - POOL SEQUENCE

Would the Heads of Departments please be aware that the following requirements would facilitate filming on the Pool Sequence:

1. Ideal Pool temperature - 92°F.
2. Chemical called Pool-clear (in USA) as a substitute for Chlorine.
3. 30 Styrofoam Floaters.
4. Underwater speakers for P.A. Address to Swimmers and Speakers for Music Playback.
5. Talkback for Underwater Cameraman to surface and to Swimmers.
6. Video relay from Underwater Camera to surface.
7. Video relay from underwater to underwater.
8. Video relay from surface to underwater.
9. Breathing system for Frank Oz that eliminates bubbles.
10. Towels, Bathrobes and Rubber Slippers for Swimmers and MISS PIGGY Doubles.
11. Waterproof make-up. Stocking caps underneath wigs.
12. Facilities on stage for:
    a) Hot room for Swimmers
    b) Drying room for wardrobe - towels, etc.
    c) Room for hairdressing and make-up.
    d) Gas heaters for these rooms.
13. All ~~corridors~~ on Stages 1 and 2 around dressing rooms to have drapes ~~inside doorways~~ to make corridors draught-free.
14. Stage 1 to be heated and kept heated over weekend during shooting weeks. Possibly, space heaters required.

ANITA MANN

3

JIM HENSON

PARACHUTE SCENE (Shot by 2nd Unit anytime)

Version A: Parachutists + Dummies

Costumed + Masked:
Dr T
Janice
Animal
Bo
Pops
Chef
Fozzie
Statler
Waldorf
Piggy
Beaker
Rowlf
Floyd
Zoot

Dummies:
* Honeydew
* Gonzo
* Kermit
* Scooter

Oscar (Can only)

19 units – 4 at least must be dummies, for scale.
Costumes – must fit people safely – take more time to make
Masks – quite elaborate

Problems:
1. What required gear for parachutists ... Helmets?
2. What wind speed (plane ab 100 m.ph. ... + fall acceleration + impact of chute opening
3. Plane to lease for shot is not a 747 or 707 – + Larger than Puppet Life guys jumping out of a smaller Than Life plane ..... ?

Version B: Dummies + Cargo or K-9 parachutes
Quicker to make – can photograph the puppets – blow up to scale, make quick sculpts in scott foam or body muslin dummies. Paint, scissor, motif the hair, etc., dye or spray foam.
– can weight feet + seat of pants for fall – also parachute harness.
– can have a few moving things like hair + scarf motifs for action, but safely attached.

4

March 9-17 VTR THE MUPPETS GO TO THE MOVIES

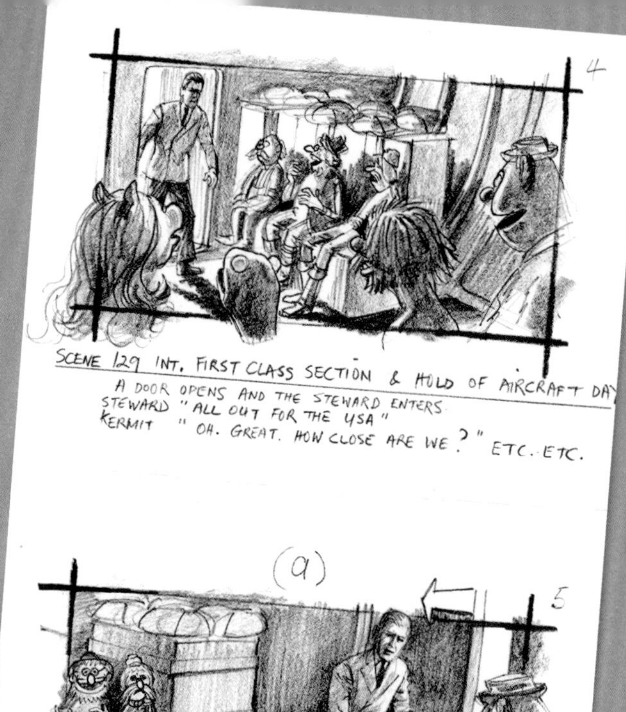

5

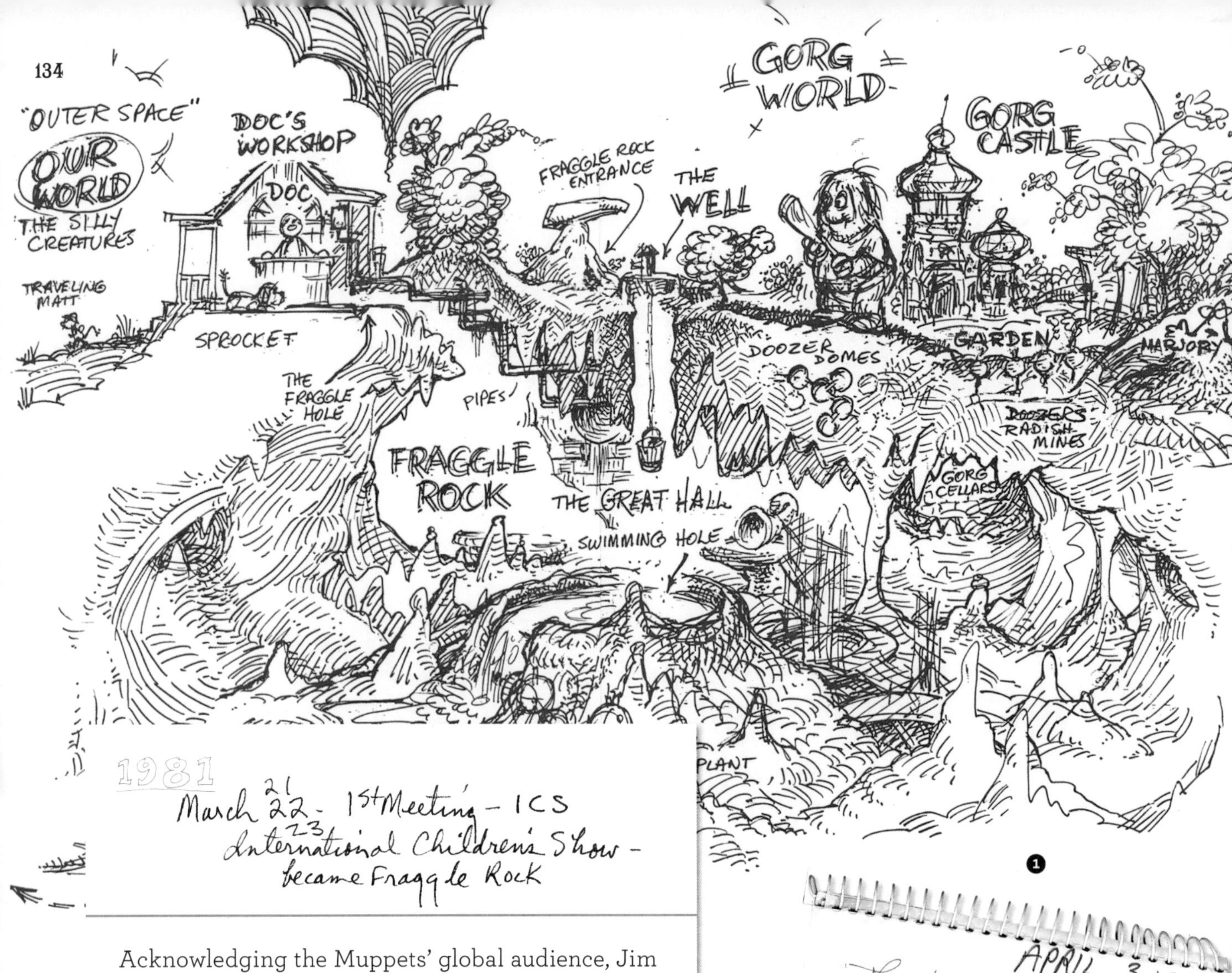

1981

March 21 22 23 - 1st Meeting - ICS
International Children's Show -
became Fraggle Rock

Acknowledging the Muppets' global audience, Jim presented an idea for an international children's television show that would celebrate tolerance for differences, recognize the interdependence of all species, and encourage environmental responsibility. His hope was that viewers would take these lessons into adulthood, making for a more peaceful world. Jim and his core development team, writers Jerry Juhl and Jocelyn Stevenson and senior art director Michael Frith, began a series of multiday brain storming sessions resulting in a concept for a series, *Fraggle Rock*. Frith remembered, "It was the most intensely creative time I have ever spent. There was amazing whooping and weeping . . . of the good kind!" A sales booklet was created describing the show in a simple, straightforward manner with, as Frith described, "a certain open-endedness and magic to be explored."

APRIL 3, 1981
The Woozle Show
or
Woozle World
or
The World of the Woozles
or
WOOZLE-WOOZLE!
concept for an international children's television show.
INSERT B goes here

❶ The world of *Fraggle Rock* as mapped by Michael Frith. ❷ The first page of Jim's Woozle World treatment that launched *Fraggle Rock*. ❸ Jocelyn Stevenson and Jerry Juhl confer on a script. ❹ Senior art director Michael Frith with Mokey. ❺ Michael Frith's Doozer sketch. ❻+❼ Michael Frith's early Fraggle designs.

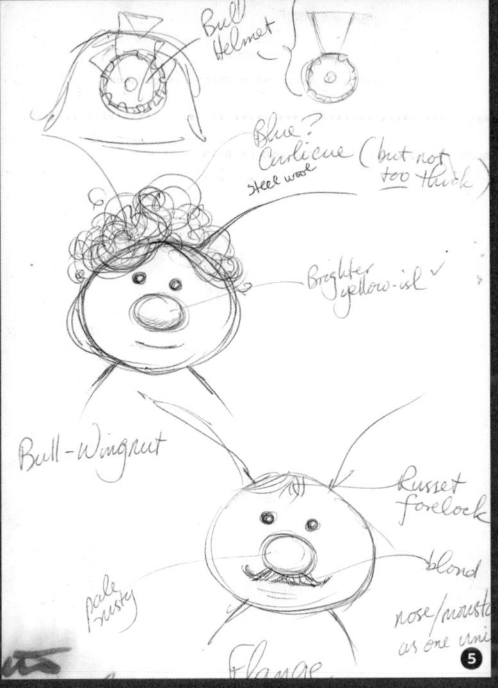

april 3 – 5 back in NY

1981

APRIL 15 BEGIN SHOOTING
THE DARK CRYSTAL

Mystic Valley first
dying Emperor
Crystal Chamber

Almost four years after Jim partnered with Brian Froud to develop a film, cameras began to roll on the set of *The Dark Crystal*. Dozens of artists, sculptors, costumers, electronics specialists, and puppet builders, working from hundreds of sketches, had created the flora and fauna of Jim's imagined world. His early outlines had grown into a full descriptive concept, providing the setting for a story crafted with script writer David Odell. An expert in ancient linguistics, Alan Garner, was asked to invent languages for the decadent Skeksis and philosophical Mystics, and the performers developed a system for the collaborative puppeteering necessary to bring the mysterious and complicated characters to life. More than a year and a half later, the film was ready for theatrical release.

❶ Co-directors Jim and Frank Oz on the set of *The Dark Crystal*. ❷ On set in the Crystal Chamber. ❸+❻ Brian Froud's sketches of Skeksis. ❹ Brian Froud's watercolor of the Chamberlain Skeksis's ceremonial banner from *The Dark Crystal*. ❺ Numerous puppeteers, including Louise Gold, Jim, Dave Goelz, and Rollie Krewson, were required to perform the disgrace of the Chamberlain Skeksis. ❼ Storyboard panel featuring a scene in the Crystal Chamber.

May 20 - AIR Muppets Go to the Movies ABC
May 18 or so - Cheryl arrives to work on D.C.

May 23 + 24 in NY to SNEAK the Great Muppet CAPER

22
DESCRIPTION SCENE 69 DATE OF
AS POWER CEREMONY IS IN PROGRESS JEN MOVES OUT ONTO BALCONY ELEMENTS

1981

May 30-31 SHOOT first POLAROID commercials

In committing to *Sesame Street* in 1969, Jim gave up what had been a lucrative career as a Madison Avenue pitchman. Not wanting to take advantage of his young audience by having their Muppet friends hawk products, he stopped making commercials. By 1981, with his *Muppet Show* characters popular across age groups, Jim felt comfortable making advertisements aimed at adults for products he believed in. Polaroid was a good fit—Jim had experimented with Polaroid cameras as a teenager in an effort to express his artistic vision and was impressed with the simplicity of the new OneStep. With the tag line, "Polaroid means fun!" the ad campaign seemed custom-made for the Muppets, although Kermit put himself in danger when he reminded Miss Piggy not to "ham it up" for the camera.

❶ Jim and his first Polaroid camera, 1956. ❷+❸+❹ Jim's Polaroid experiments from the 1950s. ❺ Miss Piggy "hamming it up" in a print ad for Polaroid.

© 1981 Polaroid Corp. "Polaroid," "SX-70," "OneStep," and "Time-Zero" ®. The
All star.
All woman.
All yours.
This could be the beginning of a beautiful relationship.
The delicious, delightful, the lovely Miss Piggy and the rest of the Muppets are now representing Polaroid Time-Zero film and cameras—the OneStep, The Button and the SX-70 AutoFocus.
And you couldn't ask for better representation. To begin with, the Muppets mean fun. So does Polaroid. And when you put the two together they mean something else: Business.
Besides being fun, the Muppets are believable. Millions buy what the Muppets say. So it stands to reason they'll buy what the Muppets sell. And lots of it.
Miss Piggy is the kind of girl we're proud to bring home to mother, father and the whole family. And you'll be glad to know that we're bringing her and the rest of the Muppets home quite often.
We're spending millions of dollars through December to generate nearly two billion impressions on network television. The fact that consumers will be seeing a lot of the Muppets means you'll be seeing a lot of consumers.
We think you'll agree that the Muppets have what it takes to continue the tradition of advertising that helped make the OneStep America's best-selling camera. And SX-70 the best-selling instant film.
Speaking of tradition, in case you're wondering about the whereabouts of James Garner and Mariette Hartley, they're introducing the new Sun cameras in one of the biggest kickoff campaigns in Polaroid history.
So, to take advantage of the big fall buying season, call your Polaroid representative. We think you'll see that, when the Muppets go to market, the market goes to the Muppets.
Polaroid
The Button
Time-Zero Supercolor
Polaroid
5
June 26 { GREAT MUPPET CAPER opens in the states
July 3-11 - second ICS meetings Michael Frith - Jerry J in for it Bonny + Wade join on 11th
July 29 - Prince Charles marries Lady Di
Oct 20 - Selfridges Muppet display opens

1981

Oct 24 – meet w/ DC costume project

Having gathered an extraordinary team of artisans to create *The Dark Crystal,* Jim sought ways to showcase their craftsmanship. An unconventional side project was the Dark Crystal Clothing Collection, which celebrated the film's distinctive costumes and their unusual materials. Jim asked the designers to create a "dramatic haute-couture collection" that reflected the "style, richness, and jewel-toned color" of the film. They created human-sized outfits for day and evening, along with hats, gloves, belts, and jewelry. Garnering a full-page spread in *Vogue* magazine, the collection was featured in Bendel's Fifth Avenue windows. In the end, the collection did not sell well, but most of the designers came back to work on *Labyrinth.*

❶ Cheryl Henson modeling the Garthim Master–inspired outfit. ❷ The designers and fabricators: (back, left to right) Cas Willing, Diana Moseley, Shirley Denney, (front, left to right) Ellis Flyte, Val Jones, Lesja Lieber. ❸ Lingerie design illustration by Neil Greer. ❹ *Vogue* feature on the Dark Crystal Clothing Collection, November 1982. ❺ Sketch of knit daywear outfit with accessories. ❻ Skeksis-inspired evening wear. ❼ Michael Frith's memo from the Dark Crystal Clothing Collection planning meeting. Michael designed the logo.

VOGUE'S View

American "Elegants": Galanos and Halston "stone washing"... new takes on velours

Edited by Mary Russell

Six young English designers were given the task of designing clothes inspired by a fantasy film

Fantasy as fashion

The dream of any young designer . . . to be given a workshop with unlimited means to design clothes that are, in fact, the stuff of dreams. Clothes inspired by a film peopled with poetic creatures living in the mysterious world of *The Dark Crystal*—fantasy and dreamchild of Jim Henson, creator of the Muppets. The puppets in *The Dark Crystal* are ethereal beings, totally captivating and romantic. The six strong designers first fashioned the actual costumes for the film creatures, then turned to making clothes for people, keeping the spirit of the film in mind. Each brought his or her expertise into play. Val Jones for knits (she has already sold designs to Missoni). Shirley Denney, puppet-costumes designer, has worked on *Spiderman, Star Wars,* and *Alien.* Cas Willing added her touch with woven textiles. Ellis Duncan is an antique-lace expert, Lesja Lieber formerly designed evening clothes, and Diana Moseley was a designer for the English National Opera. This combined talent created *The Dark Crystal* collection. Henri Bendel, NYC, was so captivated they are doing a series of fantasy windows this month.

("View" continued on page 306)

BETH BAPTISTE

The collection ranges from silk lingerie to daring leather and lace evening separates to velvet and suede sportswear. Hair: Racine for Jean Louis David at Henri Bendel; makeup, Debbie M. Details, last pages.

304

4

5

Nov 2 - recording Pigs in Space for NASA space shuttle

Dec 2 - press conference Toronto - Fraggle

Dec 13 - trapped in English Blizzard

6

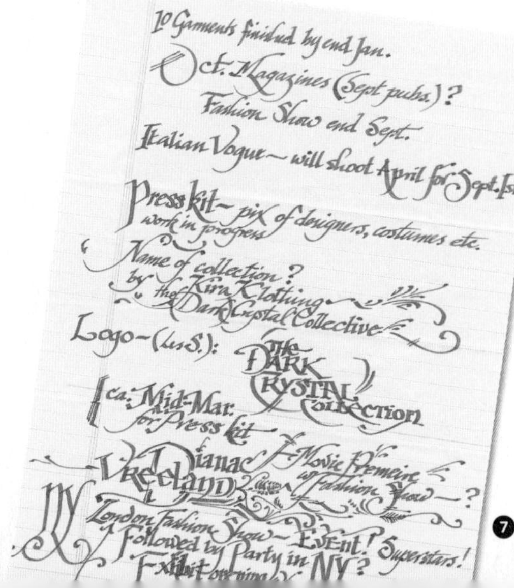

10 Garments finished by end Jan.

Oct. Magazines (Sept pubs.)?

Fashion Show end Sept.

Italian Vogue ~ will shoot April for Sept. Ish

Press kit ~ pix of designers, costumes etc.
work in progress

Name of collection?
by Kira Klothing
the Dark Crystal Collective

Logo ~ (U.S.): The Dark Crystal Collection

ca. Mid-Mar. for Press kit

Diana Vreeland

Movie Premiere w/ Fashion Show ~?

NY

London Fashion Show ~ Event! Superstars!

Followed by Party in NY?

7

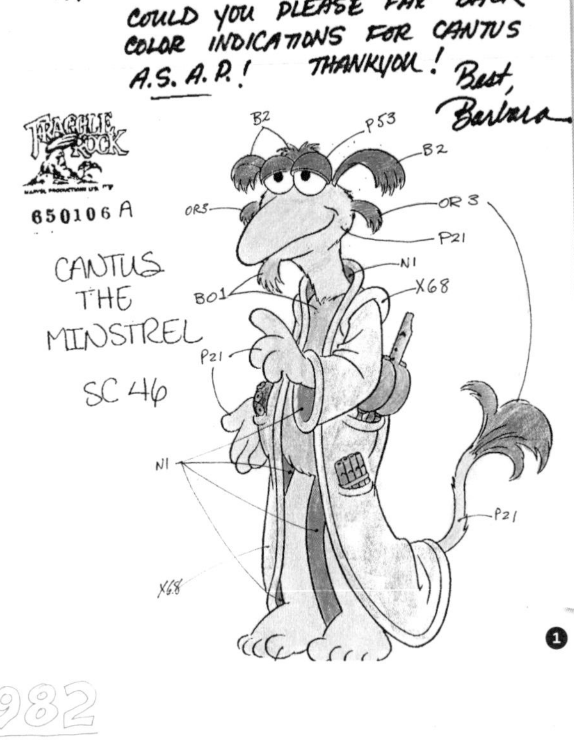

1982

March 6 – in Toronto – to begin VTR FRAGGLE ROCK VTR 3/9–13

Management of *Fraggle Rock*, under Jerry Juhl's leadership, was shared by the creative team. Jim and Frank Oz stepped away from the day-to-day production, and their longtime colleagues were cast in the main roles. Virtuoso performer Jerry Nelson was the leader of the Fraggle Five, Gobo, and Dave Goelz, best known as Gonzo from *The Muppet Show*, played Boober and Travelling Matt. Richard Hunt, whose Henson experience dated back to 1970, was ideal as Junior Gorg, while Kathy Mullen, fresh from playing Kira in *The Dark Crystal*, performed Mokey. Steve Whitmire, a *Muppet Show* veteran, was cast as Wembley, and the youthful Karen Prell, apprenticed on *Sesame Street*, performed the irrepressible Red. Jim's spirit permeated the production, and he occasionally joined in as the philosophical Cantus or the extroverted Convincing John.

❶ Cantus Fraggle as imagined for the animated version of *Fraggle Rock*, which aired 1987–1988. ❷ The Fraggle color reference guide created by the puppet builders featured the vibrant hues that worked so well on camera. ❸ Dave Goelz performing Travelling Matt in what the Fraggles call "outer space" (i.e., our world). ❹ Richard Hunt performing Junior Gorg via radio control. ❺ Jerry Nelson and Gobo Fraggle. ❻ Karen Prell and Red Fraggle. ❼ Steve Whitmire performs Wembley Fraggle, with attention from puppet builder Rollie Krewson. ❽ Jim with Cantus Fraggle. ❾ Dave Goelz and Boober Fraggle. ❿ Kathy Mullen and Mokey Fraggle.

April 5-9 – back in London working on D.C.

May 26 – 30 VTR Travelling Matts in San Francisco + L.A. – much fun

July 12 – preview Dark Crystal in Detroit a bit better

5
6
7
8
9
10

1982

July 15 - 18 in Aspen for survey & VTR
Rowlf in biplane & river for Denver

Sept - Brian attending U of Col at Boulder
Brian, Cheryl & John all drop in during
taping at ASPEN

In their second special together, *Rocky Mountain Holiday,* Jim and John Denver explored their shared admiration for the wonders of nature. The show featured the Muppet gang on a camping trip with Denver, singing songs and reminiscing about adventures in the great outdoors. While Miss Piggy stayed home, preferring the comforts of civilization, she appeared via video clips. Written by *Sesame Street* veterans Jon Stone and Joe Bailey, the program moved easily between outdoor songs and wild adventures. Comic moments included Gonzo's encounter with a giant chicken and Rowlf's ride in a biplane piloted by Denver. When the special aired the following spring, television critic John J. O'Connor said, "*Rocky Mountain Holiday* is about perfect as fare for children and all those incurably young in heart."

❶ John Denver and some singing plants on *The Muppet Show*, 1979. ❷ Jim's sketch of a family camping trip in Colorado, 1971. ❸ Michael Frith's design for the giant chicken in the *Rocky Mountain Holiday* special. ❹ Caroly Wilcox's plan for how Steve Whitmire would perform the giant chicken. ❺ John J. O'Connor's review in the *New York Times*, May 12, 1983. ❻ Color choices for the giant chicken.

Aug 9 - 24 VTR The FABULOUS MISS PIGGY SHOW in Toronto -

3

4

Nov 9-10 London 12 – Munich – 13 to Texas
check on Sesame Place 15 Houston (D.C.)

Oct 26 – lunch Neil Simon – B'way

5

TV: Muppets in Rockie Sing With John Denver

By JOHN J. O'CONNOR

THE persistently youthful John Denver joins the Muppets tonight, on ABC at 8 o'clock, in a music special called "Rocky Mountain Holiday." The program was produced by Mr. Denver and Jim Henson, creator of the Muppets, and was taped near Aspen, Colo., the spectacular mountain town that Mr. Denver calls home.

The program was completed last year, a fact that might indicate a reluctance on the part of ABC to rush it into the network schedule. The hesita- ... "Rocky Mountain ... fare

ing at their destination, Mr. Denv... and friends begin settling in for som... serious fishing and campfire camara... derie. Someone asks, "How's the TV reception up here?" but the others are generally enthusiastic about the ex... perience.

With Fozzie, Gonzo, Rowlf, Floyd, Janice, Animal, Scooter and little Robin, Kermit's nephew, in tow, Mr. Denver has a backup chorus for several songs, including "Comin' Round the Mountain," which is used as an excuse for imagining what would have happened if Miss Piggy had shown up with her noisy entourage and fans. In a flashback to the previous summ... Mr. Denver and Miss Piggy are on horseback, joining in ha... duets on "Tumbling Tumb... Trails." With...

6

1982

Dec 13 - NY Premier THE DARK CRYSTAL
Dec 14 - LA premier
Dec 15 San Francisco premier
Dec 17 - Dark Crystal opens wide

Jim spent much of 1982 in post-production for *The Dark Crystal*, completing the sound recordings, conducting test screenings, and editing the footage. By fall, focus shifted to promotional activities and a behind-the-scenes documentary. Finally, Jim was ready to premiere his film on both coasts. The industry had paid close attention to the film, featuring its ingenuity in numerous publications, but heading into theaters, reviewers didn't really know what to expect. They marveled at the artistry and praised Jim and his co-director Frank Oz for the astonishing creatures, but they weren't sure what to make of a Henson film without the Muppets. While praising the film's ambitions, initially, reviewers weren't satisfied with the story. Over time, however, *The Dark Crystal* would become recognized as an innovative triumph.

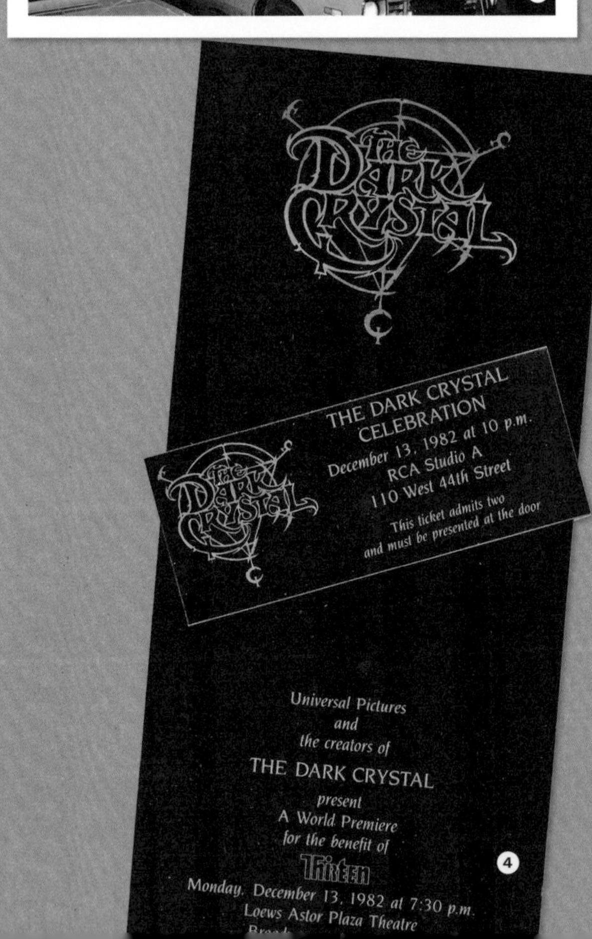

❶ Jim with an actual giant crystal at an exhibit in Paris that displayed creatures from the film with mineralogical specimens. ❷ Jim with Frank Oz at *The Dark Crystal* premiere. ❸ The marquee of the Loews Astor Plaza Theater in New York on December 13, 1982. ❹ Invitation to *The Dark Crystal* New York premiere and party. ❺ Fascination with the making of the film continued, and *Cinefantastique* featured Jim on the cover in spring 1983.

CINEFANTASTIQUE®

MAKEUP ARTIST DICK SMITH REVEALS: The Hunger

Volume 13 Number 4

$4.50
U.K. £2.75

THE DARK CRYSTAL

The Remarkable Creations of Puppet Master Jim Henson

5

Jan 10 FRAGGLE ROCK goes on the AIR HBO
Feb 20-21 at EPCOT in Fla with family

Feb 26 - to JAPAN - DC
March 2 to Australia - first time 2-Sydney 6-Melbourne

1983

March 28 - Dennis Lee - Brian F + I begin talking about Labyrinth in London

With his Creature Shop established and Brian Froud on board, Jim started planning for a second fantasy film. *The Dark Crystal* taught him that story was paramount, and he asked *Fraggle Rock* lyricist (and Canadian poet laureate) Dennis Lee to help develop a narrative. Lee produced a "poetic novella" outlining a coming-of-age story set in a Froudian world of goblins, hairy beasts, and animated masonry. This time, humans were central to the story, which was drafted into script form by Terry Jones and Laura Phillips. Focusing on the emotional journey of the main character, Sarah, Jim sought input from his producer, George Lucas, numerous Henson colleagues, and from writer/actor Elaine May. At the same time, design work progressed and Jim imagined magical encounters for his lead players.

❶+❷ Pages from Jim's idea notebook for *Labyrinth*. ❸ Jim's ambitious plans resulted in complicated scenes like the Escher-inspired one depicted here in the storyboard by Martin Asbury. ❹ Dennis Lee (left) with *Fraggle Rock* composer Philip Balsam (and Travelling Matt). ❺ Jim with his *Labyrinth* collaborator, George Lucas. ❻ Detail from cover page from Jim's shooting script. ❼ Brian Froud's concept art of a baby stolen by goblins.

the Labyrinth
the Maze
the Labyrinth Twist
The Tale of the Labyrinth

❶

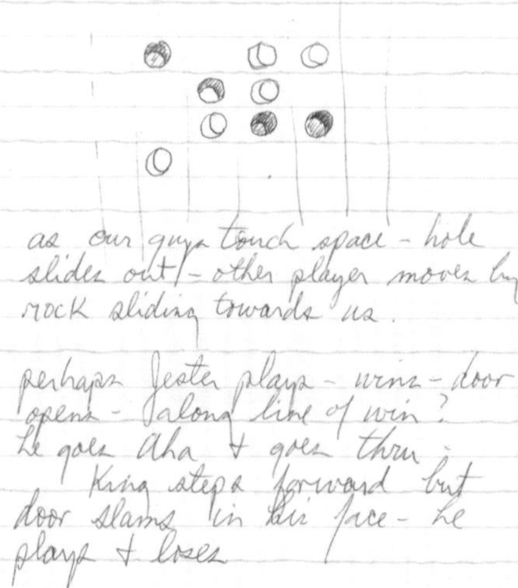

❷

❸

❹

5

LABYRINTH

6

7

April 8-10 Music Ed Meeting NYC
May 7 - 1ST MASKED BALL - second ave
Gothic House
May 12 - John Denver - CAMPING SHOW AIRS
May 21 meeting with Digital Productions
May 29 BIG BIRD in CHINA AIRS

1983

May 31 MUPPETS TAKE MANHATTAN BEGINS SHOOTING (SHOOT TIL Sept 16)

For *The Muppets Take Manhattan,* Jim's feature chronicling the Muppets' pursuit of Broadway stardom, he involved his top creative team. Frank Oz made his solo directing debut and co-wrote the script. *Sesame Street* composer Jeff Moss wrote the award-winning songs, and the central characters were given dazzling scenarios that highlighted their performers' virtuosity. Lesser-known characters, like Rizzo the Rat, were given featured roles, allowing for deeper development. Everyone contributed, and the collaborative nature of the Henson team was reflected in the film's storyline, a celebration of working together to achieve a dream. Its most famous scene, an onstage wedding between Kermit and Miss Piggy, left audiences wondering—are they or aren't they? Kermit insisted that it was simply a scene in a movie.

❶ Kermit and Miss Piggy at the altar. ❷ *The Muppets Take Manhattan* promotional postcard. ❸ Prop *Playbill* for the Muppets' Broadway show. ❹ Storyboard panel by John Davis detailing Rizzo the Rat's kitchen ballet. ❺ Michael Frith's bear designs. ❻ Sticker from the Muppets' fictional college.

CUT TO:
P. 2
PAN...
PAN WITH EGG BEARING RATS...
RATS...
PULL BACK & TILT UP AS THEY EXIT FRAME...
3
YOLANDA
& MASTERSON
SAME SHOT:
CHESTER IS RIDING
"BIDIDDLEBEE BEEP BOP! BOP! BIDOOBE
3A
PAN...
AS RIZZO CROSSES:
(HE'S SCAT SINGING...)
DANHURST
D
COLLEGE
June - working on Starboppera ideas
July 4 - weekend - go to London - launch the London shop - Connie P. in charge
July 30-31 - VTR Bruce Schwartz for J.H. Presents
July - taping for Please Don't eat the Pictures at the Met. for SS special -

4

5

6

1983

Aug 20-21 weekend meeting Rocket Ship Show - Starboppers -

Inspired by Buckminster Fuller's description of man as machine, Jim and his daughter Lisa conceived of an outer space television series featuring a digitally animated rocket ship inhabited by puppet characters, each representing facets of the human personality. Working together, the characters would teach children how to look within themselves for solutions to problems like fear or self-consciousness while pursuing exciting adventures. Australian sculptor Ron Mueck and a team of writers created the puppets and stories for *Starboppers*, producing some test footage, and Jim pitched the show to the networks. While it was not produced, the show provided an opportunity to explore advances in computer-generated animation, and Jim developed a relationship with Digital Productions who would create an animated owl for the opening sequence of *Labyrinth* three years later.

❶+❷ Ron Mueck's designs for *Starboppers*. ❸+❻ Jim's title ideas and character designs from the *Starboppers* meeting on August 20, 1983. ❹ Fabric choices for building the Cosmo puppet. ❺ Cosmo Bopper.

❶

❷

Rocket Boppers! / Space Boppe[rs]
with Bill Bopper
Brenda Bopper -
Baby Bopper
Bobbie Boppie
Big Bopper
Beverly Bopper
Star Boppers Star Dinghys
Doppler Boppers
Mach Rockets
Star Seekers Jumpin' Geminoids
Dogs in Space
Far Out Star Bopping

❸

Aug 29 - shooting Muppet Babies in Movie

Sept 13 - Dinner with Douglas Adams - 1st met.

Oct 31 - fly down from Toronto for Burr Tillstrom Museum of B'casting function

Nov 14 - in Toronto directing Fraggle

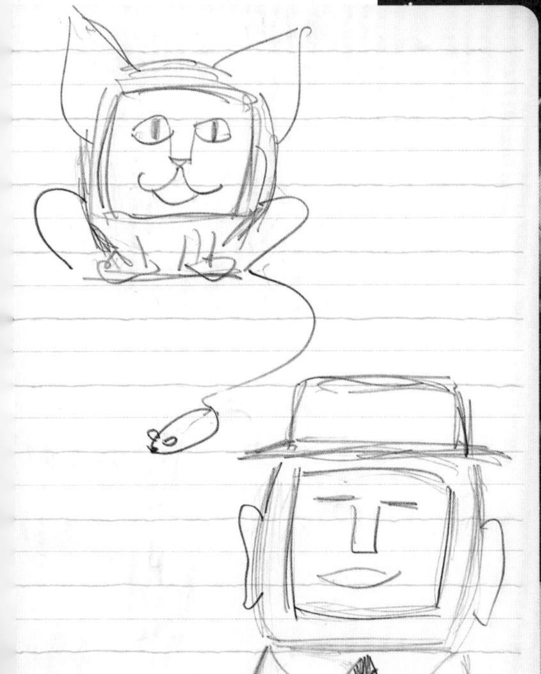

Dec 20 Henson Foundation meeting (2nd year)

Dec 31 - to Pasadena for the Rose Bowl - Miss Piggy Float - Lisa - Heather, Brian

Jim Henson's
MUPPET BABIES

1984

3/10 - Concept Muppet Babies

A delightful musical sequence in *The Muppets Take Manhattan* featured Miss Piggy's fantasy of baby versions of the Muppets. The characters as youngsters were enormously appealing, and it was immediately clear that they would translate well to other formats. Henson Associates joined forces with Marvel and CBS to create an animated series, *Jim Henson's Muppet Babies*, which celebrated imagination and creativity. Innovative techniques like the incorporation of live-action footage and photographic backgrounds highlighted the way kids interconnect seemingly unrelated ideas, stories, and characters in their dramatic play. Produced for eight seasons, *Muppet Babies* was honored with five Emmy Awards and sent the Henson licensing department into overdrive—the Muppet Babies appeared on diapers, as plush dolls, in storybooks, and on all manner of products around the world.

SAME SHOT: p. 4

SAME SHOT:

❶ Michael Frith's sketches of Baby Kermit. ❷ Baby Kermit and Baby Miss Piggy as they appeared in *The Muppets Take Manhattan*. ❸ Storyboard panel for the *Muppet Babies* promotional music video. ❹ The animated Muppet Babies. ❺ Advertisement encouraging Emmy voters to support *Muppet Babies*.

March 17 - Kermit gives speech in Atlanta - Nat'l Wildlife

March 29 - to Australia VTR Richard Bradshaw for J.H. presents til April 6

April 4 - BMW stolen - turns up several weeks later

April 10-11 shoot Muppet Babies MTV
13 - CBS - commits to M.B.

June 18 - Meet David Bowie in NY describe Labyr.

July 13 - MUPPETS TAKE MANHATTAN OPENS

1984

July 16 - Dreamchild begins shooting

Jim's London workshop, established for *The Dark Crystal*, was housed in a former postal sorting station with large open spaces ideal for creating oversized puppets and experimenting with messy materials. To keep the collaborative team busy between Henson projects, producer Duncan Kenworthy sought outside work like *Dreamchild*, a film by Dennis Potter. Exploring the friendship between Charles Dodgson (Lewis Carroll) and Alice Liddell, the inspiration for *Alice's Adventures in Wonderland*, the film included Henson-created creatures based on the original Tenniel illustrations from the books. The film opened in summer 1985 to generally positive reviews, and the writers made much of the characters from Jim's shop. The review in *The Guardian* noted, "The realization by Jim Henson and his team of the fabled creatures of Lewis Carroll's imagination is beguilingly original."

❶ Jim Henson's Creature Shop public announcement following *Dreamchild.* ❷ Inside cover of Jim's childhood copy of *Alice's Adventures in Wonderland* inscribed in his hand. ❸ Puppeteers on the *Dreamchild* set. ❹+❻ Characters created by the Henson Creature Shop under Lyle Conway's supervision. ❺ The London Creature Shop in a sketch by Michael Dixon. ❼ Script pages from *Dreamchild.*

THE HENSON ORGANISATION

announces that

following completion
of creature construction on LABYRINTH,
and after their successful association
with Thorn-EMI on the
recently completed DREAM CHILD,

JIM HENSON'S CREATURE SHOP

is now formally offering its services
to the film industry for
the design, construction and performance
of puppets or
special effects creatures
in selected motion picture properties.

In Europe, contact:- Duncan Kenworthy.
The Henson Organisation, 1B Downshire Hill, Hampstead, London NW3 1NR. (01) 435-7121.

In the U.S. contact:- Will Morrison.
Henson Associates, 117 East 69th Street, New York, N.Y. (212) 794-2400.

❶

James Henson
Stoneville
Mississippi
From Mom + Dad ❷

Alice's
...ntures

❸

Aug 19 - 24 in DRESDEN with Cheryl for
UNIMA Puppet Festival

4

5

6

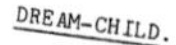

DREAM-CHILD.

Dennis Potter.

BLACK SCREEN out of which rises the very soft and evocative SWISH-SHUSH-SWISH of calm waves upon a beach, and then the distant, mysterious THROB-THROB-THROB of a SHIP'S ENGINES.

The screen slowly lightens to -

1. EXT. A ROCKY SHORE. DAY.

The ROCKS and PEBBLES of a strange, unreal shore take shape out of the darkness, and they have, especially at first, the suggestion of the folds, wrinkles and longitudinal patterns of a bed-cover or eiderdown or blanket. 1.

SOUND OF SOBBING, OFF. Hard, grieving sobbing, as of someone in real despair, seeming to come out of and then to dominate the distant Throb-Throb-Throb.

FINDING, initially in near-silhouette and not yet total light, the disturbing figures on the rock-piles of a MOCK TURTLE and a GRYPHON. It is the MOCK TURTLE who is weeping his heart out, in huge, blubbering Sobs. There is a silvery crust (of the kind a snail makes on a garden path) down its cheeks, the residue of years and years of hard weeping.

The utterly venomous GRYPHON, who has a market-stall cockney accent, sighs and shifts like someone fed-up to his back fangs.

GRYPHON (wearily)
Oh, for God's sake, shut up.

The Mock Turtle takes no notice, and continues to sob.

As suddenly and as inexplicably as in a dream, a very old woman is standing there watching them, the sea behind her. She is MRS HARGREAVES, who, seventy years before, had been the original inspiration of 'Alice'.

She contemplates the two large, weird creatures with a rather nervous interest. Then -

MRS HARGREAVES (to Gryphon)
What is his sorrow?

GRYPHON
Oh, it's all his fancy, that. This 'ere Mock Turtle ain't got no sorrow, y'know.
(to Mock Turtle)
This 'ere young lady. She wants to know your history, she do.

The Mock Turtle swallows its sobs, and speaks in a deep, hollow and very lugubrious tone.

continued

7

Sept 15 MUPPET BABIES AIRS on CBS - 9 AM

Sept 24 in San Francisco - meeting with George Lucas - Laura Phillips - Larry Mirkin & Mira V.

1984

Nov 1-5 Moscow - recce
Nov 18-24 Moscow - VTR JH presents SERGEI OBRAZTSOV
in between in London - NY - Toronto - Calif - NY - London!

Jim recognized that puppetry can be a universal language transcending national borders. Through his work and extensive travels, he met some of the world's greatest puppeteers, many unknown outside their countries, and he was eager to introduce them to a wider audience. In 1983, Jim began planning a television series highlighting master puppeteers, producing six documentaries under the banner *Jim Henson Presents The World of Puppetry.* Filmed on location in Holland, Germany, Australia, the U.S., France, and the Soviet Union, they featured Henk Boerwinkel, Albrecht Roser, Richard Bradshaw, Bruce Schwartz, Philippe Genty, and the revered Russian, Sergey Obraztsov. This was especially gratifying for Jim; as a teenager starting out, he had studied puppetry books from the library—including Obraztsov's 1950 book, *My Profession.*

Nov 25 in VIENNA with Cheryl - Great.

❶ Jim and Sergey Obraztsov. ❷ Australian puppeteer Richard Bradshaw. ❸ Jim's ideas for some unusual puppets. ❹ Jim's high school artwork captures the expressive possibilities of hands. ❺ American puppeteer Bruce Schwartz. ❻ Jim's much-used passport from the mid-1980s.

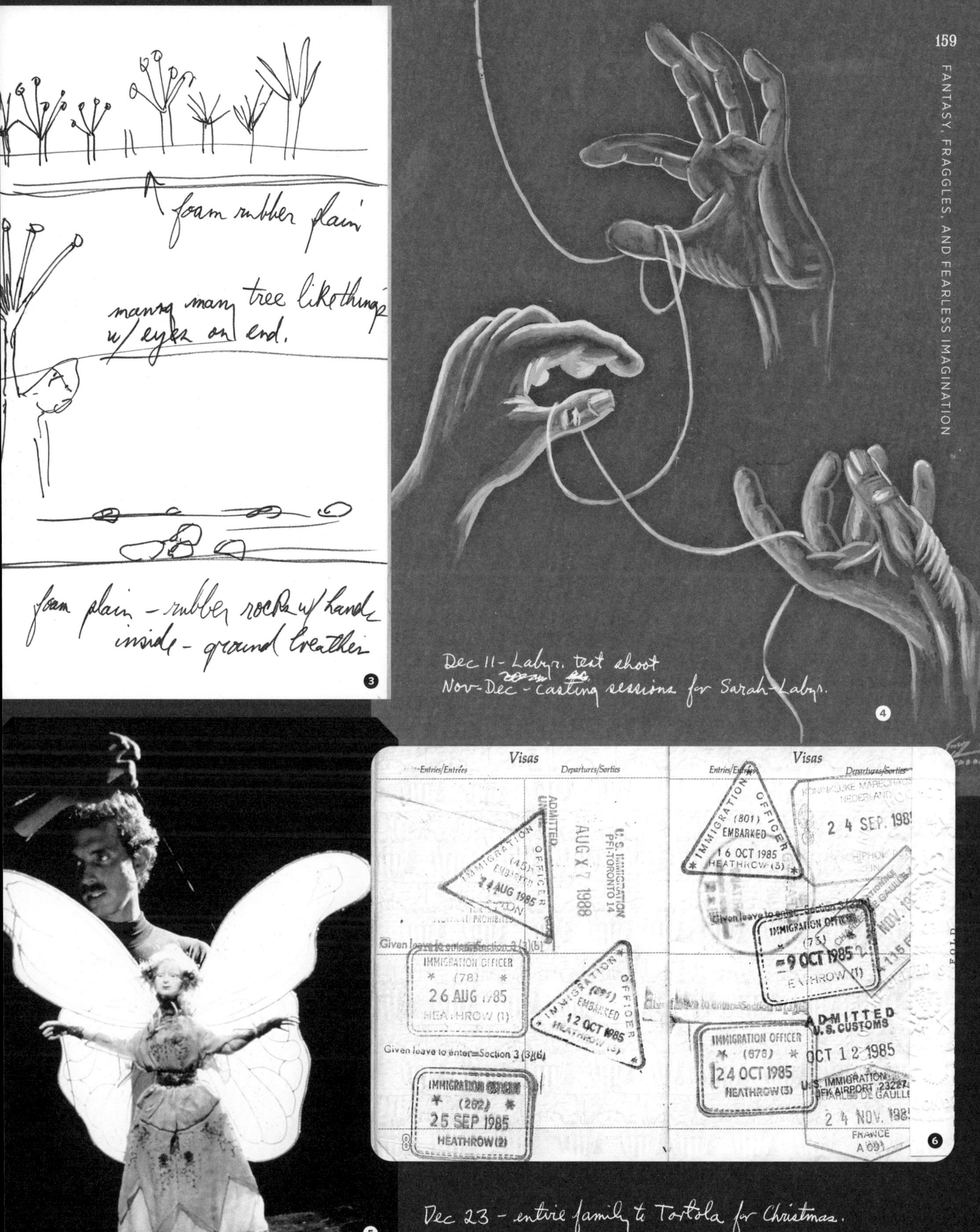

Dec 23 - entire family to Tortola for Christmas.

1985

Jan 29 - JENNIFER CONNELLY auditions for LABY, cast within a week

Feb 11 - Meet with Bowie in Gstadt - his deal is set FEB 15

Feb 16 - 3rd Annual MASKED BALL at Waldorf Astoria - w/ celebrity guests

In developing *Labyrinth*, great effort was made to retain the comic poetry of the early treatments while ensuring the believability of the characters. Much care went into casting the central role of Sarah, a mildly flawed, yet intelligent and sympathetic, character, and auditions were held on both sides of the Atlantic. Dozens of young actresses auditioned, and fourteen-year-old Jennifer Connelly won the part. She developed a strong rapport with Jim and her otherworldly co-star David Bowie. Their pivotal scene at a masked ball reflected Jim's enjoyment of masquerade parties. He hosted four masked balls, inviting his colleagues, friends, and celebrities, and his guests' inventive costumes displayed their creativity. The 1985 ball's *Labyrinth* theme inspired Jim to sport an extravagant feathered mask and goblin-like armor.

❶ Jim directing Jennifer Connelly. ❷+❸ Polaroids that Jim taped into his directing script notebook. ❹ Jim and a guest at the 1985 Masked Ball. ❺ Jim and Dave Goelz at the 1988 ball. ❻ Invitation to Jim's first masked ball in 1983.

Jim Henson
Invites
You and your guest
to a

MASQUERADE BALL

Saturday, May 7th, 1983
at 9PM

Rutherford House
236 Second Ave.
(Between 14th & 15th Sts.)

Black Tie, costume
or Festive Dress

R.S.V.P. Nancy Evans
794-2400 Ext. 304

Mask required

March 9 - Toronto on Computer Special -
Future of Fraggles - everyone wants 120

April 13 - Labyrinth - PRE-Party at 50 Downshire Hill

1985

APRIL 15- BEGIN SHOOTING LABYRINTH
Ext. Wall -
Hedge Maze
Wise Man - Knockers

Jim hosted a pre-production party to launch *Labyrinth,* and two days later, the ambitious shoot began. Directing each complicated scene, Jim worked to achieve the effects while drawing expressive performances from his characters, both human and puppet. Special care went into the Wild Things (renamed Fireys), loose-limbed characters that danced crazily, tossing their body parts and removing their eyes. The intricate routine required four weeks of rehearsal and four puppeteers for each puppet. Equally challenging was the Shaft of Hands scene taking place in a thirty-foot-high shaft with 150 hands that grabbed at and interacted with Sarah. Supplied by seventy-five puppeteers, they were augmented by an additional 200 foam-rubber hands. Jim noted it was "one of the most bizarre and unusual sequences I've ever used in a movie."

❶ Jim on set with David Bowie and Jennifer Connelly. ❷ Invitation to Jim's *Labyrinth* pre-production party drawn by Brian Froud. ❸ Concept sketch for Sarah's fall through the Shaft of Hands. ❹ Elliot Scott's scenic design for the Hedge Maze. ❺ Elliot Scott's design for Ludo's scene with the talking door knockers. ❻ Puppeteer assignments for the Fireys.

WILD THING 1

W.T. 1
Kevin Clash

WILD THING 2

W.T. 2
Karen Prell

May 4 - to NY for Muppet Monsters Meeting
May 5 - to Amsterdam
|| Forest - Wild Things
|| Shaft of Hands
May 18-19 - VTR Kermit + Piggy Dance in America
Cinderella
VTR Home Videos - Mup. Sho.

|| Oubliette
Brick Corridors
May 25-26 - Paris - buy Edgar Brant Snake Lamp
Alf + Ralph
Carved faces
Slashing Machine

1985

June 3 – David Bowie shoots
Blind Beggar scene
Jareth + Goblins

Jim was not disappointed by his choice of David Bowie as Jareth, the Goblin King. Late in the shoot, Jim told his staff that Bowie had, "added a truly magical spark as Jareth." His tall, lean presence was a perfect contrast to Brian Froud's earth-toned and compact goblins, highlighting their delightful design and eccentric personalities. Creating this population was a joy for Froud, and his imagination was overstuffed with a diversity of goblins. Inspired by the drawings and etchings of northern European artists like Albrecht Dürer, Froud produced page after page of sketches. Collaborating with screenwriter Terry Jones, he compiled a goblin catalogue complete with clever names and descriptions. Published in 1986 as *The Goblins of Labyrinth*, it gave readers a window into the depth of the film's creative thinking.

❶ David Bowie as the Goblin King among his subjects. ❷+❹+❺+❻+❼+❽ Brian Froud's goblin designs. ❸ Brian Froud with goblin puppets.

❶

June 8 – John Henson + friends over –
June 29 – to NY for Muppet Monster Shoot
July 13 – recording Muppet Show on Tour
" " LIVE AID Concert – Wembley – Bowie

❷

❸

July 13- Heather over UK for the summer

Aug 24-26- BALLOONING WEEKEND in France with 11 of us
|| Goblin Town

1985

Sept 14 - Little Muppet Monsters goes on air - also 2nd Season - Mup Babies

As a result of the stunning success of *Muppet Babies* and in an effort to extend the Henson presence on Saturday morning television, *Little Muppet Monsters* was developed for CBS. Jim and Michael Frith conceived of a show with three new Muppet monster characters: Tug, Molly, and Boo. Members of *The Muppet Show* cast appeared now and then, and the puppet scenes were interspersed with animated and filmed sequences produced with Marvel. Themes of creative play and imagination underlined the action. Despite airing as an hour-long block with *Muppet Babies*, the show did not find an audience. It did, however, provide an opportunity for some of the younger puppeteers, Camille Bonora and David Rudman, to hone their performing skills under veteran Richard Hunt.

❶ Michael Frith's design for Tug. ❷ Boo, Tug, and Molly with some chickens and penguins. ❸ Michael Frith's design for a penguin, a staple of Muppet comedy. ❹ *Little Muppet Monsters* in their basement studio. ❺ The Saturday morning lineup as advertised in *TV Guide*. ❻ The Henson licensing department's newsletter featuring the Monsters.

Sept 17 - Toronto - 30th ANNIVERSARY of MUPPETS - VTR 19-22

Oct 19 - Women in Show Business award
" 21 in Indianapolis - Art of Mups
" 26 - Geo L in UK editing
" 28 in Toronto performing in Fraggle

Nov 7-8 Geo L in NYC
" 11 David B looping 18 - Jenny Looping
Nov 20 Geo L checks out Laby - final cut
23-24 Paris - then to NY - Thanksgiving Kermit balloon dies
Dec 1 - back to UK - re-shoot Hoggle Dec 9 looping Brian

New Year's Eve - Kermit TIMES SQ

4

5

VOLUME 3 • NUMBER 3

©HENSON ASSOCIATES, INC. 1985

THE LICENSING NEWSLETTER FROM HENSON ASSOCIATES, INC.

MONSTERS • MOVE • ON CBS!

Update on Saturday Morning Muppets

As reported here in our last issue, the Muppet presence will expand to a full hour on the CBS Saturday morning lineup. Set aside Saturdays, 9am to 10am EST (8 am to 9 am CST) and watch the new fall edition of MUPPET BABIES followed by the amazing, new LITTLE MUPPET MONSTERS.

The LITTLE MUPPET MONSTERS combines puppetry, animation, live footage, cameo appearances of some of the original Muppet characters (Kermit, Miss Piggy, Fozzie, et al), lots of original musical numbers and a brand new cast of Muppet characters you'll love to love. You'll see the Little Monsters, like most kids, imagining themselves in myriad adult roles as they struggle and cope with such pertinent matters as sibling rivalry and expressing their feelings.

Says Michael Frith, Executive VP of HA! and Creative Producer of LITTLE MUPPET MONSTERS, "MUPPET BABIES is a breakthrough for Saturday morning programming. We think that the Little Monsters will continue the innovation and excitement that MUPPET BABIES began and we look forward to continued success with CBS."

The Licensing program to support the series is in development with the following manufacturers planning a unified launch at Toy Fair '86:

HASBRO. .plush; MILTON BRADLEY. .board game, puzzles; PLAYSKOOL. .puzzles; BEN COOPER. . costumes; DIAMOND TOY. .stickers; BALLOON CONCEPTS. .balloons; ALLISON MFG. .boys & girls sportswear; HALLMARK CARDS. .greeting cards, etc.; LEE BELTS. .belts; PCA APPAREL. . P.J.'s; BEACH PRODUCTS. .party unit, gift wrap

Humanitas Prize to Muppet Babies

Eight Take Away One Equals Panic, the MUPPET BABIES episode about jumping to conclusions, received the Humanitas Prize. Given by the Human Family Institute, this esteemed award is for the TV programs that "most effectively communicate enriching human values."

★

EMMY Says First is Best!

The MUPPET BABIES, Jim Henson's first production for Saturday morning TV, won an EMMY for Outstanding Animated Program. Since its 1984 debut, the show has placed in the top 5 of 42 network shows and is currently #1 on CBS-TV's Saturday morning line-up. MUPPET BABIES enters its second season this fall with all new episodes.

6

1986

Jan– in LA give Digital go ahead on titles of Labyrinth

Feb 10–22– VTR BUNNY PICNIC

Excited to incorporate the latest in computer-generated animation into his work, Jim collaborated with Digital Productions on the animated title sequence for *Labyrinth*. At the same time, encouraged by his daughter Cheryl, he went into production on an old-fashioned hand-puppet project, *The Tale of the Bunny Picnic*. Combining elements of Beatrix Potter and the can-do spirit of *Fraggle Rock*, with hints of his upcoming *StoryTeller* project, Jim presented a charming special for children populated by cute bunnies and the requisite Muppet dog. Capturing the joy of Henson picnics on the Hampstead Heath, Jocelyn Stevenson's story coupled with Diane Dawson-Hearn's visuals was well received on television and translated into a charming picture book. The interminably cute star, Bean Bunny, became a regular Muppet ensemble player.

❶ Diane Dawson-Hearn's design of the Bunny family, including the StoryTeller. ❷ Cheryl Henson and Jim examine a bunny puppet. ❸ The star, Bean Bunny. ❹ Diane Dawson-Hearn's dog design. ❺ Rollie Krewson building a bunny.

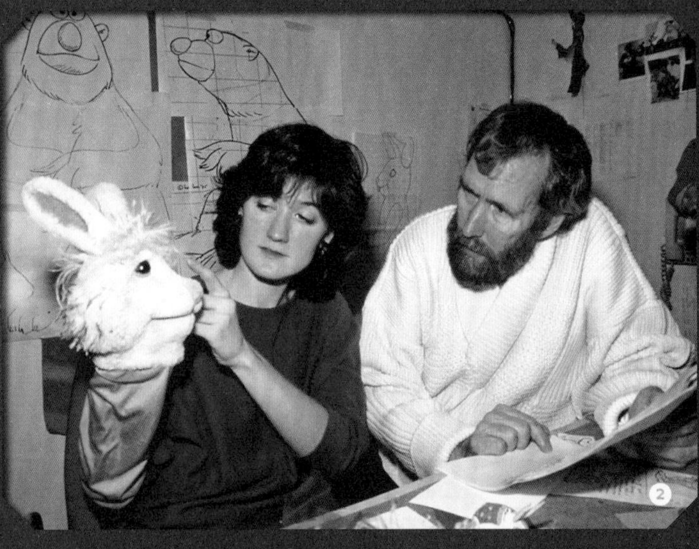

May 15 FRAGGLE ROCK ends in Toronto
May 16 - final party

June 27 - Labyrinth Opens in the US

July 19 - VACATION TRIP with Cheryl
↓ & John EGYPT -
Aug 8 Cairo - Luxor - aswan - Bang Kok -
Tokyo (July 27 - open exhibit
on Aug 1) then Jacarta - Jogja
Bali - Hong Kong

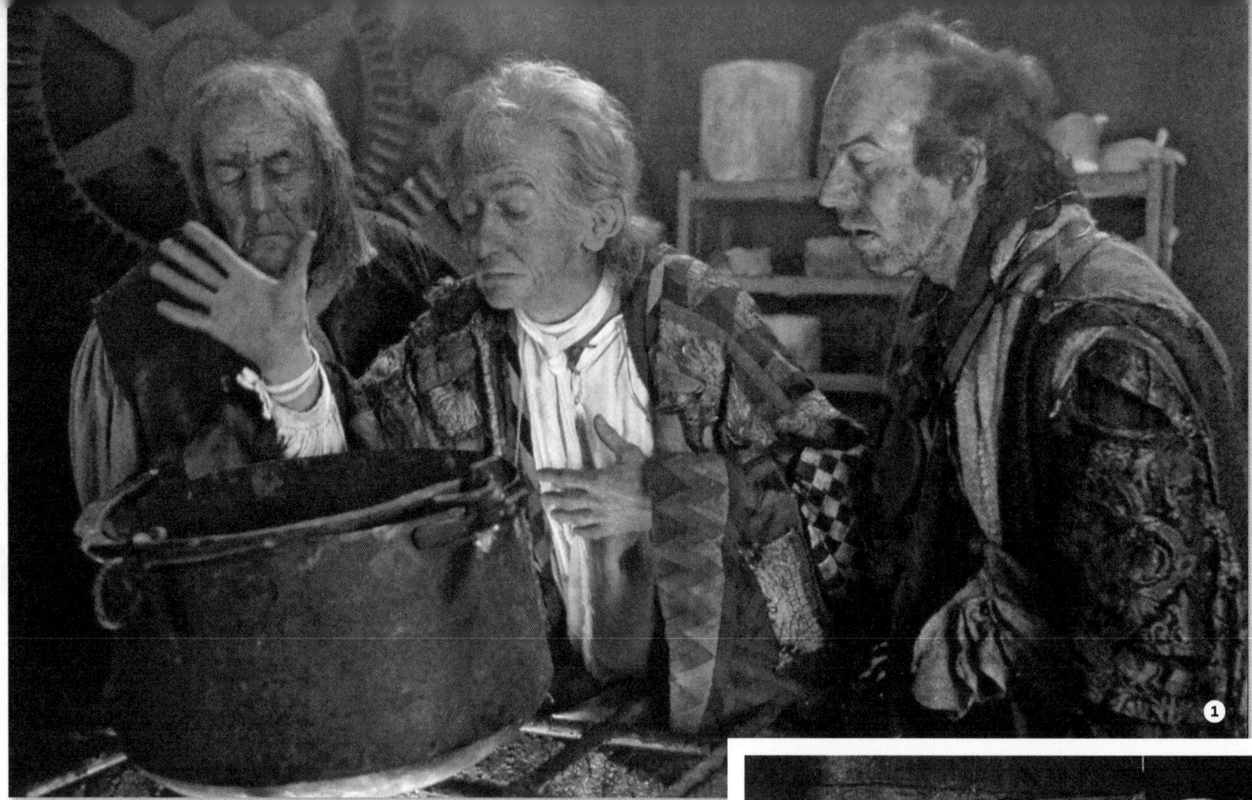

1986

Aug 26 - filming first STORYTELLER
Steve Barron directs Hans My Hedgehog

Oct 6 - VTR The CHRISTMAS TOY in Toronto
Nov - filming - VTR - test of STOOPID FLAKES

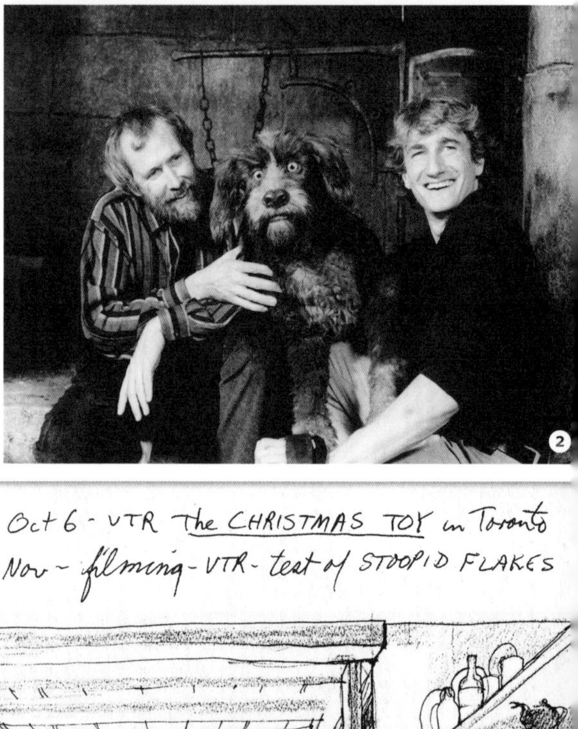

Traditional fairy tales inspired many of Jim's early projects and were parodied at length on *Sesame Street*. Building on the more sophisticated themes and visuals of *The Dark Crystal* and *Labyrinth* and a concept from his daughter Lisa, Jim began to explore a wider range of European folktales for his series, *The StoryTeller*. Recognizing the power of these timeless stories and the engaging quality of an experienced raconteur, he combined the technological and artistic talents of his Creature Shop, Anthony Minghella's captivating scripts, and John Hurt's compelling performance as the title character to conjure up nine moody and powerful episodes that propelled the viewer into another world.

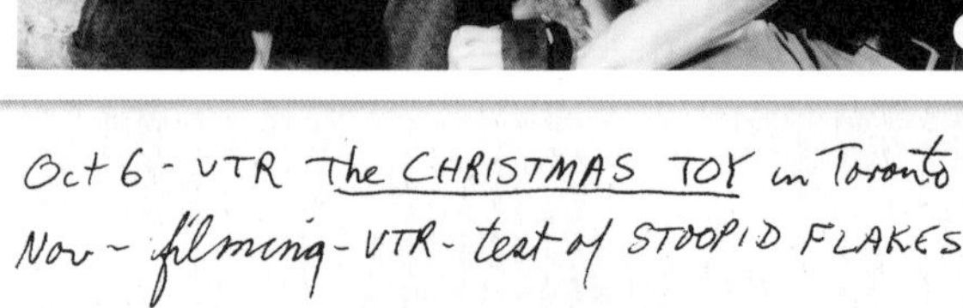

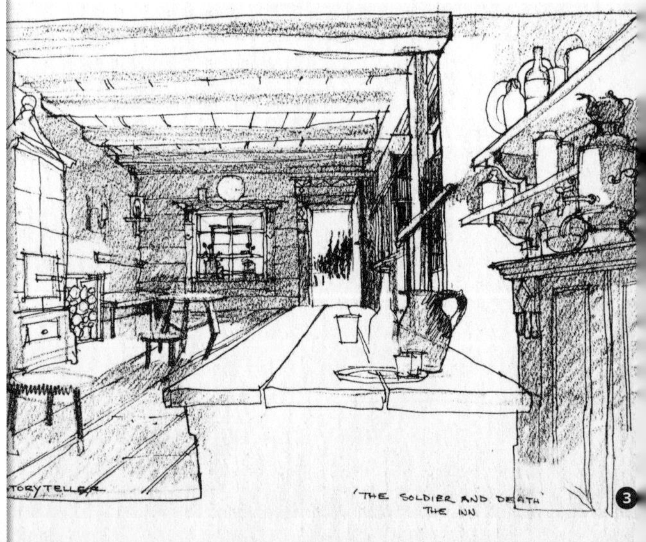

❶ John Hurt (center) plays the StoryTeller in "A Story Short." ❷ Brian Henson (with his dad) performed the StoryTeller's dog. ❸ Set design by Roger Hall for "The Soldier and Death," one of two episodes Jim directed himself. ❹ Storyboard panels from the first *StoryTeller* episode, "Hans My Hedgehog." ❺ After getting a positive response to "Hans" from NBC, producer Duncan Kenworthy solicited designs from Brian Froud for additional episodes. ❻ Hans the Hedgehog, played by Ailsa Berk. ❼ Jim valued the gift of storytelling and added storyteller characters to several of his shows. Michael Frith designed this one for *Fraggle Rock*.

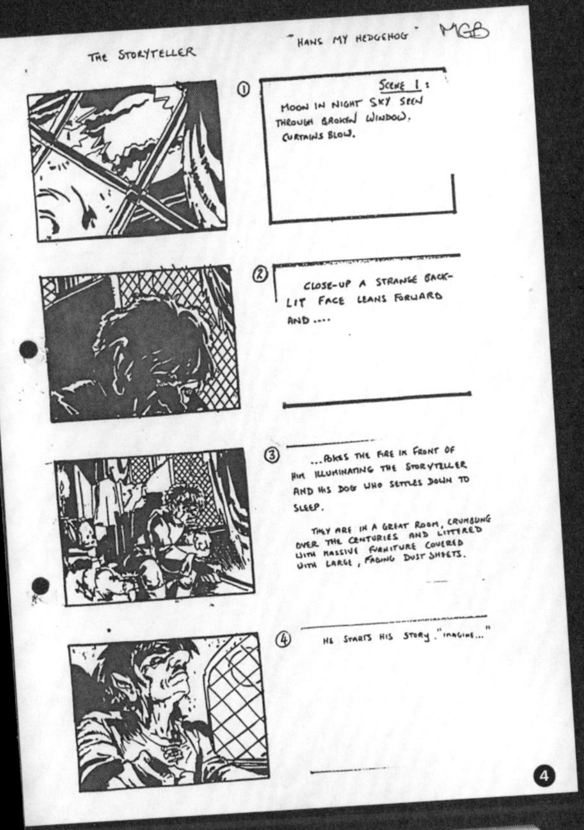

THE STORYTELLER "HANS MY HEDGEHOG" MGB

① SCENE 1: MOON IN NIGHT SKY SEEN THROUGH BROKEN WINDOW. CURTAINS BLOW.

② CLOSE-UP A STRANGE BACK-LIT FACE LEANS FORWARD AND....

③ ...POKES THE FIRE IN FRONT OF HIM ILLUMINATING THE STORYTELLER AND HIS DOG WHO SETTLES DOWN TO SLEEP.

THEY ARE IN A GREAT ROOM, CRUMBLING OVER THE CENTURIES AND LITTERED WITH MASSIVE FURNITURE COVERED WITH LARGE, FADING DUST SHEETS.

④ HE STARTS HIS STORY. "IMAGINE..."

4

5

A plume behind the "ear" becomes almost part of his hair — but drips blobs of ink down his shirt front

flippable specs — goes from sleepy kindliness to wild surmise...

pads, scrolls & misc. papers stuff his pockets

pencil stubs litter the ground like cigarette butts...

The Storyteller...
portly & kindly with patched (aesthetically) & baggy cardigan/sweat shirt/ceremonial cape (with hood), Voluminous British Army issue khaki shorts & sandals w/ socks under them. Seems merely a harmless eccentric... but with his hood up could become quite magical & mysterious...

7

6

1987

Jan 15-17 - VTR IN-TV test shoot edited at Charlex

in LA trying to sell Movie package including WITCHES

1987

March - casting in LA for Puppet Man
April VTR - Puppetman

Jim realized that the camaraderie, creativity, and occasional drama on the set of a television show might make an entertaining situation comedy, and he conceived of a show that was vaguely autobiographical, focusing on a young puppeteer starting out on local TV. While centered on the human relationships, the show was to include, "some wonderful puppet segments from backstage, not only seeing the ingenious way that it is being done, but also seeing the interaction of the puppeteers." CBS bought the pilot, *Puppetman*, and Jim cast Fred Newman and actual Muppet performer Richard Hunt as the puppeteers on *Dragontime*, a children's show. Despite the involvement of comedian and *Muppet Show* writer Jack Burns and an engaging dragon named Butane, the show's reviews were lukewarm, and the network declined a series.

❶+❹ Ron Mueck's character designs. ❷ Fred Newman in *Puppetman*. ❸ Jim with the cast of *Puppetman*: Lisa Waltz, Richard Hunt, and Fred Newman. ❺ Jim's storyboard panels for the *Puppetman* opening.

3
OPT
CL
Ea
th
(or

4

March 28 – Lisa + Heather weekend in Monterey

July 5-25 Charleville France – Puppetry/Video workshop – 21 students begin with Cheryl + Brian – Heather over for last week

Aug 10-17 I film my "Soldier + Death" Storyteller – mine the 3rd of 4 filmed at this time 1. Fearnot 2. Stone Short 3. mine 4. The Luck Child (Brian my second unit director

Sept 28 – Oct 8 VTR Muppet Family Christmas

Oct 21 VTR Dolly Parton show w/Kermit

4
GARY
DEL

interior van – shot from rear of van Del comes down – Del has been operating he has been operating Earl – all are laughing (ZACK?)

5

Clyde Dragon runs toward camera

exterior – driveway

6
DEL
ZACK

Del in mock terror jumps in van + backs away Zack in van – laughing + waving

worked
roof-
window)

5

Dec 16 - Muppet Family Christmas (AIRS)
Great Reviews - Great Rating

HENSON ASSOCIATES, INC
117 EAST 69 STREET
NEW YORK, N.Y. 10021
(212) 794-2400 TELEX-420750
PRODUCERS OF THE MUPPETS
ha! JIM HENSON

Ho Komissionooder Sjo
(1) Sneern hund de
mcenahvoo skor
herg dah Smorgas
bord lord.
Gloo das
click click en
noin filmek
den Washington

HENSON ASSOCIATES, INC
117 EAST 69 STREET
NEW YORK, N.Y. 10021
(212) 794-2400 TELEX-420750
PRODUCERS OF THE MUPPETS
ha! JIM HENSON

der Fancy Food
goôde der gritingzoo
der Kükenmenenstoof.
Yay boo thenken
svenson eet der
goo goo Per Nilsson
und der Eilert
Nassell fer yoom
yoom. BorkBork!

1987

Nov 6 VTR Chef Commercial Cereal

Nov 17-20 VTR Mother Goose - Humpty-Dumpty in Plymouth - Brian directs

The Swedish Chef was no doubt one of Jim's wackiest characters—silliness personified, a Muppet with license to do the ridiculous for the sheer joy of it. Performed by Jim with Frank Oz providing the hands, the Chef was ideal for parodies of packaged-food promotion. Jim decided to create a Swedish Chef themed breakfast cereal, inventing names like Oople-Sauceys, Croonchy Poofs, Moopettes, and the favorite (among the Henson people, not the manufacturer), Stoopid Flakes. With major contributions from art director Michael Frith, the idea evolved into a real product from Post Cereal called Croonchy Stars, landing in stores in 1988. Around the same time, Jim traveled to the U.K. to watch his son Brian directing for the first time on the set of the preschool series *Mother Goose Stories*.

❶ The Croonchy Stars cereal box. ❷ Jim's draft in mock-Swedish of a letter from the Swedish Chef to the Swedish Trade Office. ❸ Early Swedish Chef design by Michael Frith, 1974. ❹ Brian Henson directing *Mother Goose Stories*. ❺ Mother Goose.

3
4
5

1988

Jan– working on Jim Henson Hour –

The Jim Henson Hour, a thirteen-episode anthology series hosted on camera by Jim, was meant to combine Muppet antics with the experience of channel-surfing, new video technologies, and contemporary music. Jim's introductions and a weekly sequence with Muppets, old and new, preceded an array of inventive programming. This ranged from specially produced stories like the ecology-themed "Song of the Cloud Forest" and the mermaid fable "Lighthouse Island" to previously unaired episodes of *The StoryTeller* and two programs made for British television, *Monster Maker* and *Living with Dinosaurs*. Jim embraced the freedom to make any show he wanted and produced *Dog City*, a film noir parody set in a world populated solely by dogs with a script demonstrating Jim's love of groan-inducing puns.

❶ Bruce McNally's character design for *Dog City*. ❷ Michael Frith's concept for *The Jim Henson Hour* set. ❸ Storyboard panel for Anthony Minghella's story *Living with Dinosaurs*. ❹ Gregory Chisholm and the toy dinosaur, Dog, performed by Brian Henson. ❺+❻ Cheryl Henson's conceptual art for *"Song of the Cloud Forest."* ❼ Clifford, a new character designed by Kirk Thatcher for *The Jim Henson Hour*.

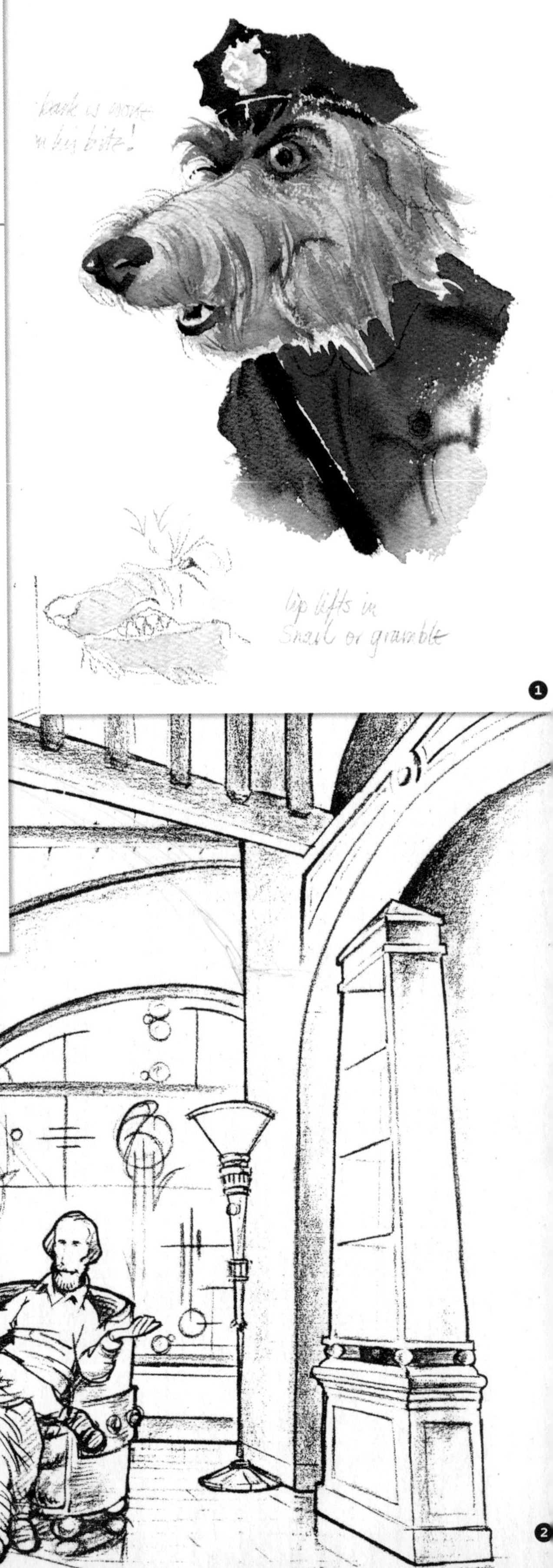

3

4

Jan 22 - A STORY SHORT - airs on NBC

Feb - VTR - Fozzie Comedy Home Video

5

6

7

Feb - creative meetings about Theme Park concepts w/ Bran Ferren

March 12 - Julie Taymore's JUAN DARIEN

1988

april – working w/ Kirk Thatcher on computer generated character – Later WALDO

Jim discovered the possibility of adapting the radio-controlled animatronic puppetry developed for *Fraggle Rock* to a system for computer-generated characters, conceiving of a digital puppet that could be performed in real time. Jim recruited designer Kirk Thatcher to work with Pacific Data Images to develop the necessary software and hardware. "After much research, experimentation and head-scratching," Waldo C. Graphic was born. Performer Steve Whitmire operated an elaborate armature rigged with motion-capture sensors, and the data was married to Waldo's digital shape. Composited into the live shot and graphically enhanced, he interacted with actual puppets being performed simultaneously. Waldo debuted on *The Jim Henson Hour* and was immortalized in Jim's *Muppet*Vision 3D* film at Walt Disney World, opening limitless possibilities for a new direction in on-screen puppetry.

❶+❷ Kirk Thatcher's Waldo designs. ❸ The Henson Performance Control System for animatronics earned an Academy Award in 1992. ❹ PDI's diagram of how the Waldo system worked. ❺ Tim Young's Waldo design. ❻ Waldo designer Kirk Thatcher.

April 12 - WITCHES begins filming in Norway

May 20 in Detroit for launch of Muppet Traffic Safety Show for Chrysler

May 23 VTR Swedish Chef for CROONCHY STARS

June 15 - VTR me skipping stones in Central PK for Neat Stuff Home Video

1988

Aug 14-17 in Newcastle for VTR of Pilot of FAFFNER HALL
Oct 26 - VTR Sesame St. 20th Anniversary Show

Typically, Jim had numerous ideas in development while continuing work with the Muppets and *Sesame Street*. *Fraggle Rock* co-creator Jocelyn Stevenson proposed a music-education television series, *The Ghost of Faffner Hall*. With eccentric characters designed by Ron Mueck, the action took place in an English mansion and featured musical guests ranging from Dizzy Gillespie to the Scottish Chamber Orchestra. At the same time, Jim looked back, celebrating the enduring relevance of his work with a television special, *Sesame Street: 20 And Still Counting*. This joyous occasion brought together the creative team, allowing Jim to reminisce with his longtime collaborators like Joe Raposo and Joan Ganz Cooney. And by featuring newer characters like Elmo, Jim demonstrated *Sesame Street*'s evolution and ability to change with the times.

❶ Ron Mueck's design for Farkas. ❷ Dizzy Gillespie on *The Ghost of Faffner Hall*. ❸ Trombonist Steve Turre on the show. ❹ Ashley Wilkinson's set design. ❺ *Sesame Street* performers (left to right) David Rudman, Camille Bonora, Fran Brill, Pam Arciero, and Noel MacNeal. ❻ Ray Charles and friends perform Joe Raposo's song "Bein' Green" to celebrate *Sesame Street*'s anniversary. ❼ Caroly Wilcox's design for Elmo, created in 1979 as an anonymous red monster. ❽ The whole gang was on hand to celebrate *Sesame Street*'s twentieth anniversary.

Aug 20-21 - visit Dad + Bobbie w/ Heather Cheryl + John

Sept 15 - Art of the Muppets opens Museum of the Moving Image in LONDON

Oct 12-13 in Peggys Cove - Nova Scotia filming "LIGHTHOUSE ISLAND

Nov 1-18 - VTR - DOG CITY - in Toronto

Dec 9-10-11 - VTR Sesame ST. 20th - last time with Joe Raposo - Ray Charles - Placido Domingo

SS SHORT RED 11/79
SS TALL
Short Red
C.W.
First sketch for ELMO.
Ernie-type head
Shaggy Grey
Caroly Wilcox

20
SESAME STREET

EPILOGUE

TO BE CONTINUED

1989–
1990

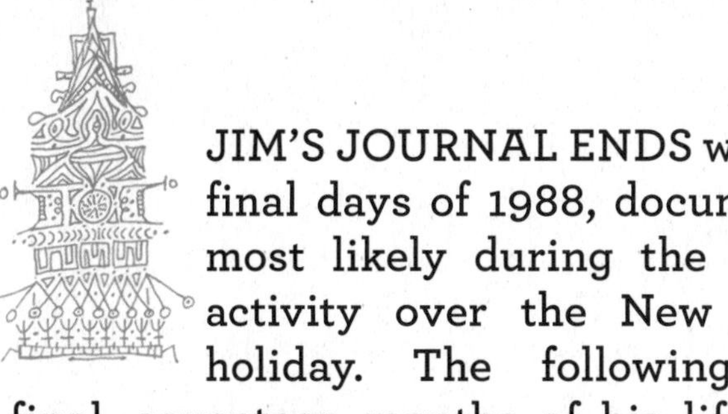

JIM'S JOURNAL ENDS with the final days of 1988, documented most likely during the lull in activity over the New Year's holiday. The following, and final, seventeen months of his life were incredibly full and provided much professional satisfaction. Like his childhood inspiration, Walt Disney, Jim became the on-camera host of his own television show, *The Jim Henson Hour,* highlighting the impressive range of work he had developed since he was seventeen. The series aired just one season, but Jim was gratified by the recognition it represented and the opportunity to explore the diverse products of his imagination.

As Jim noted in a memo to his staff in June 1989, the end of *The Jim Henson Hour* enabled them ". . . to move on to other things." These included establishing a permanent production office in Los Angeles, finalizing his film with director Nicolas Roeg, *The Witches,* creating the animatronic heads for the *Teenage Mutant Ninja Turtles* movie, developing a late-night show, hosted by two lizards, that showcased international, animated shorts, exploring a situation comedy populated by dinosaurs, and pursuing philanthropic projects with groups like Very Special Arts and A Better World Society.

Jim began talks with The Walt Disney Company, and in early 1990, with the production of the *Muppet*Vision 3D* movie, he was able to realize a longtime dream of seeing his characters as permanent attractions in Walt Disney's theme park in Florida. Jim started on the project that January, working with his closest colleagues and friends to combine his characters and his humorous, optimistic outlook with the latest technologies, many of which he helped to develop.

The demands of this ambitious production and Jim's efforts to move his company into the future were exhilarating and all-consuming. With little time for reflection or making notes in his journal, Jim did not sum up these last accomplishments on paper before his unexpected death on May 16, 1990. However, his work from that period laid a strong foundation, helping his family and colleagues build on his artistic vision. Jim Henson's impact continues today, permanently recorded in the smiles of children around the world and in the work of a new generation of creators and innovators inspired by his extraordinary life.

❶ Jim playing a cameo role in *The Muppets Take Manhattan,* 1983. ❷ Jim's concept for A Better World Society public service announcements.

The prospect of joining the Walt Disney Company and projects related to Disney's theme parks occupied most of 1989/1990 for Jim. Along with the *Muppet*Vision 3D* film, there was a television special, *The Muppets at Walt Disney World*, walk-around versions of his characters roaming the park and performing on stage there, and various television guest spots. In his usual fashion, Jim also continued to develop and produce numerous projects with a variety of collaborators. He got particular pleasure in working with his son Brian as they shared ideas for a situation comedy about a dinosaur family. The series, *Dinosaurs*, was realized under Brian's leadership, and its debut in 1991 was early evidence of Jim's lasting legacy. His company remained independent, with the Muppets not going to Disney until 2004. Today, The Jim Henson Company continues to be a home for innovation and creativity.

❶ Jim's final project, *Muppet*Vision 3D*, premiered at Walt Disney World on May 30, 1991. ❷ Jim in a promotional image for *Muppet*Vision 3D*. ❸ Jim directing *The Muppets at Walt Disney World* television special. ❹ Jim and a Teenage Mutant Ninja Turtle. ❺ Working on a Teenage Mutant Ninja Turtle head in the Henson Creature Shop. ❻ Jim's notes about *Dinosaurs*-related projects. ❼ Earl, the head of the family in *Dinosaurs*.

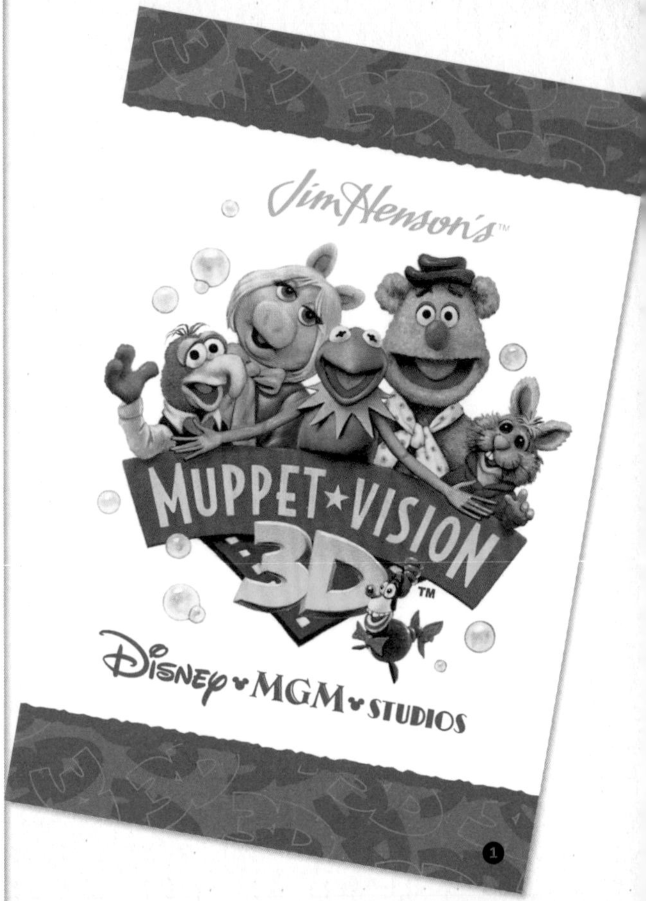

❶

❷

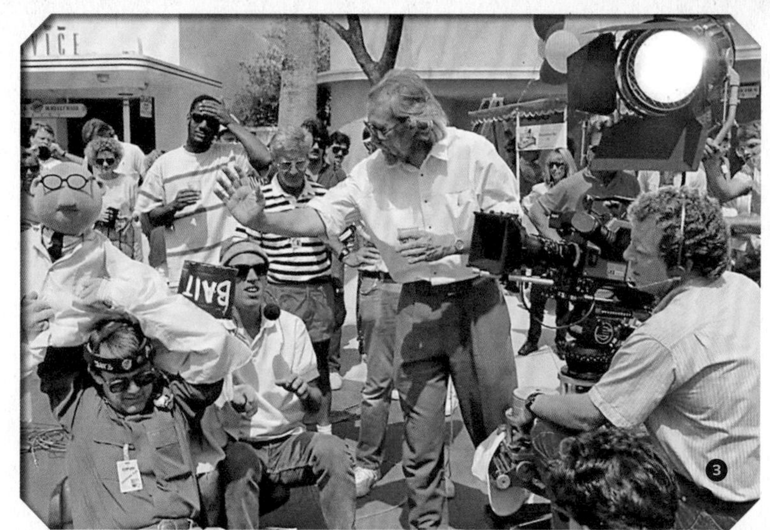

3

4

5

HENSON ASSOCIATES, INC
117 EAST 69 STREET
NEW YORK, N.Y. 10021
(212) 794-2400 TELEX-420750
PRODUCERS OF THE MUPPETS
ha!
JIM HENSON

DINOSAURS

other Dinosaur Movie
TV Documentary -
Muppets + Dinosaurs?
Museum Exhibit from Film - several
Canadian News Break -
TV special - exclusive
★ new launch PBS special - series?
exhibit - PR for them
Book Publishing -
tie in schools
Dinosaur Clubs -
merchandise
fall off - education / schools
science
Museums / Paleontologists

6

7

TIME LINE

1936
Jim Henson is born on September 24, 1936 in Greenville, Mississippi, where his father worked as a researcher for the U.S. Department of Agriculture.

1954
Jim graduates from Northwestern High School in Hyattsville, Maryland, and enters the University of Maryland.

Jim gets his first television experience on a Saturday morning show on the *Junior Morning Show*, WTOP/CBS, Washington, DC.

1955
Jim has his own five-minute show, *Sam and Friends*, with Jane Nebel. The show airs live on WRC-TV, Washington, DC, for six years.

1956
Appearances on *The Arthur Godfrey Show, The Tonight Show, The Steve Allen Show,* and *The Will Rogers, Jr. Show.*

1957
Jim Henson's first commercial, for Wilkins Coffee, is taped.

1958
Jim travels to Europe for the first time.

Sam and Friends wins a local Emmy award.

1959
Jim Henson and Jane Nebel are married.

1960
The Muppets appear for the first time on the *Today Show*, beginning regular appearances the following year.

1961
Writer/performer Jerry Juhl joins the Henson Company. Juhl (1938–2005) quickly becomes head writer for the Muppets and one of Jim's most important collaborators.

1962
Tales of the Tinkerdee television pilot is taped in Atlanta, Georgia.

Rowlf is built by puppet designer/builder Don Sahlin for a Purina dog-food commercial. Sahlin (1928–1978) is often credited with refining the Muppet look as we know it.

1963
The Muppets and the Henson family move to New York.

Jim begins regular performances of Rowlf on *The Jimmy Dean Show.*

Performer Frank Oz (b. 1944) joins the company and becomes Jim's closest performing partner.

1964
Production of Jim's Academy Award–nominated short film *Time Piece* begins.

1965
First films are developed for IBM corporate meetings, and Jim meets David Lazer.

Jerry Nelson (b. 1934) begins performing with Jim. His versatility spawned such memorable characters as The Count, Robin the Frog, Floyd Pepper, and Gobo Fraggle.

1966
Regular appearances on *The Ed Sullivan Show* begin, lasting until 1971.

First licensed products, Kermit and Rowlf dolls, are created with Ideal Toys.

1967
Cyclia, a nightclub project, begins. It is abandoned in 1970.

1968
Youth '68, a look at the youth culture of the period, is produced for the NBC *Experiment in Television* series.

The Muppets on Puppets, a PBS special, is taped.

Hey Cinderella! is filmed in Toronto and airs in 1970.

1969
Sesame Street premieres in November 1969.

The Cube, a drama coauthored by Henson and Juhl, is produced for the NBC *Experiment in Television* series.

1970
The Great Santa Claus Switch TV special.

1971
The Frog Prince TV special is produced in Toronto.

Muppets are featured in Nancy Sinatra's Las Vegas nightclub act and television special. The Muppets make guest appearances on many variety TV shows, including *The Flip Wilson Show*, the Goldie Hawn special *Pure Goldie*, and *The Dick Cavett Show.*

1972
Muppet Musicians of Bremen TV special.

1973
The Muppets Valentine Show with Mia Farrow.

1974
The Muppet Show: Sex and Violence TV series pilot.

1975
Muppets continue to appear on variety shows including TV specials for Cher and Julie Andrews, and *The Mike Douglas Show.*

Muppets make weekly appearances on *Saturday Night Live*'s first season.

1976
The Muppet Show premieres.

1977
Emmet Otter's Jug-Band Christmas TV special.

1979
The Muppets make their film debut with *The Muppet Movie.*

The Tonight Show is hosted by Kermit the Frog.

The Muppets Go Hollywood TV special.

John Denver and the Muppets: A Christmas Together TV special.

1981
Of Muppets and Men TV documentary. *The Muppets Go to the Movies* TV special. *The Great Muppet Caper* movie premieres.

1982
The Henson Foundation is established to promote, develop, and encourage public interest in the art of puppetry.

The Fantastic Miss Piggy Show TV special.

The Dark Crystal movie premieres.

1983
Fraggle Rock debuts on HBO.

John Denver and the Muppets: Rocky Mountain Holiday TV special.

The World of 'Dark Crystal' documentary.

1984
The Muppets Take Manhattan movie premieres.

Jim Henson's Muppet Babies animated TV series.

1985
Follow That Bird, Sesame Street movie premieres.

1986
The Muppets: A Celebration of 30 Years TV special.

The Tale of the Bunny Picnic TV special.

Labyrinth movie premieres.

Inside the Labyrinth documentary.

The Christmas Toy TV special.

1987
The StoryTeller TV series premieres with "Hans My Hedgehog."

Down at Fraggle Rock documentary.

Animated *Fraggle Rock* TV series.

A Muppet Family Christmas TV special.

Jim is inducted into the Academy of Television Arts and Sciences' Television Hall of Fame.

1988
The Witches movie in production.

1989
The Jim Henson Hour TV series.

Sesame Street: 20 and Still Counting TV special.

The Ghost of Faffner Hall TV series.

1990
Jim's final project *Muppet*Vision 3D*, produced for Walt Disney World in Florida.

Jim passes away in New York City on May 16, 1990, at the age of 53.

SELECTED BIBLIOGRAPHY

Bacon, Matt; with introduction by Brian Henson. *No Strings Attached: The Inside Story of Jim Henson's Creature Shop*. New York: Macmillan, 1997.

Borgenicht, David. *Sesame Street Unpaved*. New York: Hyperion, 1998.

Clash, Kevin, with Greg Brozek. *My Life as a Furry Red Monster: What Being Elmo Has Taught Me About Life, Love, and Laughing Out Loud*. New York: Broadway Books, 2006.

Davis, Michael. *Street Gang: The Complete History of Sesame Street*. New York: Viking, 2008.

Finch, Christopher. *Jim Henson—The Works: The Art, the Magic, the Imagination*. New York: Random House, 1993.

Finch, Christopher. *The Making of the Dark Crystal—Creating a Unique Film*. New York: Henson Organization Publishing/ Holt, Rinehart, Winston, 1983.

Finch, Christopher. *Of Muppets and Men, The Making of the Muppet Show*. New York: Muppet Press/Alfred A. Knopf, 1981.

Froud, Brian, and Terry Jones. *Goblins of Labyrinth*. New York: Henry Holt and Company, 1986.

Froud, Brian, and J.J. Llewellyn. *The World of the Dark Crystal*. New York: Henson Organization Publishing/Alfred A. Knopf, 1982.

Gikow, Louise; and Bruce McNally (illustrations). *Labyrinth—The Storybook Based on the Movie*. New York: Henry Holt and Company, 1986.

Gikow, Louise. *Sesame Street: A Celebration—40 Years of Life on the Street*. New York: Black Dog & Leventhal, 2009.

Henson, Cheryl (ed.), and Jim Henson. *It's Not Easy Being Green and Other Things to Consider*. New York: Hyperion, 2005.

Inches, Alison, and Jim Henson. *Jim Henson's Designs and Doodles*. New York: Abrams, 2001.

Jones, Brian Jay. *Jim Henson: The Biography. New York: Ballantine Books*, 2013.

Larkin, David (ed.), and Brian Froud (illustrations). *Land of Froud*. New York: Peacock Press/Bantam Books, 1977.

Minghella, Anthony. *Jim Henson's The Storyteller*. London: Boxtree/Muppet Press, 1988.

Morrow, Robert W. *Sesame Street and the Reform of Children's Television*. Baltimore: Johns Hopkins University Press, 2006.

Shales, Tom, and James-Andrew Miller. *Live from New York: An Uncensored History of Saturday Night Live*. New York: Little, Brown and Company, 2002.

Shemin, Craig. *Sam and Friends: The Story of Jim Henson's First Television Show*. Orlando: Bear Manor Media, 2022.

Spinney, Caroll, and J. Milligan. *The Wisdom of Big Bird (and the Dark Genius of Oscar the Grouch): Lessons from a Life in Feathers*. New York. Villard Books, 2003.

ACKNOWLEDGMENTS

I am indebted to the Henson Family, particularly Jane Henson, for giving me the privilege of organizing and caring for thousands of documents, drawings, and artifacts created by Jim Henson and his associates. Getting to know him through this material and, more importantly, through his children, Lisa, Cheryl, Brian, John, and Heather, has allowed me to witness, almost firsthand, his creativity, generosity, decency, and wit. Access to Jim's personal journal was a special gift, enabling me to know him better and providing a vehicle for sharing his inspiring story with a larger audience.

This book could not have come together without the careful management of and research into our historical collections by my Henson Archives colleagues both past and present including Carla DellaVedova, Susie Tofte, Shannon Robles, Hillary Howell, and Joshua Peach. Their work was invaluable in ensuring that the breadth of Jim's work would be presented at its best. Additional research and scanning were performed by Madlyn Moskowitz, Crystal Vagnier, Meaghan Curran, Stacie Williams, and Rachel Crowe.

The genesis of this book was my blog, Jim's Red Book, which was developed with the enormous contributions of Henson Company EVP of Branding Nicole Goldman, who supports so many archive activities, along with Allyson Smith, Maryanne Pittman, and Anna Jordan. Our publishing team, Melissa Segal, Patty Sullivan, and Jim Formanek, oversaw the move from online to print, and the new edition was shepherded by Gavin Gronenthal. Many others at The Jim Henson Company deserve my gratitude for making this project possible.

My work has always benefited from the parallel efforts of my friend and Jim Henson Legacy colleague Craig Shemin who has documented and presented Jim's work with the utmost care. I also greatly appreciate the personal reminiscences of Martin Baker, Fran Brill, Bonnie Erickson, Michael Frith, Brian and Wendy Froud, Dave Goelz, Al Gottesman, Susan Juhl, Rollie Krewson, Larry Mirkin, Ron Mueck, Jerry Nelson, Arthur Novell, Frank Oz, Connie Peterson, Karen Prell, Alex Rockwell, Jocelyn Stevenson, Kirk Thatcher, and Dick Wedemeyer that helped to enrich Jim's story and make my research such a pleasure.

The work of our partners at Muppets Studio/The Walt Disney Company and Sesame Workshop help ensure the continuation of Jim's legacy for new generations, and I'm grateful for their support and enthusiasm. Ron Howard's extraordinary documentary gives Jim's story new dimensions, and it is an honor having his thoughtful words in this book.

Steve Mockus and Michael Morris at Chronicle Books did heroic work wrestling Jim's exuberant and boundless career into the limitations of the printed page for the first edition, and at Insight Editions, Paul Ruditis is owed much appreciation for creating a renewed path to enjoying the evidence of Jim's imagination and his fascinating and joyful life. Finally, my deepest thanks go to my husband Michael Goldman and daughters Nina and Julia for their unwavering love and support.

—Karen Falk

IMAGE CREDITS

All images have been reproduced from materials in the collections of The Jim Henson Company Archives or the Henson Family Collection unless otherwise noted.

page 16: upper left: Jim Henson.

page 18: bottom: Del Ankers.

page 19: top: Del Ankers.

page 21: bottom: Del Ankers.

page 22: middle and bottom: Del Ankers.

page 27: top left and bottom: Del Ankers.

page 27: top right: Jim Henson.

page 28: top: Del Ankers.

page 28: middle: Jim Henson.

page 31: middle and bottom right: Del Ankers.

page 34: bottom left: Del Ankers.

page 35: bottom: Richard Termine.

page 38: bottom: Del Ankers.

page 41: "Money" lyrics by Stan Freberg. © Stan Freberg. All rights reserved. Used with permission.

page 41: bottom left: Jim Henson.

page 41: center right: Ted Neuhoff.

page 41: bottom right: Del Ankers.

page 42: bottom left: Del Ankers.

page 46: center: Del Ankers.

page 48: Courtesy of The Ed Sullivan Estate.

page 52: center: Jim Henson.

page 54: NBC.

page 55: bottom right: NBC.

page 58: bottom left: Robert Fuhring. Courtesy of Sesame Workshop Archives.

page 58: top right: Courtesy of Sesame Workshop Archives.

page 59: top left: Jim Henson.

page 61: top: ABC/RJ Reynolds.

page 66: Courtesy of Sesame Workshop Archives.

page 69: top: Courtesy of Caroll Spinney.

page 69: bottom left and center: Michael LeGrou.

page 75: middle: Cheryl Henson.

page 75: bottom: Courtesy of Sesame Workshop Archives.

page 85: top and bottom right: Del Ankers.

page 88: bottom left: Courtesy of Bonnie Erickson.

page 94: top: ABC.

page 101: bottom left: Nancy Moran.

page 103: top right and center: David Dagley and Still Photographic Dept. of ATV Network.

page 104: bottom left: David Dagley and Still Photographic Dept. of ATV Network.

page 104: bottom right: Nancy Moran.

page 105: top: Nancy Moran.

page 106: American Express/Ogilvy & Mather.

page 107: center and left: American Express/ Ogilvy & Mather.

page 108: top: From *The Land of Froud*, courtesy of Brian Froud.

page 109: top: From *The Land of Froud*, courtesy of Brian Froud.

page 114: top: Gail Russell.

page 116: top: Courtesy of The Center for Puppetry Arts.

page 117: top left: John Consoli.

page 118: top and center right: David Dagley and Still Photographic Dept. of ATV Network.

page 120: top: John Shannon.

page 123: bottom: David Dagley and Still Photographic Dept. of ATV Network.

page 124: right: John E. Barrett.

page 125: center right: Richard Termine.

page 125: bottom right: Courtesy of Michael Dixon.

page 127: John Brown.

page 129: all: David Dagley and Still Photographic Dept. of ATV Network.

page 130: top left: Murray Close.

page 131: bottom right: Murray Close.

page 131: bottom left: Kerry Hayes.

page 132: bottom: Murray Close.

page 135: top right and left: John E. Barrett.

page 136: top and center: Murray Close.

page 137: top: Murray Close.

page 142: center: Michael K. Frith.

page 143: all: Fred Phipps.

page 144: top: David Dagley and Still Photographic Dept. of ATV Network.

page 146: top right: Paul Schumach/Metropolitan Photo Service.

page 157: top and bottom: *Dreamchild* copyright © 1997 by Universal City Studios, Inc. Courtesy of MCA Publishing Rights, a Division of Universal Studios, Inc. All Rights Reserved.

page 157: center: courtesy of Michael Dixon.

page 160: top: John Brown.

page 161: top: Matthew Mauro.

page 162: top: John Brown.

page 164: top and bottom: John Brown.

page 166: top right: Richard Termine.

page 167: top: Richard Termine.

page 168: bottom right, David Dagley.

page 170: top and center: Stephen Morley.

page 171: bottom left: Stephen Morley.

page 172: bottom right and left: © CBS.

page 179: bottom right: Richard Termine.

page 181: top and middle left: Christie Sherman.

page 182: Kerry Hayes.

page 184: bottom: Ron Batzdorff.

page 185: center: *Teenage Mutant Ninja Turtles* Media Asia Group copyright © Star TV.

Page 185: bottom right: © The Walt Disney Company.

page 192: Courtesy of Steve Whitmire.

INDEX